Home, School, and Community Relations: A Guide to Working with Parents

Home, School, and Community Relations:
A Guide to Working with Parents

CAROL GESTWICKI
Central Piedmont Community College

Delmar Publishers Inc.©

NOTICE TO THE READER

Publisher does not warrant or guarantee any of the products described herein or perform any independent analysis in connection with any of the product information contained herein. Publisher does not assume, and expressly disclaims, any obligation to obtain and include information other than that provided to it by the manufacturer.

The reader is expressly warned to consider and adopt all safety precautions that might be indicated by the activities described herein and to avoid all potential hazards. By following the instructions contained herein, the reader willingly assumes all risks in connection with such instructions.

The publisher makes no representations or warranties of any kind, including but not limited to, the warranties of fitness for particular purpose or merchantability, nor are any such representations implied with respect to the material set forth herein, and the publisher takes no responsibility with respect to such material. The publisher shall not be liable for any special, consequential or exemplary damages resulting, in whole or in part, from the readers' use of, or reliance upon, this material.

Delmar Staff
  Administrative Editor: Karen Lavroff
  Managing Editor: Barbara Christie
  Production Editor: Christine Worden
  Design Coordinator: Susan C. Mathews

For information, address Delmar Publishers Inc.
2 Computer Drive West, Box 15-015
Albany, New York 12212

Printed in the United States of America
Published simultaneously in Canada
by Nelson Canada,
A division of International Thomson Limited

10 9 8 7 6 5 4 3

Library of Congress Cataloging-in-Publication Data

Gestwicki, Carol, 1940–
  Home, School, and Community Relations.

  Bibliography: p.
  Includes index.
  1. Home and school—United States. 2. Parent-teacher relationships—United States. I. Title.
LC225.3.G47   1988   372.11'03   86-29248
ISBN 0-8273-2646-7 (pbk.)

Contents

Section IV: Making a Partnership Work

Preface

In today's rapidly changing world, more and more families are having to learn to live with life-styles that have changed since they were children. Young children in increasing numbers are spending part or most of their daytime hours during the work week away from their parents, with other adults playing important supplemental roles in their growth and guidance. Their parents are still without question the most important people in their lives. Teachers do not become substitute parents, but in fact do many of the things parents would do for a child, if they were able to be with the child full-time; at the same time, teachers attempt to extend a child's world of experience beyond the home.

The nature of the relationship between child, parent, and teacher of young children constitutes uncharted territory today. The old concept of completely separate worlds of home and school, with minimal formal contact between parent and teacher, is inadequate considering the complex issues raised as the care of very young children is shared by adults who are related only by their particular commitment. Obviously something new needs to be considered. While teachers are committed to all children in general, parents are committed to this one particular child. It is certainly not the intent of this book to imply the necessity of a complete enmeshing of teacher and parent; such a union would be quite impossible, to say nothing of probably undesirable from a child's point of view. Rather, teachers and parents who strive to find ways to communicate and work together towards the goal of enhancing a child's development in the environments of home and school may discover that their efforts are more successful through understanding and support of the other.

This is a new world into which these teachers and parents bravely move on behalf of the children they care for. Given the changes in the structure of the world, it can be assumed that parents and teachers of the very young will continue to work in close proximity; it is for everyone's benefit to find ways of working together that feel both comfortable and worthwhile. It may be uncomfortable and awkward at times, as it often is when people are moving without models and guidelines to follow. Mistakes will be made; sometimes it will seem preferable to give up the attempt and retreat to the more familiar role of teacher or parent, working independently of others. But that is not the best answer for the children.

Working together may not be easy. There are practical problems to be worked out: finding time to talk and learn from each other when there are already so many demands on time; finding ways to include families that have myriad structures and compositions. There are more subtle, interpersonal issues: communicating ideas, questions, and suggestions to one another without impinging on each other's province; dealing with the pangs of rivalry and jealousy that arise, unlooked for. And, most difficult of all, the unique personalities, backgrounds, sets of experience and values mean that each teacher and parent has natural preferences and habitual ways of dealing with others. But there are ideas to turn into conscious actions and steps to try, or to modify, that others have tried. There will be much for a teacher to learn from each attempt. Because nurturing and communication are already aspects of a teacher's role and because the relationship is born on school territory where a teacher is most comfortable, the initiative for these efforts must come from a teacher.

In this book, we will try to heighten our awareness of what it means to be a parent—the roles and emotional responses, the needs and concerns. We will try to become conscious of what is involved in parenting, since it is only when teachers are truly able to empathize with parents' situations and feelings that they are able to communicate with sensitivity. Recognizing that today's parents are surrounded, influenced, and buffeted by a new world, we must remind ourselves of some of the facts about that world. To make concrete our points about parents, we will work from anecdotes about some fictional families, a selection from the variety of family forms and backgrounds that any teacher might encounter. Students are encouraged to use these anecdotes, as well as recollections of personal experiences with families they have observed or worked with, in order to identify with the text material. The text asks students to consider ideas from the perspective of their own reality. Students are challenged to work through these ideas actively, not passively accept them from the printed page.

As students, you may come to this study from any one of a number of positions: as a student teacher who is meeting the idea of working with parents for the first time; as a teacher who has had few experiences (or interest) in attempting to work with parents, or as one who has had some successes and some failures in your attempts. To help you consider experiences, feelings, and techniques of teachers in a variety of situations, an assortment of fictional teachers is used. Many of the examples used refer to day-care situations; indeed, as the numbers of full-time working parents continues to rise, more and more children are in group day care. Nevertheless, the techniques and ideas are completely applicable in whatever situations teachers work with young children, whether in traditional nursery school and early childhood programs, or in the early elementary years. By all means try to identify with ways you might react or substitute your own experiences to make the ideas concrete for you.

A word or two about the mechanics of writing. Happily, in the past decade or so, we are finding some men involved in preschool teaching, albeit a minority; certainly more fathers are involved actively in the day-to-day care of their young children. Some of the contexts will make it clear whether we are talking about "him" or "her." But for the sake of clear expression, in cases where it is not specific, the text uses "she" to refer to the teacher and "he" to refer to the parent, and alternately refers to children as male or female.

There are a number of people whose help and support have been appreciated during the writing of this text. I would like to thank friends and colleagues who generously read and commented on the first draft— Linda Harrison, Edith Johnson, Sally vander Straeten, Saunie Wood; Shari Blair and the staff of Open Door School; Shirley Hoots and the staff of Henderson County Child Development Center; Stephen Lehane and the staff of the Child Care Services, University of Southern Maine; Patty Hnatiuk and the staff of Thorndike Street School; Millie O'Connell, who helped me find the right school; JoEllen Wade, Mike Slade and Don Ambrose of CPCC Media Productions; and my family, who have lived with the daily accounts of this project, and especially Ron, who has now become the acknowledged MLA style and comma expert in the family.

Section I:
Introduction to Parenting

Chapter 1 A Consideration of Families

This book assumes that individuals who are currently teaching or preparing to teach will work with families throughout their career. Although the media reports that the family is a fatally wounded institution in today's world, in truth the more traditional forms of the family are diminishing while other forms are rising.

Objectives

After studying this chapter, the student will be able to

1. define family and consider several characteristics of families
2. describe seven characteristics of American life that influence the nature of modern families

What Defines a Family

The family is the most adaptable of human institutions. It is able to modify its characteristics to meet those of the society in which it lives. Certainly the family has adapted to much in recent times: industrialization, urbanization, a consumer-oriented economy, changes in traditional religious and moral codes, changes in all relationships basic to family life, between men and women, young and old. During the latter part of this century these changes have been occurring in every corner of the world, although our concern here is purely the American family.

Even before these more complicated times, it was impossible to speak with a unified voice about the American family in a society where the roots for its families were derived from diverse backgrounds. Yet those who speak persist in sounding as though there exists a homogenous family that can be described. Louise Howe says it well in *The Future of the Family:*

> *The* American family? Just which American family did you have in mind? Black or white, large or small, wealthy or poor—or something in between? Did you mean a father-headed, mother-headed or childless family? First or second time around? Happy or miserable? Your family or mine? (Howe, 1972, p. 11)

Despite the obvious fact that the phrase "the American family" is anything but truly descriptive of reality, it is used sweepingly. Generally it brings to mind a white, middle-class, monogamous, father-at-work, mother-and-children-at-home family, living in a suburban one-family house, nicely filled with an array of appliances, a station wagon in the driveway, and probably a dog in the yard. Such a description excludes over three-quarters of the country's families. It is more accurate to suggest that it is this mythical American family that is in trouble.

"Ideal" Family Images

What image comes to your mind when presented with the word *family?* No doubt people's mental images vary greatly, based in part on their individual life experiences.

Try an experiment now as you think about family. On a piece of paper draw stick figures to represent the members of the family you first knew as a young child; who represented family to you then? Then do the same to represent the family you lived in as a teenager. Had your family changed? Was anyone added or removed? What were the reasons for any changes?

Now draw the family in which you presently live. Who is there? What does this say about the changes in your life?

Now one last picture. Imagine that you could design the ideal family for yourself. What would it look like?

Sorting through your pictures may generate some ideas about family. One prediction is that most of the ideal pictures include a father, mother, and two children (probably a boy first and then a girl!) This experiment was carried out with over 200 students, primarily eighteen to twenty-one-year-old women. Almost always the ideal family included these members, no matter what the actual composition of the families in which the students had participated or presently lived. Often there were dissimilarities; reality for some students consisted of growing up with one parent, having two stepfathers, a large number of siblings, being an only child, having grandparents or others in the home. All of their real experiences were passed over in favor of the ideal two-parent, two-child home. Some students, who created more elaborate fantasy families, specified that the mother was a full-time homemaker—this from women themselves preparing for a career. The only women whose ideal family approximated the reality in which they now lived, were women who had married and had children before becoming students—unless the marriage had been disrupted by divorce. Then their ideal family included another partner.

For many, the image of an ideal family is influenced less by real experiences than by the subtle cultural messages that have bombarded us since childhood. From magazine advertisements to children's books, and even more pervasively from television shows, the attractive vision of husband, wife, and children beams at us. What has been called the "Leave it to Beaver" syndrome (Rover and Polifroni, 1985) has given several viewing generations a clear yardstick against which to measure desirable family characteristics, and measurable amounts of guilt and negative feelings when the reality does not match the ideal.

Interestingly, the students surveyed are aware that their ideal image is just that, and are also aware of the societal influences that helped produce it. They may be unaware of how insidiously this subliminal image can influence their encounters with real families. If an ideal, lurking unknowingly in the teacher's value system is considered the "good," a negative evaluation can be made of any family that did not measure up to this standard. The problem with assessing this nuclear family model as the "good" is that it may prevent us from considering alternative family structures as equally valid.

One way to become aware of one's prejudices is to make a list of the names of the families in your classroom (or neighborhood). Mark a check beside each family you would like to be friends with or those you think are doing a good job. Mark an "X" beside those families you feel most comfortable with and those you have contact with frequently. How many of these families look somewhat like your ideal family or the family you grew up in? In doing this exercise, it is important not to make value judgements about which are the "right kind of families," but merely examine your initial reactions based on prior experiences. It is all too easy for a teacher to feel more affinity and comfort with a family that approaches her idea of the desirable than with one that is clearly outside her frame of reference.

It is important for a teacher to consider these ideas actively. Recording thoughts about families in a notebook is a good starting place. Asking questions—Are there any families I feel particularly uncomfortable with? What do I think is causing this discomfort? What can I do about it? This is not to say that teachers have to give up their ideal images, but that teachers be aware lest these images become limiting factors in relationships with the variety of parents they will encounter.

Samples of Varying Family Structures

If personal images of family cannot convey a complex enough picture, perhaps brief descriptions of families you might meet and work with will help. We will meet these families now, in order to begin to consider the diversity in structure that corresponds to the differing values, customs, and life-styles that have evolved in our world. These same families will help us later when we consider different relationships and techniques in teacher-parent communication.

A. Bob and Jane Weaver have been married five years. They married the day after Jane graduated from high school. Sandra, blond and blue-eyed just like her parents, was born before their first anniversary. Bob and Jane live down the street from her parents, around the block from her married sister. Jane has not worked at all during their marriage. They are hoping to have another child next year. A second pregnancy ended in stillbirth last year. Bob earns $23,520 on the production line at a furniture factory.

B. Sylvia Ashley, twenty-nine, lives alone with her sons Terrence, nine, and Ricky, three. Her marriage to Ricky's father ended before he was born; she was not married to Terrence' father, who was in one of her classes in college before she dropped out that first semester. She has had no contact with her parents since before Terrence' birth. Although she lives in a public housing apartment, she rarely has contact with her neighbors; hers is the only white family living in the project. Before Ricky was born she worked in a department store. Since then her income has been from AFDC and food stamp payments, as well as the subsidized housing. This year she is beginning a job training program, hoping to pick up on her plan of becoming a nurses' aide.

C. Otis and Fannie Lawrence have each been married before. Otis has two sons from his first marriage—fourteen and ten—who visit one weekend each month and for about six weeks each summer. Fannie's seven-year-old daughter Kim and four-year-old son Pete see their own father who has moved out of state only once or twice a year, and have called Otis "Daddy" since their mother married him three years ago. Fannie is six months pregnant, and they have recently moved to an attractive new four bedroom house, knowing even that will still be too small when the boys visit. Fannie teaches third grade, and will take a three month maternity leave after the baby is born; she is on the waiting list at four centers for infant care. Otis sells new cars and is finishing up a business degree slowly at night. The Lawrence family income is $48,000 annually. The Lawrence family is black.

D. Salvatore and Teresa Rodriguez have lived in this country for six years. Occasionally one of their relatives has come to stay with them, but the rest of the family has preferred to stay in Puerto Rico. Right now Sal's twenty-year-old brother Joseph is here, taking an auto mechanics course; he plans to be married later this year, and will probably stay in the same town. Teresa's mother has not seen their two children since they were babies. Sylvia is seven and has cerebral palsy; she attends a developmental kindergarten. Tony is four. Teresa works part-time in a bakery. Her husband works the second shift on the maintenance crew at the bus depot, so he can be home with the children while she's at work. They rent a six-room house, which they chose for the neat neighborhood and large garden.

E. Mary Howard is sixteen and has always lived with her parents in a middle class black neighborhood. Her grandmother has had a stroke and now lives with them too. When Mary's daughter Cynthia was born last year, her mother cared for the baby so Mary could finish the eleventh grade. Cynthia is now in day care, as Mary's mother needed to go back to work with the increased family expenses. Mary still hopes she might someday marry Cynthia's father, who is starting college this year. He comes to see her and the baby every week or so. Mary's also wondering if she'll go on to train in computer programing after she finishes high school, as she'd planned, or if she should just get a job so she can help her mother out more with Cynthia and their support.

F. Susan Henderson celebrated her thirty-eighth birthday in the hospital the day after giving birth to Lucy. Her husband Ed is forty. After thirteen years of marriage, they've found adding a child both joyful and shocking. Lucy was very much a planned child. Susan felt well enough established in her career as an architect to be able to work from her home for a year or so. Ed's career as investment counsellor has also demanded a lot of his attention. Some of their friends are still wavering over the decision to begin a family. Ed and Susan are quite definite that this one child will be all they'll have time for. Money is not the issue in their decision; their combined income last year was well over $100,000. Susan's major complaint since being at home with the baby is that the condominium where they live has few families with children, and none of them are preschoolers.

G. Sam (two) and Lisa (four) Butler see both of their parents a lot—they just never see them together. Bill and Joan separated almost two years ago, and their divorce is about to become final. One of the provisions calls for joint custody of their two preschoolers. What this means right now is spending three nights one week with one parent, and four with the other. The schedule gets complicated sometimes, as Bill travels on business, but so far the adults have been able to work it out. The children seem to enjoy going from Dad's apartment to Mom in the house they've always lived in, but on the days they carry their suitcases to the day-care center for the mid-week switchover, they need lots of reassurance about who's picking them up. Joan worries about how this arrangement will work as the children get older. She works as a secretary for the phone company and needs to take some computer courses this fall, but doesn't know how she can fit them in and the kids too—let alone find time to date a new man she's met.

H. Ginny Parker and Sara Leeper have shared an apartment for two years. Ginny has four-year-old twin boys; Sara's daughter is now five. They met at a Parents Without Partners support group when Ginny was newly separated. Sara is a lesbian mother who adopted her daughter at six months. Ginny is involved in a custody battle with her ex-husband. Neither woman has any family in town. Sara is a nurse on the second shift at the hospital. Ginny works for a travel agency downtown. Sharing the responsibilities of child care, household management, and finances has made it possible for both women to live more comfortably, as well as feeling less isolated. They have a warm and supportive relationship, though Ginny is not a lesbian. She grins when asked about their sex lives, saying that with all the two mothers have to do, they might as well have sworn vows of celibacy. Privately, she expresses annoyance that many people seem to expect a divorced mother to be a social "swinger." When asked if they're worried about their children growing up without a relationship with an adult male, Ginny responds that is the reason for their active membership in Parents Without Partners. They plan to continue the living arrangement.

I. Despite the urging of some of his more Westernized friends and his wife, Chang Chik-lai has refused to change either his name or many other of his traditional ways, since he brought his family from Taiwan four years ago. His wife, formerly Chang Kuei-li, now calls herself Lee Chang, and she registered his five-year-old son (Chang Ping-sheng) at the kindergarten as Pete Chang, and his three-year-old daughter (Chang Mei-li) as May Chang. She insists that his stubborn refusal to adapt is the reason he has not yet been able to find full-time work, though he was a skilled draftsman in Taiwan. Chang has strongly resisted his wife's working too, though her job in the school cafeteria plus the day work he picks up from time to time is their only source of income. He has taken over some of the child care and housework, but is very unhappy with this arrangement, and there have been a lot of arguments at home recently. There is a plan for his parents to join them from Taiwan later this year, and he hopes the grandparents' influence will help him keep the children from losing their own cultural heritage.

J. Richard Stein and Roberta Howell have lived together for eighteen months. Richard's five-year-old son Joshua lives with them. Roberta has decided she wants no children; Richard and she have no plans for marriage at this time. Roberta works long hours as a department store buyer. Richard writes for the local newspaper. On the one or two evenings a week that neither of them can get away from work, Joshua is picked up from the day-care center by a college student that Richard met at the paper.

In this sample, as in any other you might draw from a cross-section in any preschool, the "traditional" family, with a father who works to earn the living and a mother whose work is rearing the children and caring for the home, is a distinct minority in the variety of structures; current statistics suggest that these include only 7% of American families (Rosen, 1982). How do we define *family?* The Census Bureau definition of "two or more individuals who live together and are related to one another by blood or marriage" seems too narrow to include all the dynamics of these sample families. Perhaps a more applicable definition of family is a small group of intimate, transacting, and interdependent persons who share values, goals, resources, and responsibilities for decisions; have a commitment to one another over time; and accept the responsibility of bringing up children.

Families may include more than just parents and children. Mary Howard's family includes her parents, grandmother, and child, and the Rodriguez' have Uncle Joseph. The extension of the nuclear family is more for affection and support than for a self-sufficient economic unit the traditional extended family created.

Families may include people not related by blood and hereditary bonds. The Parker-Leeper and Stein-Howell households include parents and children and others whose relationship is based on choice, not law. New relatives, such as those acquired in a stepfamily like the Lawrences, may be added.

Families may be composed of more people than those who are present in a household at any one time. The Butler arrangement and the "patchwork" (so referred to by sociologists) Lawrence family are examples of separated family structures.

Families change; their composition is dynamic, not static. It is assumed that Uncle Joseph will form his own household when he and his fiancee marry; Mary Howard hopes to marry and establish her own household. The Butler family may be added to when the parents remarry, as both say they'd like to. The Weavers hope to add another baby. Change normally occurs as family members grow and develop, particularly the children. Family members are continually adjusting to shifts within the family dynamics that challenge earlier positions.

Modern Families

Is it harder or easier to be a parent today than it was a generation or two ago? There is no question that today's parents are functioning under different conditions than their grandparents or even parents did. As LeMasters points out, social change is not synonymous with either social progress or social deterioration (LeMasters and DeFrain, 1983). Almost all of the changes discussed in this chapter have had a positive and negative impact on American parents.

Some recent trends in American life influencing the nature of families include marital instability and rising numbers of unmarried mothers, changes in role behavior, mobility and urbanization, decreasing family size, increased rate of social change, development of a child-centered society, and stress in modern living. Each of these will be discussed in this chapter.

Marital Instability and Unmarried Mothers

Statistics tell us part of the story. Since 1900, the divorce rate has increased nearly 700%. It is estimated that over 50% of marriages begun in the early 1980s will end in divorce. In 1982, 13.7 million children lived with only one parent, two-thirds more than in 1970. Of these children, one in five were white, one in two were black. According to Census Bureau predictions, it is likely that nearly half of all children born in the 1970s will spend a significant part of their childhood in a single-parent home. The majority of these single-parent families were created by divorce. But divorced parents often remarry. At least six million children presently live with a stepparent; one of every six children under age eighteen is a stepchild. (All statistics are from the Census Bureau reports on Households, Families, Marital Status and Living Arrangements, March 1984, and Current Population Reports Special Studies, Series p-23, No. 130, Population Profile of the U.S., 1984.)

In addition, some of the single-parent families are the result of a rising birth rate among unmarried adolescents. About two out of every ten adolescent girls under age nineteen gave birth in 1984; more than 50% of these were not married. These families are particularly at risk for premature births, child abuse, unemployment, and poverty (Gross, 1977).

What lies beyond these statistics is the concept that a major proportion of contemporary American parents do not operate under the optimum condition of having a partner to help in carrying out the parenting roles. There are additional difficulties to face in a single-parent family.

Poverty

Ninety percent of single-parent families are headed by women. In the most recent statistics released by the Census Bureau, the poverty rate for single-parent families headed by women with children under age eighteen increased from 36% in 1979 to 46% in 1984, including all government assistance of cash and noncash benefits (*Charlotte Observer*, Jan. 19, 1986). This low-income figure exists despite the fact that 80% of single-parent household heads are employed full-time, though typically in low-paying jobs, and provide about 60–70% of the total family income, with other resources being alimony, child support, and government assistance. Financial stress is a major complaint of divorced women. Many single-parent families are less able to provide the adequate support services they need, such as child care while a mother works, or recreation or other social relief for a parent.

Stress

A family that began with two parents and shifts to single-parent status is undoubtedly going to experience increased stress for some period of time, if not permanently. Adjustments will have to be made by all family members to the changed living patterns that include the loss of a relationship, regardless of how negative; perhaps a move, new job or school arrangements, or other changes necessitated by the constraints of a more limited budget; less contact with one parent, as well as changed behaviors in both.

The majority of single-parent families created by divorce are headed by women; a mother in a single-parent family is under the additional strain of adding the father role to her parental responsibilities. She may easily overload herself while trying to compensate for her concern induced by social attitudes that a single-parent family is a pathological family. The mixed data in this area is scarcely reassuring, and real or feared changes in children's behavior can add appreciably to a parent's burden at this time. Social attitudes towards divorce may have undergone a shift towards acceptance, but attitudes towards a "broken family" still leave many a single parent with the additional burden of guilt.

If a single-parent family is recycled to create a new blended family, additional stress may be created. A new family may begin with financial problems created when one income must support more than one family, with emotional burdens created by the multiplicity of possible new relationships as well as the striving to create an instant family, warm and close, guaranteed to make up for the earlier pain and banish the "ugly stepparent" fears. Unfortunately these burdens may be too heavy to permit survival: 40% of blended family marriages end in divorce within four years.

Changes in Role Behavior

On television, Beaver Cleaver's mom was home baking cookies, but fewer and fewer mothers today are. The Census figures for 1984 indicate the majority of women in the work force are mothers of children living at home. (To put this in perspective: in 1900, only one wife in twenty was in the labor force, but by 1950, the ratio was one out of five, and in 1984, it was about three out of five. In 1940, 8.6% of mothers with children under age eighteen worked; now nearly 50% of children under age one, half of all children under age three, and

Over half of all preschoolers have mothers working outside the home.

70% of six- to thirteen-year-olds have working mothers (Family Policy Panel Report, 1985, quoted in *Charlotte Observer,* Jan, 19, 1986).

Women's Roles

Statistics alone cannot encompass all that has occurred since the 1960s with the redefinition of women's roles. Since the publishing of *The Feminine Mystique* (Friedan, 1963), women the world over have urged each other to find equality in their relationships with men and in their place in the community and at work. This has not been an easy change for anyone involved. For women, it has meant adding new roles while often retaining much of the responsibility for household maintenance and child-rearing. If a woman tries to combine all the roles she saw her mother play at home with her new work roles, she is in danger of falling into the "Super Woman" syndrome (Time, 1980), and exhaustion and stress may spill over into all aspects of her life.

One of the difficulties for many adult women was that a change in social thinking about women's rights and roles occurred after their early impressions had been formed by examples set by their own mothers and their youthful fantasies of what life would be like as grown-up women. The female role they had learned was to nurture and care for others in their small home world; now the movement urged them to care for themselves, to expand into the world. In confusion, many women attempted to fit into the traditional pattern while expanding chaotically in all directions. Thankfully, twenty years after the beginning of the modern women's movement, many women are working out new patterns that better suit them and their situations. There is hope that children raised by women working outside the home will integrate several facets of female behavior into their sex-role perceptions with less difficulty.

Work is not the only aspect of women's lives to be reconsidered. The language of the women's movement in the 1960s and 1970s spoke of women as one of society's minorities, without rights of equality at home and personally, as well as publicly. Issues of sexuality and repro- duction, of sex-role stereotypes and limitations were discussed nation- wide. Some real changes were effected, along with much consciousness raising. The increase in marital instability may be partly attributable to this questioning of traditional relationships, and the women's movement may prove to be a major influence in the nature of families and society in years to come. Whether or not women and men agree with the push towards equality, it is virtually impossible for anyone in the country to remain untouched by the debate and its repercussions on life-styles. But change comes through turmoil, and this environment of changing relationships and role behaviors has precipitated women and men in the family into unknown territory (Seidenberg, 1973; Ericksen et al., 1979; Lein, 1984).

Men's Roles

Men's family roles are on similarly shaky new ground. Not only are they asked to share positions and power in the workplace with women, but at home more is expected of them than of their fathers before them. They may still not be carrying their equal share in the household chores, but the days of hiding guilt-free behind the newspaper until dinner is on the table are gone. Gone also are the models of paternal behavior they knew as children. But, after all, this is what happened to their fathers before them. Grandfather's role in the family was to exert authoritarian control, but after World War II, a father's major role with his children became that of playmate. As fathers received more leisure time due to changing work patterns, and as the expert advice to parents continued to change from stern rigidity to concern for children feeling loved and happy, fathers became someone with whom their children could have fun. Today's father plays with his child, but he also takes his turn sitting in the pediatrician's office, cooking dinner, supervising homework, and carpooling. Frequently he is involved before his child's birth—attending Lamaze classes with his wife to learn how to coach her through prepared childbirth. But is this involvement as pervasive as some articles in women's magazines would portray? In only a very small percentage of families where the mother works do fathers share child care responsibilities equally, though in a larger percentage, fathers assume partial responsibility (Eisenberg, 1975; Russell, 1983). According to several recent studies, men whose wives are employed are likely to increase slightly the amount of time spent doing housework, but the increase in time spent in child care is even less

Many couples share classes to prepare for childbirth.

(Eisenberg, L., 1975; Lamb, 1981; Lamb, 1982; Malmaud, 1984). One study even found that 93% of American fathers still claim never to have changed a diaper! (Russell, 1983). While some husbands may help out, the primary responsibility for both house and child care remains the wife's, perhaps due to the constraints of role behavior norms for husbands and wives (Ericksen et al., 1979). Certainly there are few models of highly participant fathers, and those few fathers who do participate equally as parents receive little recognition (Russell, 1983). But it is probably fair to say that today's father is called upon to share with his wife all aspects of the children's care, to display many of the nurturant behaviors previously associated only with mothers. To define what it means to be a man, major shifts in thinking are obviously required. However men may feel about it—and most fathers are pleased with their new roles (Yarrow, 1985)—the change in women's roles in contemporary America has changed their own.

Certainly some shifts in thinking have occurred, though many more may be required. An example of those changes is offered by the doctor who advised so many American parents, Dr. Benjamin Spock. In 1946,

Many fathers are more involved in child care today.

in his first edition of *Baby and Child Care*, he was quite definite that it made no sense for mothers to work and hire someone else to care for their children. In 1976, he stated that both parents had an equal right to a career and an equal obligation to share in the care of their children (Lamb, 1981). Slowly, society has been pushed to alter its expectations regarding the roles of family members, and individuals are caught between trying to balance the external realities and demands, and the internal psychological conflict caused by attempting a new social pattern.

The jury is still out on what impact the different patterns of family roles and parenting have on members of the family. (See discussions in Hoffman, 1974; Eiderson, 1974; Norton, 1976; Solnit, 1976; Fantini and Cardenas, 1980.) Certainly there are more opportunities for personal growth with alternatives from which to choose freely. Children have a more democratic family model as an increasing number of fathers take on the loving and serving aspects of parenthood, and an increasing number of mothers take on leadership roles outside of the home as well as inside.

Mobility and Urbanization

With increasing industrialization and employment patterns, many workers and their families move frequently in the search for new and better jobs. When asked about the period from 1975–1980, barely half of Americans were living in the same house at the end of the period that they were in the beginning (Masnick and Bane, 1980). The average American moves fourteen times in his lifetime, and 20% of the population moves every year (Talbot, 1974).

What does this mean to contemporary families? It probably means that the nuclear family, the parents and their children, are far removed from the physical presence of others who may have acted as sources of support in earlier times. A new mother coming home from the hospital with her new baby may know little about how to care physically for the infant, let alone how to deal with the anxiety that arises about 3:00 a.m. Her only support is a husband who may be as ignorant and anxious as she. In a bygone day, she may have been surrounded by her mother, mother-in-law, aunts, cousins, sisters, and neighbors who had known her since she was a baby. As time goes by, the young couple needs baby-sitters to be able to shop in peace or have some recreation time away from the child, someone to care for the sick child when the parents simply have to be at work, someone to delight along with them with the child's success at school, or commiserate and calm them when the child begins to throw temper tantrums, use bathroom talk, or anything else that may come as a shock to a first-time parent. Increasingly, parents have to turn to others to fill some of the functions that could have been performed by the extended family were they not so far removed or the need will go unmet. For example, they might hire the neighbor's teenaged daughter to look after the baby so they can have an evening out, or they might decide they can't afford the expense or the anxiety and just stay home instead. The isolation caused by moving far from traditional sources of support is a cause of stress for today's parents. Parents are totally responsible for everything, creating an ambivalent situation in their home and family. In one sense, the nuclear family so created has a special sense of solidarity that separates this unit from the surrounding community; its members feel more in common with one another than with anyone outside the family. While this may produce some warm feelings, a cold feeling of isolation may also be present.

Part of this isolation is self-induced. American families, taught to value independence, feel that seeking help beyond the family circle is an admission of failure. Today, without the traditional backup system, this lingering myth further isolates families.

> Modern suburban housing is a visual depiction of this value gone askew; separation has been mistaken for independence. Each house stands apart, fortress like, surrounded by a moat of grass . . . insulating and isolating the American family (Galinsky and Hooks, 1977, p. 1).

Rearing children in a metropolitan setting offers its own problems for parents in addition to isolation. While the diversity of cultural, religious, and racial backgrounds offers richness and variety, it can also be a potential source of conflict as children are exposed to such a pluralistic society.

Family Size Decreasing

A family unit, according to the Census Bureau, is two or more persons. Current statistics indicate the average family has decreased in size over the years, from 4.76 in 1900, to 3.67 in 1940, to 2.81 in 1978 (Masnick and Bane, 1980). This decrease is due to fewer children under age eighteen in each household—from 1.34 in 1970 to 0.99 in 1984. There are numerous reasons for this: delayed childbearing with increased standards of education and career expectations; the economic burden of raising children in times of inflation with no corresponding asset of children's economic contribution to the family unit; changing attitudes about women's role in the home and workplace; improved methods of birth control and availability of legal abortion; increased expectations for family living standards; and the move from rural to urban environments. In practical terms this means that it is possible to become a parent without ever having touched a small baby or having had any share of responsibility in caring for younger brothers and sisters. The earlier form of a larger family offered its members a little more experience as they grew with other children.

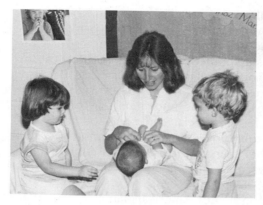

With decreased family size, many children have no experience with younger children.

Another factor contributing to the decrease in family size is the increasing absence of adults other than parents living in the home. In the 1920s, more than 50% of American households had at least one other adult living in the home—grandparents, aunts, or uncles (Croft, 1979). It was common for young families to begin married life living with their own parents. By the 1950s, this had decreased to 10%; today probably only 3–4% of homes have another adult. The Census Bureau notes the phenomenon of a marked increase in the number of persons living alone, both people older than fifty-five and people in their twenties. In the past, these would have been members of an extended family household. This implies that the smaller nuclear family is without the additional supportive resources of time, money, and companionship that other adults in the household could offer.

Increased Rate of Social Change

Parents in a relatively static society encounter less difficulty than those in a society where social change occurs rapidly and drastically, as in America for the past three decades or more. Margaret Mead poignantly pointed out what this means to parents:

> Today, nowhere in the world are there elders who know what the children know. In the past there were always some elders who knew more than any children in terms of their experience of having grown up within a cultural system. Today there are none. (p. 61) . . . Most parents are too uncertain to assert old dogmatisms. They do not know how to teach these children who are so different from what they themselves once were. (p. 66) . . . Now, in a world in which there are

no more knowledgeable others to whom parents can commit the children they themselves cannot teach, parents feel uncertain and helpless (Mead, 1970, p. 71).

There is a generation gap when parents play more complex roles in a world their own parents could not prepare them for, and try to help their own children face a world they cannot yet imagine. It is not a comfortable world where parents can just produce children like themselves, but another world where parents are unsure about their best move—a world of challenge and potential, but also of stress for today's fathers and mothers.

The rate of change is dizzying as upheaval occurs in every major institution in society. As Mead stated:

Events occurred that have irrevocably altered man's relationship to other men and to the natural world. The invention of the computer, the successful splitting of the atom and the invention of fission and fusion bombs, the discovery of the biochemistry of the living cell, the exploration of the planet's surface, the extreme acceleration of population growth and the recognition of the certainty of catastrophe if it continues, the breakdown in the organization of cities, the destruction of the natural environment, the linking up of all parts of the world by means of jet flights and television, the building of satellites and the first steps into space, the newly realized possibilities of unlimited energy and synthetic raw materials. . . . all of these have brought about a drastic, irreversible division between the generations (Mead, 1970, pp. 48-49).

Add to these global phenomena the major discontinuities in human relationships which have occurred in this country in the past twenty years as changing values, laws, and norms of behavior result in a different way of life. The Civil Rights movement, the Women's movement, the Vietnam war and the turmoil from groups opposing and supporting it, disillusionment with government leaders and with the education system, fears about drugs invading our lives and about what inflation and debt would mean to the future—an endless succession of new ideas and images bombards us. Closer to home, the structure and appearance of the family, the roles family members play, attitudes towards sexual activity, contraception, abortion—all are different now than they once were.

This means parents are unsure of themselves and worry about almost everything that touches their lives and their children's. The *General Mills American Family Report* found that parents worry about whether they're too permissive or expecting too much in a changed world; they worry about television and violence, about education, and most of all they worry because they are making decisions alone—they are reluctant to seek out advice from others (Yankelovich, 1977).

> They themselves grew up in the world of yesterday, a world
> that is now largely dead, if not buried, and this is the world
> they internalized; they rear their children in the world of
> today, a world they only partially understand and only partly
> accept; but they are rearing their children for the world of
> tomorrow, a world that nobody understands as yet (LeMasters
> and DeFrain, 1983, p. 231).

Child-Centered Society

More than one expert has pointed out how a child's role in the
family and in society has evolved over the centuries, particularly within
this century in America.

In earlier times, a child was measured harshly by the yardstick of
the adult world and restricted accordingly to fit into it.

> As early as 1820, maternal associations were formed in the
> larger cities that addressed the Calvinist idea of "breaking
> children's wills." Editorial space in newspapers and magazines
> occasionally was devoted to discussions of techniques that
> would result in children's submission to the authority of the
> mother (Bigner, 1985, p. 14).

In the late 1920s, parents were still given restrictive advice, as evidenced
by this excerpt from the writing of J. B. Watson: "There is a sensible
way of treating children. Treat them as though they were young adults.
. . . Never hug and kiss them, never let them sit in your lap" (Bigner,
1985, p. 17).

But in modern America, a child is the darling of his world. Whole
industries have sprung up to cater to his wishes—toys, children's television, breakfast cereals. The efforts of psychologists and other researchers are more directed towards telling parents what they should
and should not be doing to nurture their children. A large body of
the current state of the knowledge concerning child development now
exists and is available in forms both popular and technical (Gebay, 1981).
About one hundred books of advice to parents were published between
1965 and 1975. Parent education classes are available in almost every
community. Anyone who has taught a parent education class knows
that there are two frequently heard reactions from the parents involved:
one is to marvel that parents in earlier times did an acceptable job of
parenting without possessing this knowledge. "My mother raised five
kids and we all turned out pretty well and she never even *heard* of
Erikson or Piaget!" The other reaction is from the parent who concentrates, with guilt, on what he has already done or missed the chance
to do—"If only I'd known this five years ago." Whether the parent
decides on his own that he could have done a better job, or whether

the society around him does, the net result is that the parent comes out the "bad guy" in a culture that centers on the child.

Stress in Modern Living

Most parents today work forty hours or less a week. Modern technology and affluence have combined to provide a variety of labor-saving household appliances, therefore it would seem that the average American parent should have ample time for child-rearing.

How do we explain, then, the often-heard complaint that there is just not enough time for everything a parent has to do? Why is it that the most frequent problem of young mothers seeking medical care is exhaustion, and that some fathers spend less than an average of five minutes a day with their children?

In fact, although modern parents spend less time at the workplace and on household maintenance tasks, they have greater demands on their non-working time. There is increased pressure from society for individuals to fulfill self-centered goals. Finding and fulfilling oneself are acceptable and necessary activities which demand time. The highly organized community offers more choices and demands more participation for both adults and children. Those who point out the extremely

There are many demands on the time of modern parents.

busy life of the suburban child, moving from swimming lessons to Boy Scouts to doctors' appointments to activities organized with friends, fail to also mention that behind this busy child are parents who make all the arrangements and drive the child where he has to go! A parent who works full-time at a job has only begun to fill the expected responsibilities at the end of the working day. Chapter 2 will look more carefully at the various roles a parent plays; at this point it is important to realize that a contemporary parent's day is filled with more demands and expectations than there are hours.

The paradox about time is that while there seem to be more hours freed from working for a living, there seem to be fewer hours available to ease the hectic life of today's parent. Urie Bronfenbrenner stated this well in his statement reporting on the White House Conference on Children:

> In today's world parents find themselves at the mercy of a society which imposes pressures and priorities that allow neither time nor place for meaningful activities and relations between children and adults, which downgrade the role of parents and the functions of parenthood, and which prevent the parent from doing things he wants to do (Bronfenbrenner, 1974, p. 161).

Summary

It is interesting to note that condensing all aspects of contemporary life, there are benefits as well as negative influences for parents. The trend towards mobility that has meant enforced isolation for many American families, has at the same time brought an increased number of opportunities for employment, prosperity, and personal growth. The trend towards marital instability has brought stress and pain for many adults and children, to be sure; in many cases divorce has also brought the opportunity to find less discordant ways to live. It is not the purpose here to evaluate sociological trends; rather it is important only to stimulate the teachers who will be working closely with modern families to consider the influences in the world that impinge on those families and mold their shape and direction, sometimes without their agreement.

Modern families are beset by difficulties connected with new social patterns that have evolved from without and the psychological pressures from within that arise when individuals' life experiences differ from the model they have learned. Parenting is already a complex task and within the context of modern American culture, the challenge of parenting is heightened.

Student Activities for Further Study

1. Do your own mini-studies to consider the nature of social influences on contemporary families.

   a. Involve a group of parents of your acquaintance in an informal discussion. How do they see their lives as different from their parents' experiences as parents? Which of the aspects of cultural conditions discussed in the text do you find in their comments?

   b. With parents who are willing to discuss their lifestyles, try to learn family patterns of sex role participation—who shops, cleans, cooks, cares for the children, takes them to the doctor, to the barber?

   c. Ask several parents of your acquaintance where they were born and raised, and where their extended families now live. How do your findings agree with the text discussion of mobility?

   d. Note the family structure of all children in a preschool classroom. Figure out the percentage of traditional two-parent families, families with two working parents, single parents, stepparents, or other arrangements. What about family size? Are there additional family members in the household?

How do your findings compare with the text discussions of marital instability, changing roles of women, family size?

Review Questions

1. Define family.
2. Describe two characteristics of a family.
3. List seven characteristics of American life that influence the nature of modern families.

References and Related Readings

Bigner, Jerry J. *Parent-Child Relations: An Introduction to Parenting.* Second Edition. New York: Macmillan Publishing Co., 1985.

Bronfenbrenner, Urie. "The Roots of Alienation." *Raising Children in Modern America: Problems and Prospective Solutions.* Ed. Nathan B. Talbot. Boston: Little, Brown and Co., 1974.

———. "The Three Worlds of Childhood." *Principal 5* (1985): 7-11.

Croft, Doreen J. *Parents and Teachers: A Resource Book for Home, School and Community Relations.* Belmont, Calif: Wadsworth Publ. Co. Inc., 1979.

Eiduson, B. "Looking At Children in Emergent Family Styles." *Children Today* 3.4 (1974): 2-6.

Eisenberg, L. "Caring for Children and Working: Dilemmas of Contemporary Womanhood." *Pediatrics* 56 (1975): 24-28.

Ericksen, J., W. Yancey and E. Ericksen. "The Division of Family Roles." *Journal of Marriage and the Family* 41 (1979): 301-313.

Fantini, Mario D. and Rene Cardenas, eds. *Parenting in a Multicultural Society*. New York: Longman, Inc., 1980.

Galinsky, Ellen and William Hooks. *The New Extended Family: Day Care That Works*. Boston: Houghton Mifflin Co., 1977.

Geboy, Michael. "Who is Listening to the Experts? The Use of Child-Care Materials by Parents." *Family Relations* 30 (1981): 205-10.

Gross, Dorothy W. "Improving the Quality of Family Life." *Childhood Education* 57.2 (1977): 51-56.

Hoffman, L. "The Effects of Maternal Employment on the Child—A Review of the Research." *Developmental Psychology* 10.2 (1974): 204-28.

Howe, Louise Kapp. *The Future of the Family*. New York: Simon and Schuster, 1972.

Lamb, Michael, E, ed. *The Role of the Father in Child Development*. 2nd ed. New York: John Wiley and Sons, 1981.

————. ed. *Non-Traditional Families: Parenting and Child Development*. Hillsdale, New Jersey: Lawrence Erlbaum Assoc. Pubs., 1982.

Lein, Laura. *Families Without Villains: American Families in an Era of Change*. Lexington, Mass.: Lexington Books D.C. Heath and Co., 1984.

LeMasters, E.E. and John DeFrain. *Parents in Contemporary America: A Sympathetic View*. 4th ed. Homewood, Illinois: The Dorsey Press, 1983.

Malmaud, Roslyn K. *Work and Marriage: The Two-Profession Couple*. Ann Arbor, Michigan: UMI Research Press, 1984.

"Married Couples, Singles Discover Poverty in '80's." *Charlotte Observer,* January 19, 1986.

Mead, Margaret. *Culture and Commitment: A Study of the Generation Gap*. Garden City, N.Y.: Doubleday and Co. Inc., 1970.

Norton, Arthur J. and Paul C. Glick. "Changes in American Family Life." *Children Today* 5.3 (1976): 2-4, 44.

"The Parent Gap." *Newsweek* Sept. 22 (1975): 48-56.

Rosin, Mark. "The Family of the Future." *Parents* 57.3 (1982): 66-68.

Rover, David and Francois Polifroni. *The "Leave it to Beaver" Syndrome*. Presentation at NAEYC National Conference, New Orleans, 1985.

Russell, Graeme. *The Changing Role of Fathers*. London and New York: University of Queensland Press, 1983.

Seidenberg, Robert. "Redefining 'His' and 'Hers': A Psychiatrist Speaks on Changing Family Roles." *Parenting*. R. Markum, ed. Washington, D.C.: Assoc. for Childhood Education International, 1973.

Shorter, Edward. *The Making of the Modern Family*. New York: Basic Books, 1975.

Solnit, A.J. "Changing Perspectives About Children and their Families." *Children Today* 5.3 (1976): 3-8.

"The Super Woman Squeeze." *Time,* May 19 (1980): 73.

Talbot, Nathan B., ed. *Raising Children in Modern America: Problems and Prospective Solutions.* Boston: Little, Brown and Co., 1974.

"Workplace out of Step with Modern Family, Study Says." *Charlotte Observer,* Jan. 19, 1986.

Yankelovich, Skelly and White, Inc. *Raising Children in a Changing Society: The General Mills American Family Report.* Minneapolis: General Mills Consumer Center, 1977.

Yarrow, Leah. "Fathers Speak Out." *Parents* 60:9 (1985): 91-100.

Chapter 2 **Parenting**

In our complex modern world adults who become parents have to adjust to the various roles they are called upon to play as parents.

Objectives

After studying this chapter, the student will be able to

1. discuss seven roles that parents play and the implications for teachers
2. describe seven emotional responses of parents and the implications for teachers

Teachers working with families may become frustrated by the parents' apparent inability to focus their attention fully on matters regarding the children. Teachers may fail to remember that parenting involves many complex behaviors and roles.

Consider the following situation; does this teacher sound at all familiar?

Jane Briscoe is becoming impatient. As she describes it to her director, "These parents, I don't get it. I'm trying to take time to talk with them, and that's tough, believe me, with everything else I've got to do. But some of them just don't seem interested. Mrs. Lawrence, the other day, kept looking at the clock when I was talking. And Mary Howard this morning—she looked as if she wasn't even listening to me. I've tried, but if they don't care about their own kids, what am I supposed to do?"

The director, Mrs. Forbes, is sympathetic. She knows Jane's frustration is born partly from her concern for the children, as well as from the human reaction of wanting response when initiating communication. But she realizes also that Jane is seeing only one perspective and needs to remind herself of how life may seem from the parent's point of view, in order to be able to increase both her compassion and effectiveness. A teacher who assumes parents aren't interested decreases her effort; a teacher who recognizes the multiple pulls on the time and attention of a parent keeps trying.

"I know that's frustrating for you, Jane, when you're trying hard. There's no one easy answer, I'm sure. Sometimes I try to imagine what life must be like for some of our parents, all the things that could be on their minds when they walk in here. There's your Mrs. Lawrence—all the concerns of twenty-eight third graders at her this Monday morning, as well as her own two. And I happen to know his two boys visited this past weekend and that always makes it difficult—both crowded and hectic. And she's been looking tired now that her pregnancy's further along. Must be a lot to think about, trying to get both sets of children used to the idea of a new baby. Her husband works some long hours too—must be hard to find time to relax together, let alone finish up all the chores in that new house."

Jane looked very thoughtful. "You're right, you know. And I guess if I think about it, I can figure out some things that might keep Mary Howard's attention from being completely on me. It's exam time at the high school, and I know she's trying to do well in case she decides to go on to college. And she is still a high school kid, mother or not—I sure remember the million and one problems my friends and I had, from figuring out how to get enough money to buy the latest fashion to how to get along with our parents. It must really be hard for her to be living with her parents, as an adolescent still, as well as a young mother who needs their help in looking after her own child. There just wouldn't be room for rebellion, would there? I wonder if she gets excluded at school because of her baby. Keeping the baby must have been a big decision for her to make, and she's still so unsure of what's ahead for her."

Jane broke off and smiled ruefully. "I guess I've been spending too much time being annoyed with the parents, and too little trying to get inside their skin and see life from their perspective. Thanks, Mrs. Forbes."

Mrs. Forbes smiled as Jane went out, thinking that the young teacher would be all right; she had made the first big step in working effectively with parents.

She had begun to try to understand the experience of parenting, including the many roles a parent plays and the emotional responses of parenting.

Roles Parents Play

Although the teacher was thinking about two mothers, it should be noted that changes in social attitudes have encouraged people to think of androgynous adult roles—those that are shared by men and women and have similar functions. Recognizing that fathers and mothers may relate and interact differently with their children because of the differences in their nature and past experiences, many parents no longer separate the aspects of parenting and family living into male and female tasks. The text, following that model, will examine these roles and briefly consider the implications for teachers.

The Parent as Nurturer

The nurturing role encompasses more than the narrow interpretation of the routine care that nurtures physical development. It includes the parent's primary role of providing a psychological environment of warm emotional interaction in which the child can thrive.

For years, such nurturance has been equated with "mothering." Most early research concerning effects of parenting on personality development centered on characteristics due to the absence of normal mothering experiences or maternal deprivation. Rene Spitz (1945) studied the development of infants cared for in a foundling home with an adult-child ratio of one to eight, and those cared for by their own mothers in a prison nursery. The findings concluded that lack of attention and handling in the foundling home produced severe physical symptoms of depression.

John Bowlby (1952) concluded that all aspects of a child's development are usually retarded when children are deprived of maternal care.

Harlow's research with rhesus monkeys (1958) studied the effects of separating infant monkeys from their mothers following birth. He concluded that the absence of direct physical contact produced the

An important parenting role is to provide warm emotional nurturing.

disturbed physical and social behavioral patterns that were evident after those monkeys had grown up. His later experiments with artificial mothers stressed the importance of "contact comfort" in soft, comfortable, tactile sensations, as opposed to merely providing feeding.

Ainsworth's studies of attachment (1973), defined as the strong, affectional, mutual tie that is formed in the period following birth and endures over time, identified a number of factors that promote attachment between mother and child, by bringing the infant into close physical contact with the mother.

Little research was done on fathering until the last fifteen years or so. In fact, earlier social scientists felt impelled to explain the necessity for adding the father role to the family, implying that providing physical and economic protection was a lesser function (Bigner, 1985). Recent research indicates that earlier myths about the nature of fathering are not presently true, if they ever were.

> The consensus of research findings is that fathers do not differ significantly from mothers in being interested in infants and children, they become involved with their offspring if encouraged to do so, they are as nurturant as mothers towards children, and they may engage less frequently in active caregiving but are competent in carrying out those activities that they do perform (Bigner, 1985, p. 77).

Fathers may be as nurturant as mothers towards children.

Beginning in the late 1960s, practices related to pregnancy and childbirth permitted and encouraged fathers to become more involved at the beginning. This is a significant phenomenon in changing fathers' perceptions of their own role in the family. Several research studies conclude that the father's participation at the time of birth helps the mother assume her role; the birth itself may be a strong stimulus for nurturant behaviors from both fathers and mothers, and for reshaping attitudes (Bigner, 1985).

Most findings concur that the parenting role most crucial for a child's optimum development is the nurturing role. This is probably one of the most demanding roles a parent plays, for this includes the myriad prompt responses to an infant's needs at any hour of the day or night during the long period of infant helplessness, and the frequent setting aside of adult needs in favor of the child's requirements and demands.

The need for nurturing in its various forms does not diminish as young children become older. Parents are still the people children look to for comfort, security, and approval. Parents with several children may have differing demands placed on them at the same time—the infant crying to be picked up, the preschooler fearful of being left, the school-aged child needing comfort after an encounter with peers. It is no wonder that many parents feel "burned out" from time to time, so depleted by filling the nurturing needs of their children they have little time or energy to have some of their own needs met.

Implications for the Teacher

- Teachers can help by understanding the importance of the parent's nurturing role, and the many demands that places on the parent.
- Teachers can supplement the nurturing role without violating the parent-child bond.

The Parent in Adult Relationships

Before an individual becomes a parent, there is first a relationship with another adult. One of the demands on a parent is to foster the continuance of that relationship, or another that has perhaps replaced the original relationship.

One of the long standing-myths surrounding parenthood is that children give meaning to a marriage, improve the relationship between a couple, can help a troubled relationship, and actually prevent divorce.

In fact, the addition of parenthood roles to a marriage relationship introduces a time of abrupt transition. One researcher reported this as a time of extensive or severe crisis (LeMasters and DeFrain, 1983), though others suggest a crisis of lesser proportions (Rossi, 1968; Russell, 1974). The severity of the crisis may depend on the degree of a couple's preparation for parenthood and marriage, the degree of commitment to the parenthood role, and patterns of communication (LeMasters and DeFrain, 1983). Whether the transition is a time of severe crisis or not, a couple is unquestionably going to have to reorganize their relationship and interactions; changes will occur in a marriage with an altered lifestyle and the addition of new role images and behaviors associated with parenthood.

These changes are linked to the reported trend of a decrease in marital satisfaction. Studies report a U-shaped pattern in the degree of satisfaction, declining from after the birth of a child, as children grow older, then gradually increasing as children are raised and begin to lead independent lives (Rollins and Feldman, 1970; Rollins and Cannon, 1974; Ryder, 1973); other studies show only a decline in satisfaction with no later recovery (Burr, 1970; Bradburn and Coplovitz, 1965). One reason offered for this decline in satisfaction is role strain (Burr, 1973). This occurs when (1) there are incompatible expectations for a person holding several roles at the same time—recall our earlier discussion of the Super Woman, (2) the demands of one social role are in conflict simultaneously with those of another social role—imagine a candlelit dinner disrupted by the baby's cries, and (3) when strong demands for performance are placed on all social roles—that Super Woman image again! It is difficult

The demands of children may interfere with adults being able to pay close attention to adult relationships.

for spouses to pay close attention to the needs of their adult relationship while caring for the needs of their developing children.

All of these support the idea that using children as a means to improve a marriage is truly a myth. The parent as a nurturer of children may discover that the parent as an adult in a relationship may neglect and be neglected. In fact, the probability of divorce is doubled when couples have children during their first year of marriage; evidently many couples are too unsettled to face parenthood before they can work out some of the marital behaviors. However, if children do not improve a marriage, their presence may serve to cement it together a little longer. The median duration of marriages among childless couples before divorce is about four years; couples with several children stay together about fourteen years (Bigner, 1985). While there is statistical evidence that children stabilize marriages, this is not the same as improving them. Some married couples have their worst disagreements over their actions as parents!

Parents are people first, and there is evidence that those who are fulfilled and contented as individuals are better able to function effectively as parents than those who are disappointed in their personal lives (Gram, cited in Swick and Duff, 1978). It is evident that the support one parent gives to the other facilitates the development of the parenting role as well as optimizing conditions for nurturing the child. Although the primary adult relationship may be with a marriage partner, the adult's life may be criss-crossed with a network of adult relationships—parents, former spouses. The relationship with one's child is an extremely important relationship, but it begins out of the context of relationships with other adults.

Implications for the Teacher

- Teachers can convey encouragement and approval of parents' efforts to enhance their marriage, to engage in hobbies, to pursue personal social enrichment.

The Parent as an Individual

Americans have come to value the development of the individual person. We are now aware that this personal development is a lifelong process. (See Erik Erikson's eight ages of man, or the writings of Gail Sheehy, Daniel Levinson, or Roger L. Gould.) Parents concerned with nurturing their children's development are also encountering growth in their own lives.

From the turbulent analysis of social values in the 60s, through the more introspective consideration of personal values and life-styles in the 70s, parents expect their lives to continue to develop and change.

Many young parents are preoccupied with issues of identity. Erikson speaks of this as the fifth age, beginning in adolescence. With the prolonging of education and financial dependence on parents, and with the confusing multiplicity of roles, careers, and life-styles to select from, many identity issues are still being actively worked on in young adulthood. One measure of this may be the postponing of marriage, perhaps seen as an entry step into the adult world, a sign that a young person has settled some issues and is ready to embark on adult life. [From 1970 to 1982, the proportion of females in the age range of twenty to twenty-four who had never married rose from 36% to 53%, of males from 55% to 72% (Chulin, 1980).] The events of marriage and parenthood cause many young parents to reexamine identity issues as they take on two roles symbolic of adult life. It is not just real-life events that have to be assimilated into an individual's self-concept, but also expectations and attitudes from within an individual and from society without, that set the standards used to measure the new view of self. There are several problems here. One is that most of today's parents grew up with daily facts of life and social role expectations that are radically different from their own presently. It is difficult to let go of those early perceptions of the way life is supposed to be. When a woman's own mother was always waiting for her in the kitchen after school and had dinner cooked when her father came home from work at six o'clock, it is difficult for her to have to call her daughter daily, knowing her child has gone home to an empty house and will be alone for another two hours, sometimes beginning the supper preparations until her divorced mother comes home from work. Somehow, despite the changed circumstances, perceptions of what should be happening have not. Many parents are struggling with feeling less than successful at their patterns of life.

Many mothers find their self-esteem is being attacked, no matter whether they have chosen to fill the traditional role of homemaker or have joined the majority of mothers working outside the home. Despite the lip-service frequently given to the importance of the homemaker, the Dictionary of Occupational Titles of the Department of Labor which ranks 22,000 occupations according to the skills they require, places homemaker at the lowest possible level! Their working counterparts do not fare much better, as the media continue to indict working mothers subtly for increasing family stress now that they have added on to their traditional roles. [Results of most studies related to maternal employment are inconsistent and conflicting, primarily because of the difficulty of controlling variables (Galinsky, 1986). However, it is clear that if a mother is happy at her chosen work, in the home or out, she will do a better job of mothering (Thomson, 1980; Moore, 1978).]

A father's task of assimilating his new role into his identity is no easier. Although more recently he is gaining attention as part of the family, for many years he has been considered nonessential to the functioning of the family. Out of 444 research papers on the family presented between 1963 and 1968, eleven were devoted to data related to fathers (Levine, 1976).

**Contemporary fathers have new roles
to fit into their identities.**

The issues of identity are never finally closed. As life circumstances change, a reexamination of roles and relationships and the resulting implications for an individual is necessary. A person's identity as a parent is not fixed either. As children move through successive stages of development, parents are presented with new challenges. Skills and behaviors that served well with an infant, for example, must be abandoned in favor of new strategies to live compatibly with a toddler. Parents' feelings of competence may fluctuate as their ability to adapt with the changing child fluctuates.

The stage in the life cycle where parenting usually occurs is a time of concern with being productive. Most adults find their means to this goal in one or both of the two channels of parenting and work; the two are often in competition with each other.

Implications for the Teacher

- Parents need additional support from teachers as they develop parenting skills to match the changing needs of their developing children.
- Recognition of their skills and positive feedback helps parents develop a positive sense of themselves as parents.
- Teachers need to treat parents as individuals as well as parents, and to be prepared to work with parents of many different ages and stages of personal identity.

The Parent as Worker

About half of mothers with children under age six were employed outside the home in 1984; over 65% of mothers of school-age children were working. This was an increase of more than 10% over the previous decade, with the sharpest increase being for married women in two parent families with children under age six. There are several reasons for this increase in the number of working mothers: increased costs in rearing children and living expenses; an expanded economy with the creation of new job opportunities; earlier completion of families so that women are younger when their children are in school; reduced amount of time needed for housework; better education of women; expectations of a better life-style; and changes in basic attitudes towards roles, with new social perspectives (Auerbach-Fink, 1977).

Despite the fact that a majority of mothers are working outside the home along with fathers, much in our society indicates we are still operating on two related assumptions—that it is the natural role of men to work as providers and that it is equally natural for women to take care of children. One measure of this is that there are no national statistics kept on the number of working fathers, though careful note is made of the number of working mothers. With similar bias, studies are done on how mothers' working affects children; no such research is done when fathers work (Moore, 1978). While such attitudes may be annoying to many women in the workplace, their effect is more than mere bother; the attitudes frequently translate into equally outmoded working hours and conditions that are neither helpful nor supportive to a parent both working and carrying on home responsibilities.

The majority of these parents have an inflexible working schedule of forty hours or so per week. Only about 7.6 million employees have flex-time schedules, according to Department of Labor statistics. The option of job-sharing, eminently suited to many parents who would like to decrease the demands of their working life, is still only available to a handful. A tiny fraction of adults are able to work from their homes. But many parents are in jobs that require travel away from home. Worse yet, many American workers are asked to change their jobs and move each year, disrupting family arrangements. The average maternity leave with pay for American women is six weeks; contrast this policy with the more generous six months offered in most European countries (Curtis, 1976). Only 10% of American companies offer fathers an unpaid paternity leave. Some European countries, such as Sweden and Denmark, do offer paternity leave.

What do these employment facts mean to parents? In practical terms, parents as workers spend the majority of their waking hours going to or from work, at work, or tired from working. Their young children, who are likely to be awake during these same hours, are of necessity cared for by someone else during the parents' work day. Their older school-age children are probably in school during many of the same hours, but before and after school, the long vacations and other days off, all necessitate making arrangements for child care. There are numerous special events which parents will either have trouble fitting in or miss—the kindergarten field trip, the fifth grade band concert, the mothers' breakfast at the preschool. Employers know that they can expect an increased absentee rate for mothers of preschoolers during the winter months when colds and other infections run rampant. Parents who feel they cannot spare another day off are faced with the dilemma of leaving a sick child at school (pretending the child isn't really sick, as most centers will not accept sick children) or facing the employer's wrath. Pulled between the displeasure of the employer and the caregiver, and the needs and schedule of the child, parents may feel resentful, exhausted, guilty, and inadequate to all the tasks.

No matter what changes have occurred in the relationship of men and women and in their child-rearing participation, it is still true that in most families the "psychological" parent—the one who takes primary responsibility for the children's well-being—is the mother. This means that most women never leave for work with a clear sense of division between home and office; the concerns of home and family remain with them through the working day, and when working mothers return home they have less free time than their husbands (Booth, 1977; Backett, 1982).

> Only women who have tried to cope with both roles—mother and working woman—can understand the constant sensation of tension and fragmentation, the overwhelming complexity of living in constant uncertainty. And the sense of responsibility is enormous (Kamerman, 1980, p. 101).

No wonder it is more common to speak of stress in working mothers than in working fathers, though many women keep their stress a private matter, rather than let anyone think they are not equal to these new tasks (Curtis, 1976). Employers who see the worker is more than that one-dimensional aspect and provide for family needs in some measure are often rewarded by increased productivity and loyalty from workers relieved of some of their dilemma. Companies that provide on-site day care have found there is less absenteeism and employees stay longer in their jobs (Barud et al., 1983). Generally, American parents find that work frequently conflicts with parenting demands and they must deal with the life shaped by their work schedule. In the work world, there are institutional constraints on their ability to change and internal doubts about their right to change.

Implications for the Teacher

- Community and business attempts to alleviate stress for working parents by providing care for sick children or personnel policies which support families' attempts to care responsibly for their children need teacher support.

- Teachers can try to schedule events for parents at times that may best fit into their working schedule—conferences during after-work hours, programs during lunch hour, etc.

The Parent as Consumer

The median income of a two-working-parent family in 1981 was $29,250. At this same time, a family where the wife did not work had a median income of $20,330. This offered a buying power of 3% less than the buying power of one- and two-working-parent families in 1971, since consumer prices rose nearly 125% during the decade. Economic survival with the multiple material demands of the 1980s has been a major factor in establishing the two-working-parent family structure.

A good deal of the family income is devoted to the rearing of children. Children at one time were considered to be an economic asset—more available workers in a rural, self-sufficient family—they must now be considered economic liabilities. Recent statistics figure the average cost of raising a child born in 1980 from birth to eighteen years of age to be a mind-boggling $250,000, and this figure does not even include a college education! [The estimates include the basic provisions for basics of food, shelter, clothing, transportation, and medical care at around $3,400–3,800 per year plus a 10% annual inflation rate and the loss of the mother's income if she does not work outside the home during the child's growing years (Tilly, 1980).]

When both parents are working outside the home, a large chunk of income goes to the purchase of child care. The average figure paid by parents of infants for full-time care in a center is $100 a week, according to the Day Care Council of America, and $50 for the care of older preschoolers. A sitter would cost $130 per week, reckoned at minimum wage; a family day-care home averages $40 per week (Dreskin, 1983). In some cases, mothers find that nearly the total amount of their additional family income is spent on child care plus the purchases necessitated by employment—additional clothing, transportation, and food away from home. In this case, continuing employment is probably either for maintaining career continuity or for the mother's feelings regarding personal fulfillment.

It is no wonder that many parents feel they are on a financial treadmill. A major concern stated by most parents is money worries; a leader in the causes of marital friction is "arguing about money" (Yankelovich, 1977). The parent in the role of consumer is stretched thin; when the economic health of the nation is shaky so that many parents lose jobs temporarily or permanently as in the early 80s, the family may be thrown into a crisis.

Implication for the Teacher

- Since child care is an expensive item in the average family budget, parents often feel pressed to be sure they are receiving their money's worth. This may help the teacher understand the demands they make for nutritious foods and clean diapers, and the annoyance they express for missing mittens or damaged clothing. Teachers need to be sympathetic to the financial pressures on parents and as careful with clothing, etc. as possible.

The Parent as Community Member

With the increasing complexity of modern life, an increasing number of family functions have been taken over by community institutions and organizations: education by the school system; recreation and entertainment by the "Y" and other clubs, as well as the church, which has often expanded its purely religious function. There are as many organizations as there are interests in any given community. The community itself has become more highly structured as groups of people coming together have dictated more rules, legislation, and decision-making, both public and private. But institutions and organizations do not run themselves; there are many demands on community members for their time as volunteers, for their money and other supportive efforts. The parent is asked to support the organizations which benefit his children as well as himself. It would not be unusual to find a week where parents are asked to bake cupcakes for the PTA carnival, spend an hour manning a booth at the carnival, driving children to and from the church junior choir practice, assisting children in magazine sales to aid the efforts of the "Y" to get new uniforms for the basketball team, coaching the team, making a list of telephone calls to remind others of a local environmental group meeting, and soliciting funds door-to-door on behalf of a local branch of a national charity—as well as turning down several requests to participate in similar ways for other organizations. The broader the age range of the children, the broader and more fragmenting are the demands on parents. For most parents today, there is constant tension between outside demands on time and energy, and the amount available for personal and family needs.

Implications for the Teacher

- Any requests for parent participation add another thing to make time for. Teachers must realize this and be very sure the idea is worth what it will cost the parent in time and pressure.
- Teachers must guard against assuming that parents are too busy to become involved and so never make the effort or invitation. Parents have the right to make the decisions about how they spend their time, not have these decisions made for them arbitrarily.

The Parent as Educator

Perhaps the role for which parents feel most unprepared is the role of educator, used here in the sense of guiding and stimulating the child's development and teaching the skills and knowledge that children will need to eventually become effective adults in society. As previously mentioned, other institutions have taken over many of the family's educative functions, so that the primary task of parents is the socialization of their children (Keniston, 1977).

There are primarily two reasons why education towards socialization is such a difficult task for parents. The first was alluded to in Chapter 1. In the rapidly changing world of today, it is difficult for a parent to be sure what life will be like, even in the very near future. The childhood experiences of today's parents were quite different from what they see their children experiencing; their memories of what their own parents did will probably not serve them well in their present situations.

The second reason why parents often find the role of educating their own children to be overwhelming is that the only on- or off-the-job training most receive is through having been parented themselves. Children learn through living with parents most of the basic information they will ever get for their future role as parents. Adults tend to parent as they were parented and this pattern will likely be inadequate. A high percentage of children who received abuse from their parents become abusive parents themselves (Justice and Duncan, 1975). Studies indicate that the characteristics, values, beliefs, and most importantly, the practices of one's own parents have the greatest influence on one's child-rearing (Stoltz, 1967).

It seems ironic that our society has become skillful at imparting technical knowledge and education to prepare workers for a career, but has so far made little headway in similarly devising methods to prepare young people for the tasks in parenthood. Most parenting skills are learned by trial and error on the job, giving rise to the not-so-funny old joke about parents wanting to trade in their first-born, since that was the one they'd learned on! No wonder many parents find the enormous task of parenthood without preparation overwhelming.

Parents who do seek training (from Lamaze on) often feel pressure to become "text-book" parents, fearing that they will make mistakes or not be able to follow the experts' instructions. This can be overwhelming as well.

Implications for the Teacher

- Parents are often eager to talk with other parents, to share experiences and concerns, to discover they are not alone in their anxieties, to be supported by others who can identify with their position.

Parents are often eager to talk to other parents.

- Parents need all the information, help, and emotional support they can get as they work towards competence in their parental roles.

Parenthood as an Emotional Experience

People arrive at parenthood via a number of routes. For some, it is a carefully thought out and planned venture, an anticipated and joyful happening. For others, it is the unthought-of consequence in an adult relationship, an event possibly dreaded and resented.

Having children means very different things to different people. Hoffman and Hoffman suggest nine possible motivations at work when people decide to become parents or adjust to the concept after the fact.

1. Validation of adult status and social identity
2. Expansion of self—a continuance of the family
3. Achievement of moral values—contributing something or sacrificing in parenthood
4. Increasing sources of affection and loving ties
5. Stimulation, novelty, fun
6. Achievement, competence, creativity
7. Power and influence over another
8. Social comparison and competition
9. Economic utility (Hoffman and Hoffman, 1973).

LeMasters points out that some of our cherished beliefs, including some ideas from this list of motivations, are myths that are part of the mystique surrounding parenthood. Raising children is not always fun, nor are all children cute or necessarily appreciative and loving towards their parents all the time (LeMasters and DeFrain, 1983). All married couples should not necessarily have children, nor are all childless married couples unhappy. [Despite the fact that many adults today consider having children to be an option—which increasing numbers are choosing not to exercise—there is still considerable pressure on women particularly to consider that parenthood is an essential experience of adult life (Chulin, 1980). The increasing number of women who give birth to their first child when approaching forty is testimony to the inner pressure of what has been called the "biological clock," as well as cultural attitudes.]

So some of the assumptions people make when deciding to become parents are removed from the reality they will discover.

No matter what their motivation was to have children, there are common realities for all parents.

Irrevocability

There is no turning back. From the time of birth on, parents discover that the responsibility for the care and support of this human being will be entirely theirs for a period of approximately twenty years

The responsibilities of parenthood are there twenty-four hours a day.

or longer. Even when other institutions are available to share the task, as in education, the ultimate responsibility rests with the parents. This responsibility may be willingly and joyfully undertaken, but it is always there, twenty-four hours a day, seven days a week, constantly to be reckoned with. As one writer put it, "We can have ex-spouses and ex-jobs, but not ex-children" (Rossi, 1968, p. 32). This is a staggering thought for a parent who, when faced with the reality of the developing child's needs, may feel unequal to the task. However, it's too late—the child is here and the parenting must go on. But the feeling of total responsibility often causes parents to worry considerably about matters both large and small.

Implications for the Teacher

- Indicate your understanding and empathy for the parent's position. Many parents feel greatly burdened by the demands and responsibilities of parenthood and alone in their concerns. They will respond positively to someone who cares about their position, someone with whom they can talk freely.
- Help parents by indicating your willingness to support them and their children.

Restriction, Isolation, and Fatigue

One of the more dramatic changes in becoming a parent is the near total restriction on activity that comes with caring for a totally dependent being. Instead of acting spontaneously, a parent must make elaborate plans to leave the child even briefly. (There are periods in the child's development when it is difficult to find time to go into the bathroom alone.)

Along with this restriction in activity comes the isolation in which many parents live. Separated from extended family and by the physical housing of the modern city, hampered by the difficulty of finding free time for social arrangements, further restricted by the expenses of the child, and psychologically isolated in coming to grips with the new situation and emotions, many parents feel alone in their parenthood. Many parents are reluctant to admit they need help, since becoming a parent is supposed to be a measure of adult status.

Most young parents, especially mothers, complain of fatigue. From early morning until late at night they are responding to the needs of others—children, spouse, employer, and as many more as can be squeezed into the schedule. When mothers are asked what they want most, the common response is "time by myself." For most, it is an impossible dream.

Implications for the Teacher

- Take care not to make it seem as if you are adding still more heavy demands on the parent; parents will protect themselves and avoid such teachers.
- Realize that parents do not have excess time to waste. Activities they are involved in need to be both meaningful and streamlined.

Non-Instinctual Love

Despite the fantasies promoted by magazine advertisements and movies, many parents do not always feel love for their child. Humans operate beyond the level of instinct and much parenting behavior and response, including love, comes after time, experience, and learning. Many parents feel ambivalent about their children some of the time, with feelings ranging from exasperation to resentment, with anger occasionally overshadowing feelings of love.

Because parents labor to some extent under the delusions of the "perfect parent," many do not consciously admit these less than positive feelings about their child to themselves or anyone else, and are left concerned about their "unnaturalness," and perhaps a little guilty.

Implications for Teachers

- Offer opportunities for parents to meet comfortably with other parents. This may help them discover common experiences, so they can feel more accepting of personal responses.
- Become involved in the subtle education of parents to try to remove some of the myths and images under which many parents labor.
- Comment on the positive things you see parents doing with their children.

Guilt

It is astonishing how frequently today's parents refer to the emotion of guilt. There are many factors that precipitate this feeling: the ideal parent imaged in the various media; the changes in life-styles and role behaviors which mean that many parents live quite differently than their parents did; the prevalent feeling that parents should produce children who will do better than they have done; the social attitude that "there are no bad children, only bad parents" (LeMasters and DeFrain, 1983).

The parent most susceptible to guilt is the mother, probably because she realizes society views her as the most powerful parent. It does not matter whether she has chosen to work outside the home, or not: both employed and stay-at-home mothers are equally susceptible. The working mother may feel guilt because she is breaking a known pattern and is aware of the mixed reviews coming in from researchers and society (Howrigan, 1973). She may feel badly leaving a crying child with a substitute caregiver, being separated from her child for long hours, and even worse when she is short-tempered with a tired child at the end of her own exhausting day. Probably a good portion of the Super Mom phenomenon is fed by this guilt, pushing her to make sure her child misses no right or privilege. The degree of guilt experienced by a working mother is closely related to how hard it was to make the decision to work; to what extent she sees her parenting role as important; how supportive are the attitudes of husbands and peers; and the extent to which she feels that her performance as mother is ineffective (Lewis, 1979).

The mother who is at home with her child is not immune from exhaustion or frustration and less-than-perfect maternal behavior. She may feel she is depriving her child of the luxuries an extra income could offer, to say nothing of the worry that her child may become too dependent on her, or the feeling that society is pressuring her to be more than "just a housewife." Against the image of the ideal parent, which is impossible to match in reality, the poor parent does not stand a chance, but is left with the guilt that comes from not measuring up.

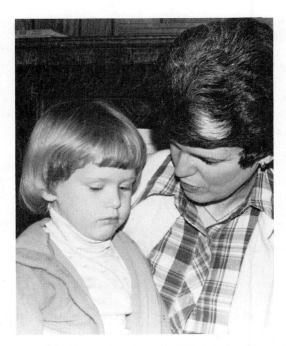

It is hard for a parent to leave a crying child.

Implications for the Teacher

- Remember that guilt may lie below the surface in many conversations and encounters with parents. Such an awareness helps the teacher consciously weigh actions and words ensuring that nothing on the teacher's part increases any sense of inadequacy that parents may feel.

- Affirm the child and parent with small appreciative comments as often as possible, since teachers may sometimes <u>have</u> to increase the guilt load by sharing something about the child.

Satisfaction

Despite the obvious negative aspects of total responsibility and restriction, most parents find much to rejoice in. There is great satisfaction in watching children grow and develop, especially when one has played a large part in the nurturance of that growth. For many parents, the achievements and characteristics of their children give feedback to be incorporated into the parents' own self-esteem; to some extent, the degree to which the child does well (or badly) is a reflection of how well the parents feel they are doing. Most parents feel no one else can know their child as well as they do and care for him/her quite as well.

Another source of parental satisfaction is the affectionate mutual attachment that forms between adult and child (Russell, 1974). It is a very positive feeling to know that you are the most important person in the world to the other. And because it is so important, many parents fear any event or person which could be conceived of as disruptive to that relationship. Many parents experience jealousy or resentment when others become important in the loved child's life, although frequently these emotions are disguised and not recognized by the parent.

Implications for the Teacher

- Respect the closeness of the parent-child bond. Ensure that classroom attitudes and practices nurture and preserve attachment.

- Be aware that jealousy may lie behind some of your encounters with parents so that no actions on your part increase these feelings.

- Present comments in ways that avoid personal evaluation and reaction. Parents frequently react defensively if they feel their child (and therefore their parenting skills) is criticized.

- Offer tangible and reassuring evidence that the child is cared for adequately by the supplemental caregiver—and at the same time, reassurance that the child still needs the parent!

It is sometimes hard not to feel jealousy when others become important in the child's life.

Uncertainty

Each child has a unique response to the world; no matter how well-read a parent is on child development and parenting skills, it is often a different matter putting principles into practice in specific situations with a specific child! As children change, parents must also, so that parenting techniques that worked well at one point must be discarded and new ones learned. Usually a parent does not feel totally confident that he is performing the task correctly. With the changes within the family and the surrounding culture, (discussed earlier in Chapters 1 and 2) today's parents are doing the job without role models, clear directions, or firm approval from society. No wonder most parents often feel unsure of the situation.

Implications for the Teacher

- Parents need someone who understands the uncertainties involved in the situation. They do not need someone who believes there is only one right answer in child-rearing or who conveys the impression that she is totally certain of her own actions at all times.

- Conveying the impression of looking for answers together is a helpful teacher response.

Real Concern for Children

However it may appear to an outsider, most parents do learn to love and care for their children. They want the best for them, whether it concerns physical care, education, or future plans.

Implications for the Teacher

- Understand that parents genuinely do care and are concerned for their children. Even when parent behavior strikes you as indifferent or uncaring, believe that caring exists. Many factors may cause behaviors that convey negative impressions. (Some of these will be discussed in Chapter 6 and Chapter 15.)

Summary

In the area of interpersonal relationships and communications, most breakdowns occur because of insensitivity to the other's position and feelings. There is no question that teachers bring their own needs and emotional responses to the encounter, and these must be reckoned with, but an awareness of the possible roles and emotional responses that accompany parenthood will help teachers to work with parents.

Several distinct roles make up a parent's life. These include

1. the parent as nurturer
2. the parent in adult relationships
3. the parent as an individual
4. the parent as worker
5. the parent as consumer
6. the parent as community member
7. the parent as educator

Despite the fact that every parenting experience is unique to the individual, there are several common experiences that have implications for the teacher working with parents. Most parents experience

1. irrevocability of parenthood
2. restrictions, isolation, fatigue
3. non-instinctual love
4. guilt
5. satisfaction related to self-esteem

6. uncertainty
7. real concern for child

Student Activities for Further Study

1. Read a personal account written by a parent, or someone considering becoming a parent. Suggestions:

   Friedland, Ronnie and Carol Kent, eds. *The Mother's Book: Shared Experiences.* Boston: Houghton Mifflin Co., 1980.
   Gansberg, Judith M. and Arthur P. Mostel. *The Second Nine Months.* New York: Tribeca Communications, 1984.
   Greene, Bob. *Good Morning Merry Sunshine: A Father's Journal of His Child's First Year.* Boston, Mass.: G. K. Hall, 1985
   Whelan, Elizabeth. *A Baby—Maybe?* New York: Bobbs-Merrill, 1976.
   Heffner, Elaine. *Mothering: The Emotional Experience of Motherhood after Freud and Feminism.* Garden City, NY: Doubleday and Co., 1978.
   McBride, Angela Barron. *The Growth and Development of Mothers.* New York: Harper and Row Pubs., 1973.

2. Talk with several parents. Choose parents whose children include infants, toddlers, and preschoolers if possible. Talk with at least one father. Discuss their reactions to parenthood: adjustments, negative aspects, positive aspects, changes in adult relationships and lifestyle. Share your findings with your classmates.

3. Talk with a professional in an agency that works to support and/or educate parents. What are some of the major concerns, difficulties, and needs of parents that he/she reports?

4. Learn what agencies in your community work to support and educate young parents. Learn everything you would need to know to refer a parent to the service.

Review Questions

1. List seven roles that parents play.
2. Discuss the implications of these roles for a teacher working with parents.
3. List seven emotional responses of parents.
4. Discuss the implications of these emotional responses for teachers.

References and Related Readings

Ainsworth, M. "The Development of Infant-Mother Attachment." B. Caldwell and H. Ricciuti, eds. *Review of Child Development Research.* Vol. 3. Chicago: University of Chicago Press, 1973.

Auerbach-Fink, Steveanne. "Mothers: Expectations of Child Care." *Young Children* 32.4 (1977): 12–21.

Backett, Kathryn C. *Mothers and Fathers.* New York: St. Martin's Press, 1982.

Barud, Sandra L., Raymond C. Collins, Patricia Divine-Hawkins. "Employer Supported Child Care: Everybody Benefits." *Children Today* 12.3 (1983): 2–3.

Bigner, Jerry J. *Parent-Child Relations: An Introduction to Parenting.* 2nd. Ed. New York: Macmillan Co., 1985.

Booth, A. "Does Wives' Employment Cause Stress for Husbands?" *Family Relations* 28 (1977): 445–49.

Bowlby, John. *Maternal Care and Mental Health.* Monograph series no. 2. Geneva: World Health Organization, 1952.

Bradburn, N. and D. Coplovitz. *Reports on Happiness.* Chicago: Aldine, 1968.

Burr, W. "Satisfaction with Various Aspects of Marriage over the Family Life Cycle" *Journal of Marriage and the Family* 32 (1970): 29–37.

———. *Theory Construction and the Sociology of the Family.* New York: Wiley, 1973.

Chulin, A. "Postponing Marriage: The Influence of Women's Work Expectations." *Journal of Marriage and the Family* 42 (1980): 355–65.

Curtis, Jean. *Working Mothers.* Garden City, New York: Doubleday and Co., 1976.

Dreskin, William and Wendy Dreskin. *The Day Care Decision: What's Best for You and Your Child.* New York: M. Evans and Co., 1983.

Galinsky, Ellen. "How do Child Care and Maternal Employment Affect Children?" *Child Care Information Exchange.* Issue 48. (1986): 19–23.

Harlow, H. "The Nature of Love." *American Psychologist* 13 (1958): 673–685.

Hoffman, L.W. and M.L. Hoffman. "The Value of Children to Parents." J.T. Fawcett, ed. *Psychological Perspectives on Population.* New York: Basic Books, 1973.

Howrigan, Gail. *The Effects Of Working Mothers on Children.* (reprint) Cambridge, Mass.: Center for the Study of Public Policy, 1973.

Justice, B. and D.F. Duncan. "Physical Abuse of Children as a Public Health Problem." *Public Health Review* 4 (1975): 183–200.

Kamerman, Sheila B. *Parenting in an Unresponsive Society: Managing Work and Family Life.* New York: The Free Press, 1980.

Keniston, Kenneth. *All Our Children: The American Family Under Pressure.* New York: Harcourt, Brace, Jovanovich, 1977.

LeMasters, E.E. and John DeFrain. *Parents In Contemporary America: A Sympathetic View.* 4th ed. Homewood, Illinois: The Dorsey Press, 1983.

Levine, James A. *Who Will Raise the Children? New Options for Fathers (and Mothers).* Philadelphia: J.B. Lipincott, 1976.

Lewis, Michael A. and Leonard A. Rosenblum, eds. *The Child and Its Family.* New York: Plenum Press, 1979.

Moore, Shirley G. "Working Mothers and Their Children." *Young Children* 34.1 (1978): 77–82.

Rapoport, Rhona and Robert and Ziona Strelitz. *Fathers, Mothers, and Society.* New York: Basic Books, 1977.

Rollins, B. and H. Feldman. "Marital Satisfactions over the Family Life Cycle." *Journal of Marriage and the Family* 32 (1970): 20–28.

Rollins, B. and K. Cannon. "Marital Satisfaction over the Family Life Cycle: A Reevaluation." *Journal of Marriage and the Family* 36 (1974): 271–281.

Rossi, A. "Transition to Parenthood." *Journal of Marriage and the Family* 30 (1968): 26–39.

Russell, C. "Transition to Parenthood: Problems and Gratifications." *Journal of Marriage and the Family* 36 (1974): 294–302.

Ryder, R. "Longitudinal Data Relating Marriage Satisfaction and Having a Child." *Journal of Marriage and the Family* 35 (1973): 604–607.

Spitz, R. "Hospitalism." O. Feichel et al., eds. *The Psychoanalytical Study of the Child.* Vol. 1. New York: International Universities Press, 1945.

Stoltz, Lois M. *Influences on Parent Behavior.* Stanford, Calif.: Stanford University Press, 1967.

Swick, Kevin J. and R. Eleanor Duff. *The Parent-Teacher Bond.* Dubuque, Iowa: Kendall/Hunt Publ. Co., 1978.

Thomson, Elizabeth. "The Value of Employment to Mothers of Young Children." *Journal of Marriage and the Family* 42 (1980): 551–66.

Tilley, T. "Your $250,000 Baby." *Parents* 55.11 (1980): 83–87.

Yankelovich, Skelly and White, Inc. *Raising Children in a Changing Society: The General Mills American Family.* Minneapolis: General Mills Consumer Center, 1977

Chapter 3 A Day in the Lives of Two Families

This chapter examines the hypothetical lives of two of our fictional families introduced in Chapter 1 to heighten our awareness of the demands and stresses in the lives of parents with young children. The more sensitive a teacher is to the complex lives of different families, the more she can approach them with the kind of understanding that can lead to a true partnership.

Objectives

After studying this chapter, the student will be able to

1. list several external factors causing stress in the families portrayed.
2. list several emotional responses evidenced in the parents portrayed.

You first met Jane Briscoe as she tried to imagine what life was like for some of the families of her acquaintance, unique in the circumstances of their lives but related by the common roles and experiences of parenthood. No one who is just an onlooker to the living drama of any family can come close to appreciating the thousands of details, interactions, and emotional nuances that compose a family's experience. Researchers (or teachers) frequently do not have the opportunity to record the actions of family members as they live their daily lives, but it is probably only through such methods that the individual threads of the family fabric can be perceived and appreciated. Here is a closer look at two of our fictitious families as they move through a day.

The Lawrence Family

When the alarm went off at 6 a.m., no one moved. Fannie stayed quite still, hoping Otis would remember it was his morning to get the children up and start the dressing and breakfast process. She felt so tired, she couldn't get up yet anyway, she told herself, stifling the guilty reminder that it was eleven the night before when Otis got home from his class and he must be pretty tired too. But this past month she'd seemed to be completely exhausted to start each day. She wondered how she would get through the next three months, and thought again that it might be a mistake to work right up until the birth, but that was the only way she could get the three months off afterwards. In her head she reviewed the whole decision, but there appeared to be no other way out. Their income looked fine on paper, but when you subtracted the $500 a month that Otis sent for the boys—more now that Danny had to get braces—there just wasn't any extra for her to take additional unpaid leave.

She groaned, but Otis still didn't move. In a burst of exasperation she maneuvered out of bed and banged the bathroom door louder than was necessary. Otis stretched and turned over, feeling guilty about Fannie, but also telling himself he needed the extra after the late night at class, and the late night he would have tonight at work. He'd get up in just a few minutes and help Fannie get the kids ready.

Fannie laid out breakfast things and went back up to waken the children. Pete was tired and hard to get moving so she practically had to dress him, and Kim was impatient to get her hair done. By the time they were eating breakfast, Fannie looked at the clock and realized she'd have to skip hers and dress quickly, or she'd be late again. In the still darkened bedroom she fumbled for clothes and shoes, then went into the bathroom to shower quickly and dress. She returned to the kitchen to find the TV blaring and the table a mess of cereal and milk. "Kim, when I leave you in charge, I don't expect you to let Pete watch TV; just look at this mess. Turn that off and at least put the milk in the fridge and get your teeth brushed, and Petey, see if you can't tie your shoes to help Mamma out today."

Kim said, "Mamma, I want a lunch packed. It's that dumb fried chicken for lunch at school today and I hate it."

"Kim! I told you before, I have to fix lunches at night. I don't have the time. We've got to leave right now, so don't start that." Kim's lip trembled and Fannie turned abruptly away. She did not have time for one of Kim's scenes now; besides, she was getting pretty sick of them, as often as Kim was doing this. Last night she'd spent an hour whining that she didn't have any friends in her class and she hated Miss Johnston. This wasn't like Kim, Fannie thought distractedly. She'd always been a happy child.

Otis appeared in the kitchen just in time to see Kim burst into tears. "Hey, what's the matter here?" he asked cheerily. Fannie glared at him, as Kim sobbed that Mamma wouldn't make her a lunch and she couldn't eat the lunch at school. "Oh won't she—" Otis began teasingly, but Fannie snapped quickly, "Just be quiet, Otis, I haven't had one second this morning. I haven't even had time for breakfast, so if she wants a lunch, you'd have to make it, but we have to leave right now!"

Otis handed some change to Kim and said, "Well, at least you can eat some ice cream, OK? Now leave your Mamma alone." He patted Fannie's shoulder apologetically. "Slow down, babe. You'll make it. You shouldn't be skipping breakfast. Have a good day. Come on Petey, hurry up, your Mom's in a hurry. Don't forget I work late tonight, Fannie. See you by ten. Try to be awake," he joked, patting her again.

"Fat chance," muttered Fannie and hustled the children to the car, Kim still sniffling loudly. As she drove along, Fannie thought to herself that sometimes she wondered why they'd gotten married. Otis was never home in the evenings, what with work and the college classes. Instantly she stifled the thought and wished she'd at least given him a hug. He did work hard.

She dropped Kim off at her school, with a determined smile. Kim walked off sullenly and Fannie tried not to mind. She noticed that there was no one else entering the door along with Kim. It was early, she knew, but she had to drop Kim off, then Pete, and still arrive at her own school by 7:45 a.m. She just wouldn't have felt right leaving Kim to wait for the bus, but this was one of the things Kim complained about—all the other kids got to ride the bus. She made a mental note to try to see Kim's teacher soon and ask her whether Kim was justified in saying she had no friends. Perhaps she could arrange for a girl to come with Kim after school, on a day when her own schedule allowed Kim to skip going to after-school day care. Anyway, she'd have to ask Miss Johnston if Kim being dropped off early created a problem; she was a little afraid to do that, since the teacher was a young single woman who probably wouldn't understand the morning schedule. Heaven knows it would be worse next year, since Pete's center did not offer care for infants; that would mean three stops before 7:45 a.m. She sighed, then realized they were at Pete's center. Thank goodness he'd been quiet, unusual for him.

"Oh, no," she whispered as they passed the classroom bulletin board with its reminder that the teachers needed toothpaste. "I forgot again," Fannie helped Pete take off his jacket and smiled toward a teacher who approached her.

"Oh, Mrs. Lawrence, I see Pete's got one of his cars again. We really can't let the children bring their own toys, it creates such problems. Please take it with you." Confused, Fannie looked down and realized Pete had been clutching a tiny car in his hand. She started to explain to the teacher that she hadn't realized he'd brought it, and fell silent as she realized that made her sound like a pretty careless mother. Pete grabbed his hand away, and Fannie looked for help to the teacher, who looked away. Fannie realized she would have to take the car away. She thought a nasty thought about the teacher and pried the car out of Pete's fingers. Pete burst into tears and Fannie's stomach tightened.

She gave him a quick hug and muttered a few words in his ear, looked appealingly at the teacher—who now seemed even more annoyed—and quickly dashed down the hall. She felt like crying herself as she listened to Pete's wails and thought about what a horrible morning it had been for all of them. She was so preoccupied with thinking about the kids' reactions and making resolutions for a tranquil evening that she walked right past another parent, who called hello after her. Sheepishly, she waved back and then hurried on, her face hot with embarrassment. The trip to her own school was punctuated by stoplights and blocked lanes, and she found herself almost running from her parked car, aware that several busloads of children had already arrived.

The day went fairly smoothly for Fannie, although with twenty-eight third graders to look after, plus her turn at playground duty, she was very tired by the time the final bell rang. A parent who came to pick up her child wanted to talk about the new reading program, but Fannie had to cut her off to get to the weekly faculty meeting on time. As she hurried down the hall, she reminded herself to make an appointment with Kim's teacher, so she wouldn't start off by annoying the teacher. The faculty meeting dragged on, and Fannie found herself glancing repeatedly at her watch, estimating how long it would take to pick up Kim and get her to her dancing class.

At last the meeting ended and she rushed out to her car, noticing with longing the group of young women who stayed back, chatting and planning to go out for a drink.

Her heart lifted when she saw Kim playing happily with another girl at the after-school day care where the bus dropped her each afternoon. The college student in charge of the group apologized for not having remembered that it was Kim's dancing class day and having her already changed. Fannie swallowed her irritation, but it became more difficult to control as Kim dawdled in play with her friend to the point where Fannie had to brusquely order her to leave and hurry up and change. Kim began to whine, but stopped when she saw the look on her mother's face.

Fannie tried to relax and make pleasant conversation about Kim's day as they drove to the dancing class. Kim chattered happily about her new friend at day care and asked if she couldn't come to her house to play one afternoon. Fannie promised, thinking uneasily of the logistic problems of rides and permission that might entail. She dropped Kim at the door, promising to try to be back in time to watch the last few minutes of the class. Checking her watch, she tried to organize her errands to fit them into the hour time slot—drop off the cleaning, cash a check at the bank, pick up a few groceries and get to the post office for stamps before it closed. That would cut it pretty close for picking up Pete and she hated his day to be so long, but she knew from experience it was worse to drag a tired child with her. Trying to ignore her own fatigue, she hurried on.

Pete looked up hopefully as she walked into his room at the day-care center, and she realized with a pang he'd probably been doing that as each parent entered the room for the previous half hour. His teacher said he'd had a good day, after the upsetting beginning. Fannie was annoyed that she'd brought that up again. She just wished this young woman could understand that it was bad enough having to rush Pete in the morning, let alone strip him of all his favorite things for the day.

There was an accident holding up traffic on the road back to Kim's dancing studio, and by the time they'd got there she was waiting in the parking lot with the dancing teacher, who looked in a hurry to leave. Kim's face was stormy as she accused Fannie: "You promised." Fannie tried to explain, but felt both helpless and angry before the eight-year-old's indignation. Impulsively, changing the mood and giving in to her own fatigue, she suggested supper at McDonald's. Amidst the kids' squeals of glee, she thought glumly about the nutritional consequences and decided she wouldn't ask them what they'd eaten for lunch. Some mother, she thought, conjuring up an image of her own mother's plentiful dinner table. And what's more there'd be nothing to keep warm for Otis. Well, maybe she could fix him a nice omelet, if he wasn't too late.

The kids were cheerful and chatty over hamburgers, so Fanny relaxed and enjoyed their stories. "We're doing OK," she told herself. "They're really fine."

It was after seven when they got home. Fannie put Pete in the bathtub, started Kim on her reading homework in the bathroom to watch him so Fannie could unpack the groceries and put a load of laundry in. At least Otis had had time to clean up the breakfast mess; that was more than she could have stood, twelve hours later!

She read Pete a bedtime story and then tucked him in. He was tired and settled in quickly. Fannie looked back at him tenderly. He was growing so quickly; pretty soon he wouldn't be the baby any more. For the thousandth time she wondered how he'd feel when the new baby arrived.

Kim wanted to watch some television, but Fannie reminded her first to find her clothes for the morning and decide if she wanted a lunch, which she did. Making the sandwiches, Fannie thought, "Maybe tomorrow will be a better day." At bedtime Kim asked her to be sure to give Daddy a kiss for her. Fannie wished again that Otis could be home more at night, so they could feel like a real family. She knew what Otis would say if she brought it up again. "The classes are important, if I'm ever going to be able to stop selling cars at night. It's only a couple more years. And in the meantime selling cars is giving us a good living." He was right, of course, but the kids practically never saw him. Well, for that matter, it was tough on all of them.

Fannie folded the laundry, washed her hair, spread out her clothes for the morning, and lay down on the bed to read the morning paper. Within ten minutes she had fallen asleep. When Otis came in at 10:00 p.m., she was still asleep. He sighed, turned out the light, and went to see if there were any leftovers in the kitchen.

The Ashley Family

Sylvia Ashley got up quickly when the alarm went off at 6:00 a.m. She had washed out Terrence's shirt the night before and wanted to iron it before it was time for him to get up. Anyway, she liked having time in the early morning, when the building was still quiet. The rest of the day there was hardly a moment when someone wasn't yelling or throwing something. She turned on the kitchen light cautiously, knowing the roaches would scurry away from the sink.

She ironed carefully. She felt badly that Terrence had to wear the same clothes over and over, but at least he was always clean and tidy. She hoped the teacher would notice that and not treat him badly. The way some people treated people without money—she hated it for herself and she didn't want her kids to grow up thinking they weren't as good as everyone else, just because they lived in public housing and didn't have a father to back them up.

She sighed, remembering she had to go back to the social services office today to talk to the social worker. She dreaded that, but since their allowance had been cut two months before, she simply hadn't been able to make it on the reduced amount. Last week she'd had to borrow three dollars from her neighbor across the hall to get some macaroni and milk for the kids' supper, and she knew she couldn't do that again—the woman barely spoke to her anyway. And with trying to get into that job-training program, she knew she'd have to get herself a new pair of shoes. Ricky's sneakers had a hole right through the toe too.

She unplugged the iron and glanced at the clock. Time to get the boys up. They were cheerful and chattered away, Terrence helping Ricky get dressed. Ricky ate a bowl of cereal, and Sylvia gave Terrence a glass of milk to have something in his stomach until he got to school. He preferred to have breakfast at home and she'd always let him until things got so tight. Since he was eligible for the free breakfast at school, it made a little place she could save.

She dressed quickly and then cleaned the kitchen up. Terrence was ready at the door, hair neatly combed, when she got there. He grumbled a bit every day about his mother and little brother having to go with him to school, but she didn't like the idea of him walking alone six blocks through this neighborhood. Ricky struggled to keep up. They waved to Terrence from the street as he climbed the school stairs by himself. Sylvia worried about him—he never mentioned a friend, and after school she and Ricky walked him home and then he played with Ricky. She knew he needed friends his own age, but she kept him in the apartment unless she could go to the playground with them. She'd seen and heard plenty of fights and wildness from some of the kids in their building, and she knew some of them were already in trouble with the police. She was going to keep her boys free of that. Terrence was a good student, a smart boy—he would grow up differently than those other kids.

She and Ricky waited at the bus stop for the bus that would take them downtown to the square where they could transfer to the one that would take them out to the Social Services building. She barely heard Ricky talking away and pointing out cars and asking questions as they rode along, as she rehearsed what she had to say.

The waiting room was full; she found one chair and held Ricky on her lap for a while, until he got wiggly. Then she let him sit on the floor beside her. She kept listening for the woman to call her name, knowing that Ricky was getting restless. He asked her for something to eat, as he watched a man eating crackers he'd bought from the vending machine. Sylvia didn't want to waste fifty cents on that, and wished she'd thought to bring something for him. Fortunately, they called her name just then, and Ricky was distracted by moving into the small office.

At least this social worker was better than the last one, who'd positively sniffed every time Ricky moved. Sylvia had always been furious underneath, since this woman had to know there was no money for babysitters and nobody that could help them out, but it wouldn't have done to let that anger show.

By the end of the discussion, Sylvia felt very depressed. She always hated the questions about whether she'd heard from either of the boys' fathers; she always wanted to say she was thankful she hadn't, and wouldn't take a penny from either of them anyway. It didn't look like there would be any increase in her monthly check because the social worker pointed out that social services would have to pay for Ricky's day care when the job training started in four weeks. Sylvia didn't know how they'd manage, knowing there'd be more expenses with her in the program. But she'd do it. Then maybe she'd be able to make enough to get them into a little apartment somewhere nicer, and she'd have some friends from work and Terrence could have friends to play with and things would be better. She had to do it. Her kids deserved more.

Ricky was tired and cranky as they waited for the bus home. He started to cry and she spanked him, not very hard, but she just couldn't stand to listen to that right now or have the bus driver stare at her when she got on with a crying child.

He fell asleep on the bus and she pulled him against her shoulder, knowing he'd wake up when they had to transfer. Poor thing, it had been a long morning for him. Neither of them said much as they rode the last bus and walked home for lunch. Ricky finished his soup and she put him in bed for a nap. She sat, thinking about Ricky starting in day care and about herself starting in the training program. She hoped she could do it. It had been a long time since she'd been in school and then she didn't have kids and everything else to worry about. She worried about how it would be for Ricky; he'd never been away from her at all. The social worker had told her that the center was a good one, but that didn't reassure her that Ricky would not get upset.

She glanced at the clock. Just a few more minutes until she'd have to wake up Ricky to take him while they got Terrence. Poor thing was so worn out she'd like to leave him sleep, but there was nobody to ask to stay with him. She worried briefly about Terrence who would have to come home and be by himself for a couple of hours until she finished her class, picked up Ricky, and arrived home. She'd already lost sleep a couple of nights worrying about that, but there was nothing else to be done. She'd warn him about answering the door, not using the stove, and everything else she could think of, and then just hope he'd stay in the apartment, safely, by himself.

Terrence was quiet coming home. In the apartment he unfolded a note and handed it to her. It was a reminder that parents needed to send a dollar the next day to pay for a ticket to a play at the children's theater next week. Sylvia avoided Terrence' eyes as she said that she couldn't send the money, so he could stay home from school the day of the play. Terrence said nothing.

She gathered up the laundry and her wallet and keys, and took the boys with her down to the basement laundry room. The children sat, listlessly arguing. When another woman came in, Sylvia snapped at the kids to be quiet, and they sat glumly until she asked Terrence to help her match the socks. Back upstairs, the boys watched cartoons while she made hamburgers for supper. After supper, Terrence did his homework at the kitchen table and Ricky sat beside him and colored in a coloring book she'd bought in the drugstore. She put them in the bath together while she tidied the kitchen. After the children watched some more TV, she put them in bed and sat by herself in the living room, on the couch where she'd sleep. There was nothing she wanted to see on TV, but she left it on to keep her company. After an hour or so, she turned out the light to sleep.

Working With Parents in the Classroom

It is a good idea to try to comprehend the lives of the families with whom you will work. Perhaps this has been a useful consciousness-raising exercise for you.

Both of these families have unique living circumstances and experiences, but in both there is a common thread of stress with the roles and responsibilities, the isolation that comes from concentrating on children's care, and the deeply felt concerns for the children's lives.

You may or may not yet be a parent yourself. If you are, then you have had daily experiences from the parent's perspective and do not need further convincing of the astonishing task of blending and fulfilling these various roles. Separately and on the printed page, they appear demanding; when experienced together, in the context of daily life, they can be staggering.

For those of you who are not yet parents, recollections of your parents' lives during your childhood may be faint and will not do justice to the enormity of the life demands. Even acquaintance with your classroom parents probably does not fully expose you to the extent of the demands on them. An active imagination will help you best here. On a sheet of paper, jot down any facts you know of several of your families' lives—the family members and ages, jobs and what is involved, hobbies and interests, special family circumstances.

Now mentally take yourself through a sample of their days—and nights. (Parenting does not have a neatly prescribed limit on working hours!) Remember to include the details of daily life such as doctor's visits, haircuts, trips to the library and bank, as well as the unforeseen emergencies that pop up—the car breaking down, the baby-sitter getting sick, the additional assignment at work. Choose a cross-section of families to contemplate; remember that the socioeconomic circumstances of any family may add additional strains, whether they be the daily struggles of a poverty-level family or the demands on an upwardly–mobile professional family. If you're doing this right, you will likely soon be shaking your head and tired in your imagination.

This might be a useful exercise to repeat whenever you find yourself making judgements or complaining about families. It is virtually impossible for a teacher to work effectively with classroom families until she is able to empathize with them. Remember this is only an attempt to mentally understand possible situations; no outsider can fully appreciate the nature of what really goes on in any one family. Every family truly stands alone in its uniqueness.

Summary

No one can truly understand all of the emotional implications of parenthood, for each parent comes to this point with a particular set of needs, experiences, and motivations. Nevertheless, it is important to realize the potential emotions involved in parenthood, so that teachers do not unwittingly ignore or exacerbate strong emotional responses.

Student Activities for Further Studies

1. Re-read the summaries of the ten fictional families in Chapter 1. Select another family to create an imaginary day in their life. Work

with a partner, brainstorming to stimulate your thinking. Share your account with the class.

2. Invite a parent of preschoolers to your class discussion. Ask him/her to come prepared to give a sample diary of their family's daily life.

3. Read an account of an American family, or other material that might increase your understanding of various cultures or segments of society. For suggestions, refer to the section of References and Related Readings.

Review Questions

1. List several external factors causing stress in the families portrayed.
2. List several emotional responses evidenced in the parents portrayed.

References and Related Readings

Bohen, Halycone H. *Balancing Jobs and Family Life.* [case studies] Philadelphia: Temple University Press, 1981.

Duberman, Lucille. *The Reconstructed Family: A Study of Married Couples and their Children.* [case studies] Chicago: Nelson-Hall, 1975.

Glazer, Nathan and Daniel P. Moynihan. *Beyond the Melting Pot: the Negroes, Puerto Ricans, Jews, Italians and Irish of New York City.* Cambridge: MIT Press, 1970.

Lewis, Oscar. *LaVida: A Puerto Rican Family in the Culture of Poverty.* New York: Random House, 1966

Schneider, David M. and Raymond T. Smith. *Class Differences and Sex Roles in American Kinship and Family Structure.* [case studies] Englewood Cliffs, New Jersey: Prentice-Hall, 1973.

Section II: Teacher-Parent Partnerships in Early Education

Chapter 4 What is Parent Involvement?

The term *parent involvement* is used to define a number of things in a variety of child development programs.

Objectives

After studying this chapter, the student will be able to

1. describe three patterns of parent involvement and explain the ideas that underlie each

Perspectives on Parent Involvement

Jane Briscoe again. "You know, I'm really confused. At a meeting I went to recently, the subject of parent involvement came up. After several people discussed what they thought about parent involvement, I realized I have been using that term differently than most of them. One of them implied that parent involvement was parents meeting together and making the decisions in a program. Another spoke as if parent involvement meant parents working as aides in the classroom. Somebody else mentioned the early intervention programs where parents are being taught more about their children, so they can expand the ways they help their own children develop. And I've been thinking parent involvement is when I try to let parents know as much as I can about what's going on in their children's classroom lives."

Small wonder that Jane is confused. In program descriptions, research, and in conversational usage among teachers, the term *parent involvement* is used to describe all of these patterns of parent participation in early childhood education. Sometimes the phrase seems limited in scope.

> By focusing on parental involvement, we tend to confine our thinking about day care-family relations to specific roles that parents can play in the operations of a day care center. We think of parents attending meetings, raising money, painting a room, baking cookies, and perhaps making policy decisions and hiring personnel. We generally think of parents not individually but as a group, a constituency that needs to be involved in perpetuating a child care program. What the concept of parent involvement typically does not include is consideration of daily one-to-one interactions between parents and staff, parent relationships with other parents . . . (Powell, 1977, p. 4).

Powell goes on to suggest that parent involvement is really concerned with solving the problems that families and child-care programs encounter when working together to care for young children, including defining the boundaries of family-day care interaction and the roles of parents in coordinating the relationship between the family and the child-care program. This is indeed a larger issue than is suggested by some descriptions of parent involvement. To get a perspective on this issue, it may be useful to examine some of the various approaches to working with parents.

The assumption in this text is that the majority of American teachers working with young children are not working in programs that have mandates to include parents specifically, as do most federally funded enrichment or intervention programs. In addition to the traditional nursery school programs, the rising numbers of private-for-profit child-care centers, including day-care franchises and family day-care homes, and of nonprofit church-sponsored day-care programs, place many teachers on the front lines as the contact between home and preschool. Some teachers are convinced that working with parents will help them create a more supportive environment for the children in their care. Mandated programs, specially designed to involve parents, provide valuable information about the effects of certain techniques and strategies on families and teacher-parent relationships. For teachers who are defining their own methods, these programs offer interesting models to examine. Even more important than any method may be the philosophy behind why teachers consider it important to support families. Therefore, the text offers a brief overview of the varying concepts of parent involvement and suggests further readings should the student wish to pursue a particular interest.

Three Patterns of Parent Involvement

Except for the parent-cooperative nursery school movement within the traditional middle-class nursery school concept, parents were excluded from much of the early childhood education in this country until the mid-sixties. Substantial research provided data that precipitated the increase in the amount of parent involvement. These studies suggest that the early years are of the utmost importance in setting learning patterns for children and families; that parents' style (particularly mothers') is the key to children's learning style; and that mothers' aspirations and self-confidence are the key to children's sense of confidence and competence as well. Since the mid-sixties, these beliefs have given rise to three patterns of parent involvement.

Intervention Educational Programs

Intervention educational programs are deliberately designed to improve children's total learning environment by stimulating changes within key elements of that environment, particularly in parental behaviors. Research evidence suggests that there is a close connection between the development of children's IQ scores and learning potentials to opportunities within the home to learn, explore, use language, and to have these learning activities positively reinforced. Without enlightening parents on how to best stimulate and nurture the development of their children, valuable time and opportunities for preschool children will be lost. They could be the children who are unprepared for the language, social, and cognitive experiences of an elementary school setting, and may drop even further behind their peers in these skills. Realizing this, a body of empirical data from educational and sociological research was used for the persuasive arguments that led to the establishment of the Head Start program as part of President Johnson's War on Poverty, and of other center-based intervention programs, all of which include components of parent education and involvement. Data from subsequent studies continues to justify parent participation.

Why is parent participation considered to be a necessary component of an intervention program? Studies confirm the assumption that early experiences of young children, including their relationships and interaction in the home environment, have an important and lasting impact on their cognitive growth, educational achievement, and psychological development. A substantial amount of research on specific factors in the home that influence children's behavior, found that maternal warmth, high levels of emotional involvement and interaction, and parental interest are positively associated with children's achievement (Bing, 1963). It is also suggested that differences in academic performances among children are related to the value in the home placed on school learning (Bloom, 1964). While studies indicate that low-income mothers value achievement and conformity (Hess et al., 1968), they focus less on developing problem-solving skills, give less positive feedback and fewer verbal directions (Bee et al., 1969; Brophy, 1970) than mothers from higher socioeconomic levels.

From these studies came the belief that intervention programs for young children in the economically disadvantaged and cultural minority segments of society will help them to succeed in the established educational system. And, since the home environment is identified as important, programs are designed to involve parents. Programs consider parents, especially mothers, as a major factor to be worked with, not compensated for (Bruner, 1972). Such models, designed for *Family Impact* as Gordon calls it (1977), offer parent education so that families and children can orient themselves successfully towards school. This approach assumes that the educational system is sound, that success in it is desired by a family although they may not know how to achieve it, and that offering chances for new knowledge and attitudes to parents is the key to that success.

In addition to the national Head Start program, other model intervention programs include seven programs studied by Bronfenbrenner in 1976 to analyze the long-term effects of working with parents and their children. He found that there are considerable gains in children's IQ scores during the first years of a program, but the gains disappear after children leave a program. However, Bronfenbrenner argued that the full impact of a program on children, families, and

Parents involved in their children's preschool classrooms learn new skills.

communities cannot be assessed on the basis of these scores alone (Bronfenbrenner, 1976).

Some research indicates that the involvement of parents over a period of time in a program is a critical factor in the gains made by children. Rodin found that, of three groups of children whose mothers were not involved, moderately involved, and intensely involved, there was no significant difference between the three groups after one year in a program, but significantly greater gains for both groups where mothers were involved after two years (Rodin, 1972).

Although early studies specific to Head Start suggest an excessive optimism in its evaluations of gains in cognitive development (Cicerelli, 1969), there is affirmation that parent involvement is positively related to children's scores, academic achievement, verbal intelligence, and self-concept, as well as to parental feelings of success and involvement in community activities (Midco, 1972). [Current studies offer more optimistic findings about the long-term effects on school performance, confidence, and self-image, up to fifteen years after children participated in the preschool intervention program (Lazar and Darlington, 1979; Mann et al., 1978; Collins and Deloria, 1983).] The effectiveness of Head Start is still being questioned, due to the inconsistencies in various studies of IQ scores and subsequent progress in school, despite obvious individual successes (Schweinhart and Weikart, 1986).

As well as center-based programs, some intervention programs involve parents directly in educating themselves through home visitation programs. Studies indicate that scores not only improve over a period of time with this method, but are maintained for several years after the intervention has been discontinued. Effects may be present even in younger children within the family, who had not been directly involved (Bronfenbrenner, 1976).

In the intervention programs, the emphasis for parent involvement is on (1) parents as learners, increasing parental knowledge about children and their needs, and ways that child development can be nurtured and supported, and (2) parents as teachers, working with professionals in the classroom and/or in the home, to enhance the professionals' efforts. The schools seek out parents and include them in order to increase the effectiveness of their efforts to educate children.

Parents were active in preschool classrooms with teachers prior to the intervention programs, notably in nursery schools associated with the parent-cooperative movement. Such schools appeared first in 1916 as the forerunner of a growing movement through the 1930s, 1940s, and up to the present, mostly around middle-class enclaves such as universities and suburban towns. These schools welcomed mothers, who often underwent some training, to share in their children's classroom life, in order to learn, grow, and enrich the lives of their children and themselves. (For a full description of the philosophy, goals, and organization of the parent-cooperative preschools, see Taylor, 1967.) But in the intervention programs, the implication may be that low-income families, especially black and other ethnic minorities, are inadequate to rear children in a complex urban society. Parental involvement should not be a euphemism for the involvement of low-income parents. This has the potential of developing paternalistic and exploitative patterns (Knitzer, 1972).

Parents Involved in Decision Making

Backed by social and political organizations created during the rise of ethnic nationalism in the mid-sixties, parents have demanded the move toward parent involvement. They want a participatory voice in the decisions made regarding educational policies affecting their children and communities. In this model of parent involvement, referred to as the *School Impact Model* (Gordon, 1977), parents desire a part in the planning, operation, and overall evaluation and direction of the program.

> The rationale for parent participation in decision making is based on the belief that people will not be committed to decisions in which they had no involvement. Furthermore, it is believed that the process of considering information, decision making, and implementation are, in themselves, educational, and aid in developing leadership skills. It also is argued that parents know their own situation best, and hence must be involved in planning for their children's education (Hess, 1971, p. 277).

Parents involved in decision-making may have a real impact on the direction of the programs.

Allowing this initiative to the community is a means of activating parents to do something for their children (Bruner, 1972).

In practice, the involvement of parents in decision making along with professionals frequently leads to the question of how to reconcile conflicting views about what is good for children, potentially a difficult and time-consuming process. But parents continue to be involved in varying degrees, in various programs.

In the federally funded Head Start, Follow Through, and Parent and Child Center programs, parent participation in policy making is mandated. Parents set the standards for the hiring of professional staff, often interviewing and selecting staff. They also participate in decisions on budgetary matters.

Today there is a growing movement among all citizens, not just ethnic minorities, to press for the community's right to both criticize and support the schools. Parents are learning that their voices can have impact (Buskin, 1975). The existence of "anti-expert" feelings in American society today, possibly as a result of a mistrust of bureaucracy, is partially responsible for parents pushing for the right to be involved. Therefore, this second pattern of parent involvement came largely as a result of parents' demands on the schools, rather than schools' attempting to involve parents.

Parents Viewed as Partners

The form of parent involvement that exists most widely is the effort to increase communication between parent and teacher using methods and experiences most appropriate for a particular set of circumstances. This is true no matter how extensive the cross section is of families served, or whether or not a program is publicly funded with the accompanying mandates for parent participation. The motivation behind such an effort is the philosophy that a preschool functions in a partnership with, or as an extension of, the home, with corresponding rights and duties for parents. This presumes a mutual involvement, rather than a one-sided pulling or pushing of parents into the educational system.

Most parents have complete responsibility for their children, but little control over some of the larger social forces impinging on their children's lives (Keniston, 1977). In the past, when the use of day care was primarily by families who could not provide for their children, rather than families in the mainstream of American life, it was easier to feel that parents needed no say in what others thought desirable for their children. However, as day care is used increasingly by middle-class parents who choose it as a component of their life-style, parents are increasingly having a say about what they want for their children. This demand for input will continue to increase as the entry age into supplemental care becomes earlier (Schickedanz, 1977).

In carrying out the multitude of duties involved in child rearing, parents receive little moral or psychological support from society (Kamerman, 1980). The preschool's chief role is to confirm the importance of child rearing and the parents' role in it, not as a substitute for the family, but as a support for and supplement to the family. One author exploring the issues involved with the increase in day-care use suggests the following:

> The greatest danger of day care to the family is not that day care exists, but that it will be organized in such a way as to foster the kind of division, intrusion and separation that have already attenuated the ties between parent and child (Steinfels, 1973, p. 238).

Parents who express a wish to know more about what their young children do during the day are really stating something far more complex, related to the bonds and shared experiences between parent and child, and an extension of the relationship between a family and a child's school (Smith, 1980). The center that shares in child-rearing endeavors with parents may act as a reconstituted form of the extended

Parents want to know as much as they can about their child's school life.

family, offering parents an escape from the isolation of child rearing (Galinsky and Hooks, 1977).

The separation or integration of parent and teacher responsibilities is seen by some to be one of the main issues in preschool centers, since the question is asked, "Who will raise America's children?" (Steinfels, 1973, p. 114). There are private citizens and public voices (such as Richard Nixon's as he vetoed a bill that would have enabled increases in the amount of funding for day care in 1971) who fear that "family-centered child rearing would be replaced by community child rearing, to the further detriment of the traditional family patterns." But perhaps it does not have to be such a clear-cut issue of having all the control or none of it. There is no argument that traditional family patterns have already changed; the majority of families do have two working parents and single-parent families have increased dramatically. Neither of these trends seem likely to reverse. Since an increasing number of parents seek child care for their preschoolers, why not create the environments and philosophies that permit parents and teachers to work in supportive partnerships that are mutually beneficial to home and school, rather than put children totally under professional care, and only minimally inform parents of progress or problems. From this perspective, the kinds of parent involvement that increase communication and sharing of experiences are an essential, not optional, part of a preschool program.

Preschools have chosen to address the issue of parent involvement in a variety of ways, ranging from a low level to a high level of parent involvement. Centers with a low level of parent involvement allow parents to take part in activities that do not challenge the expertise of a teacher or the decision-making power of the school. Activities such as newsletters, parent meetings, or individual parent conferences, tend

Teachers can reassure parents that they do not have to handle it alone.

to keep parents at a distance, learning secondhand about their child's life at school. Schools with a high level of parent involvement provide opportunities for parents to make their presence known, particularly in the educational setting, by parent visits and observation, or visits to volunteer assistance; here parents are perceived as a source of help. The highest levels of parent involvement occur in schools that believe both teachers and parents have expertise, and both parents and the school have decision-making rights. Communicating via many channels, parents have the power to make decisions concerning education of their children (Schickedanz, 1977). These channels of communication will be explored in Section III.

Presently, except for subjective accounts from parents, (Steinfels, 1973, Chapter 6; Galinsky and Hooks, 1977, Chapter 4) much is unknown about the effects of different types of parent involvement. One implication from early studies on intervention programs can be generalized to all patterns of parent involvement: parents' confidence in their own abilities and worth is a crucial component of parental competence and, it follows, of functioning positively within the family (Brody, 1969). Parents enrolling their children in preschool programs are in a transition time of parenthood, helping their children move into a larger world while adjusting to changes in dependency and new roles themselves. If they are supported and brought into a partnership, their feelings of competence in this new phase of parenting will increase.

Because teachers in most situations can work towards this parent-teacher partnership, the emphasis in this text is on attitudes, behaviors, and techniques that foster constructive working relationships.

As Jane Briscoe pointed out earlier, "parent involvement" has a variety of meanings. There are variations in the attitudes and emotional responses to these concepts from teachers who are primarily responsible for creating both the atmosphere and activities that may help or hinder such endeavors.

Listen to several teachers in a child development center; we'll see them again later in various activities with parents.

You've already met Jane Briscoe. Jane is twenty-seven years old, single, and has been teaching four-year-olds since she graduated from the Child and Family Development program at State College five years ago. She describes herself as an extrovert, the oldest of a family of four girls. She believes wholeheartedly in working as a partner with parents; her only complaint is that many of her parents seem too busy to spend much time in the classroom. But she keeps on trying.

Anne Morgan is thirty-five, a divorced mother of a ten-year-old daughter and eight-year-old son. She has been working at the center since her divorce four years ago; before that her only teaching experience had been doing student teaching. Anne is often heard to criticize some of the behaviors of parents at the center, who seem to her to be less than conscientious about their parental duties. She does not encourage or invite parents into involvement in her classroom or much conversation with her, though she is always polite when she sees them. When a parent with a problem called her at home in the evening, she complained bitterly to her director about the infringement on her private time.

This is John Reynold's first year of teaching preschoolers. He's had to endure a lot of kidding from friends, since they feel it's an unusual career choice for a black man who played football in college. He is deeply involved with the children, conscientious about observing them and making individual plans to fit in with their developmental needs and interests. However, he feels very uncomfortable in his contacts with parents, feeling that they are always watching him. He is unsure how much he should tell them about some of his concerns about the children. One of the parents asked for a conference next week, and he's afraid this means she wants to criticize. He and his wife expect their first child this year, and he's hoping that may help some of the parents accept him as competent. It's not so much that anyone has questioned his competence with the children, but he's sure that's what they think.

Connie Martinez is enjoying teaching in this center, which she chose because of the good masters program at the university nearby. She is working hard to finish her degree, and says that although she believes in parent involvement, she just doesn't have any extra time beyond her planning and preparing activities for the children. She has never told anyone, but she really thinks too many of the parents are letting the center do too much for their young children, and she doesn't think this should be encouraged. Last week a mother brought in a child who had just come from the doctor's office, and asked if the teacher could give the first dose of the prescribed eardrops, since she had to get right back to work; Connie was very annoyed with this demonstration of parents shifting their own responsibilities to the teacher. She simply says she's too busy to spend much time with parents, when asked if she believes in parent involvement.

MiLan Ha came to America as a six-year-old. When she graduated from high school, she was second in her class. After a year of college, she took the job in the preschool, which she enjoys. MiLan is a talented artist, and encourages lots of creative art with her children. She is a very quiet young woman, with no close friends on the staff. She lives at home with her parents, an uncle and two nieces. She dreads the conferences and meetings which are scheduled at her preschool, and uses the excuse that her English is not good. In fact, her English is excellent. She is just extremely uncomfortable in social encounters. When parents enter her room, she smiles, and quickly turns to the children. The parents feel she is a good teacher, but are uncomfortable with her also.

Dorothy Scott has been teaching for thirteen years; she took about five years off when her own son was a preschooler. She has quite definite ideas about child-rearing and feels most parents don't handle things with their children as well as they should. She believes it's important to hold conferences and meetings to tell parents what they should be doing, and doesn't mind spending extra time to do these things, though finds it very discouraging when parents don't attend or disregard her advice. Some of the parents have asked the director privately if it was necessary for their children to be in Mrs. Scott's room, but, unaware of this, she states proudly that she has never had a parent complain.

Six different teachers and six different attitudes that clearly determine the responses and relationships each would offer to parents.

Summary

Parent involvement may refer to either or all of three patterns of working with parents.

1. Parents may be involved as part of planned intervention programs, designed to stimulate optimal developmental conditions for children by involving and educating parents to more effectively teach their own children.

2. Parents may be involved in making decisions that affect the structure of the educational systems that serve their children.

3. Parents may be involved through a variety of techniques and activities used to enhance teacher-parent communication in programs that value parents and teachers working as partners for children's welfare.

It is time to go beyond personal preferences and performances to explore questions related to what everyone stands to gain from a constructive parent-teacher partnership.

Student Activities for Further Study

1. Find out if your community has a parent-cooperative preschool program. If so, visit and discover in what aspects parents are involved.
2. Interview several preschool teachers. Find out
   a. how they define parent involvement,
   b. what activities and strategies they use to involve parents, and
   c. how much time each week or month they spend in working with parents.
3. Talk to several parents who have children in preschool programs. Find out what they want in terms of their own involvement with the programs and teachers, and what they have actually experienced.
4. Find out if there is a Head Start or Parent and Child Center in your community. If there is, visit and discover how parents are involved in the program.

Discuss all of your findings with your classmates.

Review Questions

1. Describe the three most typical patterns of parent involvement.
2. Explain the underlying ideas for each of the patterns of parent involvement.

References and Related Readings

Bee, H. et al., "Social Class Differences in Maternal Teaching Strategies and Speech Patterns." *Developmental Psychology* 1 (1969): 726–34.

Bing, E. "Effects of Childrearing Practices on Development of Differential Cognitive Abilities." *Child Development* 34 (1963): 631–48.

Bloom, B.S. *Stability and Change in Human Characteristics.* New York: John Wiley and Sons, 1964.

Brody, G.F. "Maternal Child Rearing Attitudes and Child Behavior." *Developmental Psychology* 1 (1969): 66.

Bronfenbrenner, Urie. *Is Early Intervention Effective? A Report on Longitudinal Evaluations of Preschool Programs.* (U.S. Dept. of Health, Education and Welfare, Office of Child Development) Washington, D.C.: U.S. Govt. Printing Office, 1976.

Brophy, J.E. "Mothers as Teachers of their own Preschool Children: The Influence of Socioeconomic Status and Task Structure on Teaching Specificity." *Child Development* 41 (1970): 79–94.

Bruner, Jerome S. "Poverty and Childhood." *The Preschool in Action: Exploring Early Childhood Programs.* Ed. Ronald Parker. Boston: Allyn and Bacon, Inc., 1972.

Buskin, M. *Parent Power: A Candid Handbook for Dealing with Your Child's School.* New York: Walker Co., 1975.

Cicerelli, V., et al. *The Impact of Head Start. An Evaluation of the Effects of Head Start on Children's Cognitive and Affective Development.* Westinghouse Learning Corporation and Ohio University. Washington, D.C.: Government Printing Office, 1969.

Collins, R.C. and Dennis Deloria. "Head Start Research: A New Chapter." *Children Today* 12.4 (1983): 15–20.

Galinsky, Ellen and William H. Hooks. *The New Extended Family: Day Care that Works.* Boston: Houghton Mifflin Co., 1977.

Gordon, Ira J. "Parent Education and Parent Involvement: Retrospect and Prospect." *Childhood Education* 54.2 (1977): 71–78.

Hess, R.D. "Parental Behaviors and Children's School Achievement: Implications for Head Start." *Critical Issues in Research Related to Disadvantaged Children.* Ed. E. Grotberg. Princeton: Educational Testing Service, 1969.

Hess, R.D. and Virginia Shipman. "Early Experiences and the Socialization of Cognitive Modes in Children." *Child Development* 36 (1965): 869–86.

Hess, R.D. et al. "Parent Involvement." *Day Care: Resources for Decisions.* Ed. Edith Grotberg. Washington, D.C.: Day Care and Child Development Committee of America, 1971.

———. *The Cognitive Environments of Urban Preschool Children.* U.S. Dept. of Health, Education and Welfare, Children's Bureau, Social Security Administration, 1968.

Kamerman, Sheila B. *Parenting in an Unresponsive Society: Managing Work and Family Life.* New York: The Free Press, 1980.

Keniston, Kenneth. *All Our Children: The American Family Under Pressure.* New York: Harcourt, Brace, Jovanovich, 1977.

Knitzer, Jane. "Parental Involvement: The Elixir of Change." *Early Childhood Development Programs and Services: Planning for Action.* Ed. Dennis N. McFadden. Washington, D.C.: NAEYC, 1972.

Lazar and Darlington. Consortium for Longitudinal Studies. *Lasting Effects After Preschool: Summary Report.* Washington, D.C.: U. S. Dept. of Health, Education and Welfare, 1979.

Mann, A.J., A.V. Harrell, and M.J. Hunt. "A Review of Head Start Research since 1969." *Found: Long-Term Gains from Early Intervention.* Ed. B. Brown. Boulder, Colo.: Westview Press, 1978.

MIDCO. *Perspectives on Parent Participation in Head Start: An Analysis and Critique.* Washington, D.C.: Project Head Start, 1972.

Powell, Douglas R. *The Interface Between Families and Child Care Programs: A Study of Parent-Caregiver Relationships.* Detroit: The Merrill-Palmer Institute, 1977.

Rodin, N. "Three Degrees of Maternal Involvement in a Preschool Program: Impact on Mothers and Children." *Child Development* 43 (1972): 1355–64.

Schickedanz, Judith A. "Parents, Teachers and Early Education." *Early Childhood.* Eds. Barry Persky and Leonard Golubchick. Wayne, New Jersey, Avery Publishing Group, Inc., 1977.

Schlossman, S.L. "The Parent Education Game: The Politics of Child Psychology in the 70's." *Teacher's College Record* 79 (1978): 788–808.

Schweinhart, Lawrence J. and David P. Weikart. "What Do We Know So Far? A Review of the Head Start Synthesis Project." *Young Children* 41.2 (1986): 49–55.

Smith, Teresa. *Parents and the Preschool.* Ypsilanti, Mich.: The High/Scope Press, 1980.

Steinfels, Margaret O. *Who's Minding the Children: The History and Politics of Day Care in America.* New York: Simon and Schuster, 1973.

Taylor, Katherine W. *Parents and Children Learn Together.* New York: Teacher College Press, Columbia University, 1967.

Chapter 5 Benefits of Teacher-Parent Partnerships

This chapter explores the benefits of establishing a positive working relationship for children, parents, and teachers.

Objectives

After studying this chapter, the student will be able to

1. list three benefits for children when parents and teachers work together constructively
2. list three benefits for parents when parents and teachers work together constructively
3. list three benefits for teachers when parents and teachers work together constructively

Let's go back and listen to Anne Morgan again. She seems quite definite about her position.

> "Look, I'm not their parent, I'm their teacher. There's a lot of difference between the two. All I can do is work with the children for the eight hours or so they're in my classroom at the center. After that they're the parents' responsibility. Goodness knows some of those parents could use some help—some of the things they say and do! I do get annoyed when I work so hard with a child, and then see the parent come right in and undo everything I've tried to do. But it's really not my business, I guess. Let them do their job and I'll do mine."

Anne Morgan apparently has decided that there is no purpose in establishing a working partnership between teachers and parents. Chapter 6 looks at her attitudes as barriers to the relationship, but first let's examine the areas Anne is overlooking: the benefits to children, parents, and teachers as the adults learn to communicate and cooperate.

Children can move more easily into new situations from the secure base of that first important attachment.

Benefits for Children

In their early years, children are dependent on the key adults in their lives to foster first a sense of security, and then feelings of self-worth. Children develop a sense of trust in the people and world around them as they perceive a predictable and consistent response from their parents. Parents are, of course, of primary importance here. An attachment is made to specific people that an infant associates with comfort and warm sensory contact; the attachment is a long-lasting, emotional, learned response. It is this attachment in a parent-child relationship that forms the basis for a child to trust or not trust her environment. Erikson (1963), Bowlby (1966), Ainsworth (1969), Klaus and Kennell (1976), and Brazelton (1981) conclude that this parent-child attachment is crucial for the development of a healthy personality. The presence of the mother or other primary caregiver to whom a child is attached, serves as a secure base from which to move out and respond to other environmental aspects. Preferably, when a child moves into the school world, that first important attachment provides a base of security that can be extended to other adults.

This task is made easier if familiar, trusted adults are comfortable with the new adults. Contrast the effects, for example, on these two young children.

Susan's mother feels nervous around the new teacher. She feels that the teacher is looking critically at some of the things she does, and does not seem like a friendly person. As a result, she spends little time talking to her, hurrying in and out of the classroom when picking Susan up. She's made some negative comments to Susan's father at home about the classroom situation. Susan's teacher is perturbed by this avoidance behavior, and feels both annoyed and uncomfortable when Susan's mother darts in and out. Susan, puzzled but aware of the strain between the adults, does not allow herself to relax and feel secure in her new classroom world.

Jenny's parents, on the other hand, looked long and hard before they found a preschool that seemed to match their beliefs about child rearing. They took the time to talk with the teacher at length; they discovered that they shared some leisure time interests. Both parents and teacher now feel comfortable and trusting as they share conversations daily. Jenny seems to feel that her circle of loved and trusted adults has widened; she moves easily back and forth from home to school.

A young child's anxiety in a new school experience may be lessened if there is not an abrupt division between home and school. Children thrive when they feel a continuity between parents and teachers that can only be present when the adults have reached out to understand and respect each other. Just as a teacher's first task in relating to a young child is to build a sense of trust and mutual respect, so it is this

Children feel more secure when their parents appear comfortable with their teachers.

same task that is important first in working with parents. It is not realistic to expect teachers to like all parents. However, it is essential that teachers respect parents for their caring and efforts. In most cases, parents do care.

Obviously it is not entirely possible to maintain continuity in all areas, nor is it necessarily advantageous to do so. In the case of young children, however, it is believed that such continuity serves to support optimal development by providing the child with a consistent, predictable, social world (Belsky et al., 1982, p. 101).

Children also gain in feelings of self-worth if they perceive that their parents are valued and respected by others. A child's sense of who she is is closely connected with the sense of who her parents are. If her parents receive positive feedback, she also feels worthwhile and valued.

> Jenny beams when her teacher comes over to greet her father in the morning and ask how the weekend camping trip went. In her eyes, her teacher and father are friends, and this means her father is somebody special in her teacher's classroom. This transfers to Jenny herself feeling she has been treated in a special way and is therefore valued.

The presence of parents and their acceptance by a teacher is especially valuable in affirming for minority children a sense of value for and integration of their own culture in the classroom world (Joffee, 1972).

The welcome and acceptance of her parents is especially valuable for the minority child.

Another benefit for children in a constructive parent-teacher partnership is the increased ability of all adults to guide and nurture a child's development knowledgeably. Parents and teachers who can comfortably share personal observations and insights, general knowledge and ideas, and specific incidents and reactions, expose each other to a wealth of information that may help them provide the most appropriate response for each child. A child is surely benefitted by such an exchange of information.

Last month Jenny missed her daddy very much when he was out of town on a long business trip. At home she became clinging and demanding of her mother. Miss Briscoe noticed lots of crying at school, and easy frustration with everyday tasks. At first she was puzzled by the sudden change, but when Jenny's mother shared her description of the behavior at home and the temporary change in the family pattern, she was able to help Jenny talk openly about her concern for her daddy. She read a story book at group time about a daddy who sometimes had to go away; Jenny took it off the shelf almost daily to read it by herself. How lucky for Jenny that her teacher knew, so didn't simply respond to the new crying by seeing it as an undesirable behavior, and either ignoring or punishing it.

Some of the gains for children resulting when parents and teachers cooperate, share information, and expand their skills, are measurable. Research reveals that children gain in academic skills, positive self-concept, and verbal intelligence when extensive parent participation with teachers is required (Honig, 1975).

When teachers and parents share information, the child benefits.

The three benefits to children are

1. increased security in the new school environment,
2. increased feelings of self-worth, and
3. increased number of helpful responses and appropriate experiences due to adults' sharing of knowledge.

Benefits for Parents

What do parents gain from developing a working relationship with their children's teachers?

An immediate benefit is the feeling of support in carrying out the responsibilities of parenthood. As discussed earlier, the changing nature of American life means that many parents are removed from the natural supports of family and roots, traditions, and models, when they begin the usually unprepared-for task of parenting. The many questions and uncertainties that occur in everyday activities often make parenting lonely, worrisome, and indeed overwhelming. Galinsky writes of the

A parent-teacher relationship can give parents the feeling of being not quite alone in their responsibilities.

contemporary myth that each modern isolated family feels it should be able to do everything for itself, to be complete on its own (Galinsky and Hooks, 1977). In reality, parents can never be totally independent; they need others to watch their child while they work or go to the store, or just to talk to, to make it all less overwhelming. Having an adult who cares about their particular child, to share both the good and the not-so-good times of day-to-day life, is extremely helpful in alleviating anxieties. It has been noted that after mothers have a chance to express their feelings and concerns to others willing to listen with an empathetic ear, they often exhibit more patience with their children, listen more carefully to them, and are more responsive to their needs than before the opportunity to unburden themselves (Kunreuther, 1970). A parent-teacher relationship can offer much needed support to parents.

In addition, teachers provide a background of information and skill from their expertise and experience in dealing with a variety of children, as well as a model for positive guidance techniques. There is no question that parents possess firsthand knowledge about their children, but frequently the experience of living with their children is their only

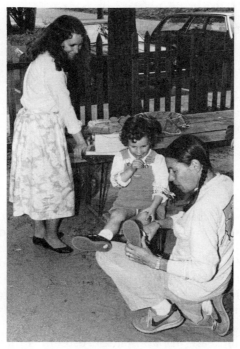

Parents may learn new skills by watching and listening to teachers working with the children.

opportunity to learn about child development. Many parents never have the opportunity to learn relevant developmental information and often misunderstand the nature of developing children. They may be unaware of the appropriate nurturance at each phase, as evidenced by the current tendency of many parents to push their "hurried children" into early academics, assuming that "sooner is better," rather than understanding that young children are not ready for such learning. When teachers share their knowledge of child development, they help parents respond more appropriately to their children's developmental needs.

Teachers have a specific education in the principles of child development and are trained in effective guidance techniques. When parents converse with teachers, and watch and listen to teachers working with children, they can expand their knowledge and ideas, and become more effective as parents.

"You know," says Jenny's mother, "I sure am glad to have you tell me most four-year-olds tend to get a little out of bounds; when she began to spit last month, I was horrified. Jenny's the first four-year-old I've ever known. My sister's family lives in California, so I never had a chance to see much of her children at that age. It makes it a little easier to live with Jenny to know that it's not just her, or to think we've done something wrong. And it's also been helpful to watch you dealing with some of that behavior in the classroom. It would never have occurred to me to be so calm and suggest she go into the bathroom to spit."

It is essential that parental self-esteem develops in a positive way. Parents who believe in themselves are far better able to develop and use appropriate parenting skills; parents who feel self-confident are far better able to provide their children with a secure environment and foster positive feelings of self in their children (Morrison, 1972). Studies indicate that there is a definite impact on the development of feelings of competence and self-esteem in parents involved in their children's programs (Miller, 1968).

Perhaps one reason for the increase in parental self-esteem is that parents can get specific positive feedback on their functioning as a parent, and feedback that is especially meaningful because it comes from an "expert" in child rearing.

"You know," says Miss Briscoe, "I admire the way you talked with Jenny this morning. You were sensitive to her feelings, but also quite definite that you had to go. That approach helped her see where the limit was. Good for you."

Preschool teachers are powerful people, because in many cases they are the first people outside the family to see children and their parents on an ongoing basis; their approval is important to parents.

A positive feeling of parental self-esteem is also nurtured when parents feel they are a vital part of their child's school world as well as home world. Teachers who help parents feel included in the edu-

All parents may enjoy the feeling that they are part of their child's school world.

cation process contribute to feelings of competency in parents. Parents feel they are in control, sure that their children are getting the kind of care they want, rather than feeling that control is elsewhere, and they are powerless to provide what their child needs. This is helpful for all parents, especially fathers, who often feel cut off by our culture, unimportant to the overall needs of the child.

"You know, Miss Peters," Jenny's father said at a recent conference, "I'm very glad you suggested I'd be welcome to come and spend some time any afternoon I can get off work a little early. I really like knowing who the kids are that Jenny talks about at home—just to see what part of her day here is like. It's important to me not to feel as though I have nothing to do with part of her life."

The three ways parents benefit from positive teacher-parent relationships are

1. feelings of support in the difficult task of parenting,
2. knowledge and skills gained by parents to help them in child-rearing, and
3. enhanced parental self-esteem from receiving positive feedback on their parenting actions and feeling included in their child's life away from home.

Benefits for Teachers

What about teachers, whose efforts to develop a positive working relationship may be the greatest? Are there benefits to justify such efforts? Again, the answer must be yes.

Anyone who has worked in a preschool classroom is aware of the uniqueness of each child's personality and needs. Teachers have learned much that is applicable about the general characteristics of children at particular ages and stages, but in order to be effective with each child, there is additional information to learn. Each child comes to the classroom with a past history—years of reactions, experiences, and characteristic styles of behaving that are unique. Each family has its own dreams and expectations for its children, its own patterns of behavior and mores related to the specific cultural or ethnic ethos from which it comes, its own structure, relationships, and needs. Teachers need to know all this and learn it early in their associations with children and families. With this specialized knowledge, parents are in a position to assist teachers in working with their children. One way of describing the difference in the kinds of knowledge that parents and teachers have of children is that parents' knowledge is vertical, having developed longitudinally through the child's life; teachers' knowledge is horizontal, encompassing everything about a particular age-group. At the point where these two lines intersect, teachers and parents can support each other in a partnership of knowledge. To leave untapped such a resource would reduce teachers' abilities to really work to optimum capacity with each child. Teachers who build an effective communication with parents are less likely to be frustrated while working with the many unknowns in children, and are more likely to meet realistic goals for each child, and support each family in reaching their own particular goals.

At the same conference Miss Peters commented how helpful it had been for her to know, before Jenny's entrance to the classroom, that she was a quiet child who normally took a long time to warm up in a new situation—"Otherwise I'd have been concerned. But that helped me give her lots of time and support and not to expect too much talking until she was comfortable. I was also glad to know she especially liked puzzles—that way I could plan something special for her during those first days."

Teachers' self-confidence will grow as positive feedback is received from others regarding their job performance. To have their efforts valued and respected, as demonstrated by parents' positive response and desire to cooperate, is an important contribution to teachers' sense

Teachers benefit when they see their efforts are valued and respected.

of professional well-being. There is no question that teachers have frustrating and negative experiences as they work with parents; there is no such thing as one hundred percent success in such complex endeavors involving human personalities, needs, and other foibles. But for teachers who honestly and warmly try to reach out to parents, there is enough success for them to realize that their efforts are effective and appreciated.

Parents involved in schools and centers learn so much about the functioning of preschool teachers that they often become advocates for teachers, urging communities and centers to establish working policies and personnel conditions that benefit teachers.

> "For all you do, that's what they pay you? I think that should be brought up with the board."

Teachers have only the resources of one person, with their own limitations on time, energy, knowledge, creativity, experiences, and other resources. Parents may offer additional resources in all these commodities and others as well. The learning experiences teachers can offer children in the classroom are multiplied and enhanced by parents who feel invited and included in the educational process. Parents learn a good deal about interacting with their own children and often "teach" very well. Parents as a classroom resource will be discussed further in Chapter 12.

A review of the research on the importance of involving parents in the education of their young children strongly suggests that the effectiveness of teachers and their programs is reinforced and increased by an active involvement of the families of preschool children. (See Chapter 4 and Bronfenbrenner, 1974; Gordon, 1971.)

The three benefits for teachers are

1. increased knowledge which enables teachers to be more effective with each child,
2. positive feedback which increases their own feelings of competence in their profession, and advocacy of their interests, and
3. parental resources to supplement and reinforce their own efforts in providing an enlarged world of learning.

Summary

Since there are benefits for all—teachers, parents and children— it should also be stated that it is difficult to discover any disadvantages in forming a healthy sense of working together. Why, then, are not more teachers and parents involved in constructive partnerships? The answer may lie in examining attitudes and behaviors on both sides that act as barriers to effective teacher-parent relationships.

Student Activities for Further Study

1. Talk with a preschool teacher about what she feels she has gained and/or learned from her working relationships with parents. Compare your findings with the benefits to teachers discussed in the chapter.
2. Ask a preschool teacher to think of one specific child in her class. What are some of the things she has learned about that child that could only have been learned through the parents?
3. Talk with a parent whose child has been in a preschool classroom this year. What are some of the things the parent feels he/she has gained from the teacher?
4. Ask both teachers and parents for examples of situations regarding children where the adults have been able to work as partners, coordinating plans and information.

Review Questions

1. List three benefits for children when parents and teachers work together as partners.
2. List three benefits for parents when parents and teachers work together as partners.
3. List three benefits for teachers when parents and teachers work together as partners.

References and Related Readings

Ainsworth, M.D. "Object Relations, Dependency and Attachment: A Theoretical Review of the Mother-Infant Relationship." *Child Development* 40 (1969): 969-1026.

Belsky, Jay, Lawrence Steinberg and Ann Walker. "The Ecology of Day Care." *Non-Traditional Families: Parenting and Child Development.* Ed. Michael Lamb. Hillsdale, New Jersey: Lawrence Erlbaum Assoc. Pubs., 1982.

Bowlby, John. *Attachment and Loss.* Vol. 1. *Attachment.* New York: Basic Books, 1969.

Brazelton, T. Berry. *On Becoming a Family: The Growth of Attachment.* New York: Dell Publishing Co., 1981.

Bronfenbrenner, Urie. *A Report on Longitudinal Evaluations of Preschool Programs: Is Early Intervention Effective?* Vol. 2 DHEW Publ. No. (OHD) 74-25.

Conant, Margaret M. "Teachers and Parents: Changing Roles and Goals." *Childhood Education* 48.3 (1971): 114-118.

Erikson, Erik H. *Childhood and Society.* 2nd Ed. New York: W.W. Norton and Co. Inc., 1963.

Galinsky, Ellen and William Hooks. *The New Extended Family: Day Care That Works.* Boston: Houghton Mifflin Co., 1977.

Gordon, Ira. *A Home Learning Center Approach to Early Stimulation.* Gainesville, Florida: Institute for Development of Human Resources, 1971.

Hendrick, J. "What Mothers Need." *Young Children* 4.12 (1969): 109-114.

Honig, Alice S. *Parent Involvement in Early Childhood Education.* Washington, D.C.: NAEYC, 1975.

Jackson, Nan. "The Teacher Profits Too." *Parents, Children, Teachers: Communication.* Washington, D.C.: ACEI, 1969.

Joffee, Carol. "Child Care: Destroying the Family or Strengthening It?" *The Future of the Family.* Ed. Louise Howe. New York: Simon and Schuster, 1972.

Klaus, M.H. and J.H. Kennell. *Maternal-Infant Bonding.* St. Louis: C.V. Mosby, 1976.

Kunreuther, S.C. "A Preschool Exchange: Black Mothers Speak and a White Teacher Listens." *Children* 17. (1970): 91-96.

Lane, Mary B. "The Needs of Parents." *Education for Parenting.* Washington, D.C.: NAEYC, 1975.

Miller, J.O. *Diffusion of Intervention Effects in Disadvantaged Families.* Urbana: University of Illinois Co-ordinating Center, National Laboratory of Early Childhood Education, 1968.

Morrison, G.S. *Parent Involvement in the Home, School and Community.* Columbus, Ohio: Merrill, 1972.

Safran, Daniel. "Making the Parents Feel At Home." *Day Care and Early Education* 1.4 (1974): 11-14.

Scheinfeld, D. "On Developing Developmental Families." *Critical Issues in Research Related to Disadvantaged Children.* Ed. E. Grotberg. Princeton: Education Testing Service, 1969.

Chapter 6 Potential Barriers to Teacher-Parent Relationships

Chapter 6 explores the attitudes and behaviors existing in teachers and parents that may act as obstacles to communicating openly and comfortably and establishing working relationships.

Objectives

After studying this chapter, the student will be able to

1. discuss several attitudes of parents and teachers that may create communication barriers
2. discuss several emotional responses of parents and teachers that may cause communication barriers
3. discuss several external factors in the lives of parents and teachers that may create communication barriers

Why Are There Barriers?

Chapter 5 explored the potential for parents and teachers to offer each other strength, support, and knowledge as they work together for children's benefit. But why is it that sometimes the relationship never gets off the ground?

Some of the parents and teachers introduced earlier may help demonstrate the reasons.

John Reynolds is quite ready to admit it: he's frankly terrified of the prospect of his contacts with parents in this first year of preschool teaching.

"Look, I'm just feeling my way with the kids this year. I'm sure those parents are wondering what's going on, and I'm not comfortable with them asking many questions. And I don't even have any kids of my own, to draw on that experience. I'm sure they wouldn't even listen to me. What's more, some of these parents are well-established in their own professions—I'm not even sure how to talk to them."

Connie Martinez shares his negative feelings about the parent involvement philosophy at the center, but for different reasons.

"Enough time goes into running a good classroom for young children without asking teachers to spend even more time on trying to do things for parents. And if you ask me, the whole idea is wrong, anyway. Parents today are pushing their responsibilities off on someone else, always asking the government or somebody to do more for them. Many of my parents live in public housing and get their child care subsidized already. It's just wrong; the more you do for them, the more they'll let you do. How will they learn to do a good job with their own kids that way, if we're helping them every step of the way. My parents raised six children without any preschool teacher working along with them."

Dorothy Scott shares her pessimism.

"I've been working with young children for thirteen years now and believe me, the majority of parents just don't seem to care. I've knocked myself out planning meetings to teach them the things they ought to know and most of them never show up. You tell them what they should do, and they keep on doing the same old ways. It can be pretty frustrating, let me tell you."

MiLan Ha won't say much about her feelings.

"I really wish I could just work with my children without anyone suggesting I should also be working with the parents. When parents begin to talk to me, I just freeze up and can't think of a thing to say. With the children I'm fine."

These teachers are expressing strong attitudes that clearly will influence any interactions they have with parents. But some of the parents have equally potent viewpoints.

Sara Leeper says: "That teacher can hardly stand to talk to me. You can see her disapproval written all over her face. I'd like to know who she thinks she is, sitting in judgement over me. I'm a good mother."

Jane Weaver is very uncomfortable around the teacher, but for different reasons.

"She just knows so much. I never went to college and sometimes I don't quite understand some of the words she uses when she talks about what she's trying to accomplish with the children. I'm afraid I'd show my ignorance if I said anything. And she's so very expert—she always knows what to do with those children. She makes me feel—dumb."

Mary Howard explains her biggest problem with the teacher: "I feel like a nuisance. I mean, she's always so busy I hate to bother her to ask her anything. I just feel like I'm butting in, and that makes me feel kind of bad. Cynthia's with her all day long and sometimes I just feel left out."

These comments exemplify some of the attitudes that will be explored. Consider these ideas and emotions in light of your experiences; think of parents and teachers you have observed.

To identify familiar attitudes and behaviors from personal experience is not a negative evaluation of the individuals involved. Many of the reactions are very natural human behaviors that constitute a problem only when they are unrecognized and unattended interferences between parent and teacher.

When considering parent-teacher communication, remember that the initiative should come, in most cases, from a teacher. Since this communication takes place in school, a teacher's home territory, it gives her the advantage of her own environment, and with this advantage comes the burden of responsibility. A teacher is responsible for creating an atmosphere open to dialogue. She must recognize not only those experiences and feelings of parents that might stand between them, but also analyze her own attitudes and behaviors so that she does nothing to exacerbate parents' discomfort.

In one sense, parents and teachers can be described as natural adversaries, not because of the dynamics of any individual relationship, but because of the nature of the relationship that emerges from the roles defined by the social structure of society. Parents and teachers generally have different perspectives in how to approach and view a child, a difference that evolves from the definitions of their social and cultural roles. Our culture defines parents as ultimately responsible for their children's well-being. Because of their attachment, parents tend to be protective and highly emotionally invested in their child. They can be described as individualistic, having particular expectations, goals, and intense feelings for their child. Teachers are given the cultural role of rational guide; their perspective can be described as universalistic, concerned about a child in the context of broad goals of socialization and education (Lightfoot, 1975). A teacher can be affectionate and still be able to regard a child with an objectivity not possible for a parent, what Katz calls a "detached concern" (Katz, 1980). Katz distinguishes between mothering and teaching in several dimensions.

Distinctions Between Mothering and Teaching in Their Central Tendencies in Seven Dimensions.

ROLE DIMENSION	MOTHERING	TEACHING
1. Scope of Functions	Diffuse and Limitless	Specific and Limited
2. Intensity of Affect	High	Low
3. Attachment	Optimum Attachment	Optimum Detachment
4. Rationality	Optimum Irrationality	Optimum Rationality
5. Spontaneity	Optimum Spontaneity	Optimum Intentionality
6. Partiality	Partial	Impartial
7. Scope of Responsibility	Individual	Whole Group

Source: Lilian Katz, *Current Topics in Early Childhood Education,* v. 3 (Ablex Publishing Corp., 1980), figure 1, p. 49.

Perhaps one of the greatest difficulties encountered when an increasing number of very young children are cared for by other adults, usually called "teachers," is the overlapping of parents' and teachers' spheres of influence. The institutions have not yet moved to define clearly the roles within this new context.

The ambiguous, grey areas of authority and responsibility between parents and teachers exacerbate the distrust between them. The distrust is further complicated by the fact that it is rarely articulated, but usually remains smoldering and silent (Lightfoot, 1978, p. 27).

An acceptance of the differences and, perhaps, conflicts in the relationship between parents and teachers should not also imply an acceptance of distancing, mistrust, and hostility as inevitable. These responses result from a lack of communication and from mistaking differences for complete alienation.

More powerful influences than these culturally suggested roles impel parents and teachers as they develop a working relationship. It is important to remember that when people come together, they do so as individuals whose personalities, past experiences, present needs and situations all determine their perceptions and reactions. "Humans of all ages get caught in a powerful web spun of two strong threads;

the way they were treated in the past, and the way the present bears down on them (Hymes, 1974, p. 16). Teachers need to examine sensitively the words and behaviors that pass between parents and themselves; to do so requires positive self-esteem and a sense of competence, or else teachers will be reluctant to undergo so searching an examination.

Lombana suggests that most of the barriers to effective parent-teacher relationships can be separated into three categories: (1) those caused by human nature, (2) those caused by the communication process, and (3) those caused by external factors (Lombana, 1983). It is worthwhile to consider these in more detail.

Barriers Caused by Human Nature

There is a strong desire in most people to preserve their self-image; anything perceived as a threat to an individual's self-image serves as a barrier, as an individual avoids the source of the threat. It is interesting to note that the behavior that one person in the parent-teacher relationship might use to protect her self-concept might trigger an equally defensive behavior in the other person, setting up a cycle. For example, the teacher who remains coldly professional to hide her own insecurities and keep a parent at a distance may cause the parent to become hypercritical and demanding in order to get the teacher to pay attention to him. Fears related to protecting self include:

Fear of Criticism

As John Reynolds expressed, many teachers dread parental criticisms and so avoid any possible source of these. This is particularly true of young teachers who fear that their position may not be accepted because of a lack of teaching experience or because they have not experienced parenthood firsthand. Teachers unsure of their own abilities fear any negative feedback that may confirm their inner doubts. They put an invisible "Do Not Enter" sign on their classroom door, that conveys to parents that their presence and opinions are not welcome.

Parents are also particularly vulnerable to criticism. Aware of the cultural myths and facts that place the burden for children's success and positive functioning squarely on parents' shoulders, most parents dread any indication that they are not doing a good job. With many parents uncertain that what they are doing is "right," yet feeling they must prove it is right in order to be accepted as fit parents, a defensiveness against any suggestion of change often results (Taylor, 1967). If a teacher gives the impression of evaluating parents' efforts, it may be easier to avoid her or be defensive, rather than hear the results of her evaluation.

> Jane Weaver admits: "When I saw the teacher watching me scold Sandra the other day, I felt as nervous as a kid myself. You could tell by the look on her face she didn't like it. Well, I don't care—she doesn't have to live with her and I do. What does she know about children anyway—she never had any of her own twenty-four hours a day."

Regardless of their personal outlook and how they view their parenting performance, most parents find it difficult to seek outside their home for professional advice, even under serious circumstances (Yankelovich, 1977). It is incorporated into the self-image of most American parents that they should work things out for themselves as a sign of personal strength and parenting success. Therefore, for many parents, reaching out to share responsibilities with teachers is contrary to their self-image.

Many parents see their children as extensions of themselves; to comment negatively on one is akin to commenting negatively on the other.

> "It really bothers me when the teacher says Sandra is shy. I've always been pretty quiet myself, and it just hurts to hear her say that."

Chilman (1971) suggests that when children go to school, both parents and children are meeting their first big test: "How will he—and therefore we—do?" Parents have made a heavy emotional investment in their children and may avoid a teacher as a source of possible hurt.

Fear Hidden Behind a "Professional" Mask

An insecure teacher may depend too heavily on the image of the professional person who knows the answers and is all-important in the task of caring for children. This exaggeration of professional behavior intimidates parents and keeps them at a distance, which may be a teacher's unrecognized goal. Such a teacher has a hard time acknowledging the importance of parents' contributions or the right of parents to be involved. When one's sense of being in control is shaky, it is difficult to share power.

> "After all, I've been trained to do this. I frankly don't see why parents who haven't should be able to plan policies, make suggestions or interfere with what I do in my classroom."

Exhibiting the aloofness of false professionalism or the unwllingness to recognize and respect parents' significant role masks a teacher's uncertainties she hopes will go unchallenged.

Parents perceiving a teacher's self-imposed distance of excessive professionalism, withdraw behind fear and resentment.

> "Well, she may be quite a teacher, but does she have to let us know how wonderful she is *all* the time?"

It is hard to communicate comfortably across this distinctly cold gap. Parents are reluctant to spend energy in a situation where they feel they are not really needed or wanted (Auerbach-Fink, 1977).

> "Who's she trying to kid? She really thinks she does a better job with them anyway—why does she even bother to ask parents to come in?"

Another possible reaction of parents faced with a teacher's excessive professionalism is to become aggressive in trying to bridge the gap, further alienating or frightening a teacher by demonstrating "pushy" behaviors.

Fear of Failure

Working with parents is an ongoing process; it takes time and effort to build a relationship and that relationship is only the beginning. Teachers looking for immediate results from their efforts will be disappointed. If teachers are not prepared to accept the idea that it is an ongoing process and expect immediate evidence of effectiveness, they might be tempted to abandon all attempts, rather than leave themselves open to a sense of failure (Ade and Hart, 1976).

> Hear Dorothy Scott again: "Well, I'm certainly not going to bother planning another open house. Fifteen children in my room, and five parents show up. It's a big waste of my time."

Certainly no one wants to feel unsuccessful in their efforts, and teachers who define parent involvement only by numbers physically present at any one event may protect themselves in the future by withdrawing.

Fear of Differences

The majority of teachers are "hopelessly middle-class" (Mc-Candless, 1968). Teachers encountering parents from a variety of backgrounds, experiences and viewpoints may fall into the all-too-human tendency to stereotype people, their conditions and actions. This creates barriers that preclude true openness to an individual and his actual personality, needs, and wishes. The barriers may arise in as many directions as there are classes and cultures.

> Connie Martinez talks about some of her families. "Well, of course, the Butlers are college-educated and pretty well-off, so I expect them to do a good job with their children. They really don't need much advice from me. (The Butlers are inexperienced and uneducated in child development and guidance, and are very shaken by the breakup of their marriage. They hunger for advice and support.) Sylvia Ashley's on welfare, so I don't suppose she'll make the effort to come to a parent conference." (Sylvia Ashley has never yet missed an opportunity to talk with any teacher who offered it.)

It is easy for human beings to attend selectively to information that is consistent with their beliefs and self-concepts (Lombana, 1983).

> Ignoring all the good parenting Sara Leeper does, Connie continues to complain, "I really don't see why they let her adopt a child. I certainly wouldn't have, if I'd been making the decision. What kind of environment can a lesbian offer a child?"
>
> "And speaking of environments, Joshua's father lives with his girlfriend. I've heard Joshua refer to her that way: 'My dad's girlfriend.' Now what does that teach a child?"

Parents, in turn, may avoid contact with teachers whose manner, communications style, and expectations are uncomfortably different from their own.

> "That teacher, I don't know, she talks too *good*," explains Mr. Rodriguez.
>
> "You know," says Mary Howard, "just because I'm black, she talks to me like I live in a ghetto or something."

Chang Chik–lai is angry. "She's never tried to find out how our children live at home, what *we* want. I don't want my children losing everything from our culture, and if you ask me, she's ignoring the fact that we have a culture!"

Often, there are differences in background between teachers and parents, but these distinctions can be less divisive when teachers are careful to behave in ways that diminish the importance of the differences, and make the effort to know parents as individuals, not as members of a particular ethnic group or social class.

Barriers Caused by the Communication Process

Verbal and nonverbal messages sent and received by teachers or parents may be distorted through a filter of feelings, attitudes, and experiences. The words used or interpreted may widen, not close, the gap. (Chapter 7 will discuss ways in which the communication skills of a teacher can foster positive relationships with parents.)

Reactions to Role

Strong reactions are often aroused by the very role of the other. Parents have their own childhood encounters with teachers and learning experiences. Some of these may be positive, causing the parent automatically to consider a teacher as a friend. But in many parents, the unconscious response to a teacher is someone to fear, someone who will disapprove, correct, or "fail" the parent (and child). With such an underlying assumption, many messages from a teacher may be interpreted more negatively than the sender intended. Some parents, particularly in lower socioeconomic classes, have had numerous encounters with case workers, social workers, and other figures with authority. A parent who has a history of dehumanizing or disillusioning experiences with professional people may already have erected barriers in the form of negative expectations (Samuels, 1973).

Teachers need to realize how their unconscious reaction to parents is influenced by their relationships with their own parents. A teacher who has unresolved hostilities in the relationship with her own parents may have real difficulties relating comfortably to others who bear the label "parent" (Taylor, 1967). A teacher's experiences that have shaped her values about family life may conflict with the reality for parents with whom she works (Travis and Perreault, 1980). For example, a teacher who feels that mothers really should be at home may not be able to relate sympathetically to a working mother. People alienated by unconscious emotional responses can never really hear or speak to each other clearly.

Other Emotional Responses

Parents may have fears of antagonizing teachers by their questions or comments, with the effect that a teacher could single out their child for reprisals when they are absent.

> "I'd like to tell his teacher that I don't like the way she lets the children do such messy art activities, but if she gets mad she'll just take it out on Ricky when I'm not around. I'd better not."

A recent study found that 50% of all parents, 59% of minority parents, were not sure how well their child was treated in a center (Yankelovich, 1977). With such feelings of uncertainty, it is not surprising that parents fear speaking out might have a negative effect.

Another fear promoting parents' feelings of being adversaries of teachers is the fear that they will be replaced by teachers in their children's affections. Attachment is a mutual process and the affectionate relationship with their children satisfies many emotional needs of parents. Despite evidence to the contrary (Galinsky, 1986), many parents fear this loss and are inhibited from forming relationships with teachers because of their feelings of jealousy and competition with teachers for their children's regard.

> "I'll tell you, it makes you wonder. She comes in to give the teacher a good morning hug, and not so much as a good-bye kiss for her own mother who's going to be gone all day. I get pretty sick of hearing Miss Ha this and Miss Ha that, I can tell you."
>
> "How do you think I feel when she cries at the end of the day and just doesn't want to go home?"

There are often ambivalent emotions here: a mother wants her child to be independent and happy away from her, but resents the perception that a teacher is taking over.

Teachers themselves are not immune from competing for children's affections, especially if their own emotional needs are not being met in their lives beyond the classroom. A warm affectional bond with each child is important, but when a teacher finds herself thinking that she "can do a much better job with him than his own mother" or "would like to take the child home with me, he'd be better off," she has slipped over into dangerous territory of identifying with a child so completely she sees him only as a child she loves in the classroom, not as a member of the more important world of his family (Travis and Perreault, 1980). Parents are naturally the most important people in their children's lives and need to be supported as such. A teacher who begins to confuse her role with being a "substitute" for parents engenders fear and suspicion. A teacher who needs to feel more important to a child than his parents may find it too easy to blame the parents for the child's shortcomings and convey such an attitude in her choice of words, as in the following:

> "The way you're reacting each time he has a temper tantrum is really causing Pete to have more outbursts."

Teachers need to realize these emotions of jealousy and fear are hidden factors limiting much of what is truly said and heard. If teachers ignore the likely presence of these emotions, they may unwittingly fan the sparks into destructive flames.

> "Oh, she was just fine, Mrs. Weaver. She plays as happily as can be all day and never asks for you once. You don't need to worry about her missing you."

This may be intended as reassurance, but will simply confirm the mother's worst fears. Most parents believe that no one else can do the job for their child as well as they can (Yankelovich, 1977) and teachers who help parents feel they are not being displaced from this important position prevent barriers from being raised between them.

> "She did go to sleep well at naptime today. That was an awfully good idea you had to bring her blanket from home. I know she misses you especially then, and it helps to have that blanket as connection for her."

The word "guilt" creeps into many conversations when modern mothers have a chance to talk freely. The many demands on parents, coupled with an unrealistic image of perfection and a feeling of not doing what should be done, result in guilt feelings. This parental emotion may operate as a hidden barrier; parents feeling inadequate to the task may avoid all possible reminders of this, including the person doing things for their child that parents feel they should be doing.

Resentment can creep into the relationship from both teacher and parent.

Preschool teachers have extremely demanding jobs that use enormous amounts of energy, creativity, and emotion for long hours each day. In most cases, preschool teachers are paid much lower salaries and fewer benefits than their counterparts in schools for older children. They are accorded less professional status and recognition, even when they have completed the same number of years of training. Therefore, it is easy for teachers to feel they are taken advantage of by the community in general and parents in particular.

> "I don't see why they can't pick their kids up on time—don't they know I have other things to do in my life?"
>
> "Do you realize she had Easter Monday off and she went and played tennis and brought him to my classroom just like any other day?"

Parents have their own reasons for resenting teachers. In families where both parents work, child-care arrangements are the most critical component for the smooth running of the entire enterprise. This places parents in the ambiguous position of recognizing how important a preschool teacher is to their way of life, but resentful of having a person outside the family play such a necessary role in their lives. Contradictory, to be sure, but enforced dependence often breeds not gratitude, but resentment.

Parents and teachers who resent each other will be unable to communicate clearly.

Personal Factors

There are teachers who explain their lack of communication with parents by their own personalities or their discomfort in social situations. These factors require special efforts on the part of teachers and they should not be accepted as justification for failure to take the initiative in reaching out to parents.

> MiLan Ha knows that she doesn't have nearly as much contact with parents as many of the teachers in her center, but she says she just can't help it. She says it shouldn't make a difference since she works so well with the children, but she does wonder what she might do to help the situation.

Teachers aware of their introverted personalities need to find ways of pushing their own efforts: perhaps setting specific goals, such as talking to a certain number of parents each day, or approaching a parent they have never talked with much, or saying one sentence beyond "Hello, how are you." Teachers having difficulty getting started may need to pre-plan their comments to parents. (Thinking of one thing each child has done or been interested in may be a good place to start.) It may help to share feelings of discomfort with co-workers and be encouraged by their support. Some initial success in getting to know a few parents makes subsequent encounters a little easier.

Teachers need to remind themselves frequently that part of a preschool teacher's responsibility is to work with parents and that parents, because of a lack of familiarity with a school situation, may be far more uncomfortable than the teachers themselves. As the leader in a classroom, teachers are automatically placed in the role of hostess. Just as a hostess does not allow guests to flounder, unspoken to and uncomfortable, in her own living room, so a teacher must take the initiative to converse with parents.

Awareness will help; pushing oneself a little extra will help; a little success will help. Personality and social discomfort must not be allowed to interfere with the communication process.

Barriers Caused by External Factors

As well as internal feelings and experiences, the external circumstances in which teachers and parents find themselves may act as barriers.

Time

Both parents and teachers are undoubtedly under time constraints. If school philosophies and administrative actions do not support working with parents, teachers may not receive either the staffing arrangements or the compensatory time that is needed to respond with flexibility to parents' life-styles and working patterns. Parents never have enough time for the demands of their lives, but they will find the time for parent involvement if they feel it is really important (Auerbach-Fink, 1977). There is a variety of ways to maneuver around time as a barrier (see Chapters 9 and 10), if working together is perceived as important to parents and teachers. It is more productive to consider time as a real problem and search for creative solutions, than to interpret the other's lack of availability as a lack of concern for the child (Swap, 1984).

"Busy-ness"

Another external factor that may function as a barrier is a teacher's appearance of being always busy. This may result from the realities of caring for the needs of a group of children or from an unconscious desire to keep parents at a distance. But whatever the reason, the perception that a teacher has too much else to do to be bothered by a parent keeps many a parent from more than the briefest greeting. As teachers try consciously to dispel this impression of being busy, there are things that can be done. At the beginning of the day, preparations for classroom activities can be made before the children arrive or by another staff member, leaving a teacher available to talk. Teachers need to plan, and have ready for use, activities which children may begin by themselves that require little supervision: puzzles on the table; dried beans and cups to fill in a basin; several lumps of playdough waiting in the art area. When children begin to play, parents and teachers will be free to talk. A classroom should be arranged so that when parents enter they have easy access to a teacher (Herwig, 1982). Staffing arrangements and physical locations at the end of the day should provide enough teachers to care for children so that some are free to talk with parents (Powell, 1977). Planning and attention to details conveys the message that teachers are there for parents.

Old Ideas of Parent Involvement

The changes in family structure and living patterns over the past two decades demand changes in the timing, content, and form of parent involvement, activities, and expectations (Lillie and Trohanis, 1976). If a teacher or school continues to offer nothing more than the traditional forms and meeting times, conferences, etc.—what Swap calls *institutionalized rituals,* that are so obviously unsupportive of good relationships (Swap, 1984)—they are failing to recognize a family's current needs. Examples of *institutionalized rituals* are parent-teacher conferences scheduled at 4:00 p.m., on the teacher's break, or meetings held every first Tuesday at 6:30 p.m. Sometimes the old ideas are adhered to as an unconscious punitive attitude towards parents deviating from traditional lifestyles—mothers who now work, instead of being available to come in for a conference at 10:30 in the morning. Directors and teachers must be aware that their own values may contribute to any reluctance to change forms of parent involvement.

Administrative Policies

Some schools and centers have policies that discourage or forbid contact and discussion between parents and staff other than supervisory personnel, perhaps on the grounds that unprofessional contacts may take place. The major difficulty here is that parents are denied the opportunity to build a relationship with a child's primary caregivers, and that the designated supervisory personnel are often not available in the early morning or late afternoon when parents need to talk. Such policies effectively deter any meaningful parent involvement.

Personal Problems

From the parents' side, the pressure from personal problems can act as a barrier to the parent-teacher relationship. As much as a parent cares about his child and how he is functioning in the classroom setting, too many concerns about other life matters may necessarily require a parent's primary attention. This parent should neither be condemned for indifference nor ignored because of absence, but shown continued support and understanding from a teacher concerning the demands on parents.

These external barriers may be more easily toppled than some of the internal ones. Jesse Jackson is credited with saying:

> Parents must make room in their hearts and then in their house and then in their schedule for their children. No poor parent is too poor to do that, and no middle-class parent is too busy (quoted in Croft, 1979).

In the same way, no teacher who believes in the importance of working as a partner with parents will find the problems so immovable as to abandon all attempts.

Summary

The key to removing many of the barriers to parent-teacher relationships is a teacher's mind-set (Ade and Hart, 1976; Powell, 1977). When teachers believe that there is value in working with parents, they will find the time and energy to commit themselves to identifying and dealing with potential barriers. To sum up, these barriers "include the intense feelings, ego involvements, deeply held attitudes and values, past histories and current concerns" (Chilman, 1971, p. 124) that parents and teachers bring to the process of communication. It is an interesting reminder that each group sees the main obstacle in the other: teachers note parents' unwillingness, and parents note teachers' distant behavior (Tizzard et al., 1981). But rather than blaming others, it is more productive to examine personal attitudes and behaviors. The barriers can be broken by "a bit more relaxation, a bit more empathy, a bit more recognition of the many complex factors that shape life for all of us" (Chilman, 1971, p. 125).

Student Activities for Further Study

1. As you work in your classroom or internship placement, keep a journal of your experiences and encounters in working with parents. Use the journal to be honest about your emotional responses. How does your awareness compare with some of the emotional responses in the text?

2. Examine your own biases. Is there a style or kind of family with which you would be less comfortable working than with others? Discuss this idea in small groups.

3. Wherever possible, observe teachers and parents talking together. What nonverbal signs do you see of comfort and discomfort?

4. Talk with several preschool teachers. Ask them to recall negative experiences in working with parents. Afterwards, try to analyze which of the barriers discussed in the text might have been at work.

5. Talk with several parents whose children are involved in preschool programs. Do they recall negative experiences in relationships with teachers? Try to analyze which of the barriers discussed in the text may have been present.

Review Questions

1. Identify three kinds of fears in parents and teachers, related to human nature, that may act as barriers to the development of effective relationships.

2. Describe four emotional responses that may break the communication process.

3. List four external factors that may act as barriers.

References and Related Readings

Ade, William and James L. Hart. "Parent Involvement: Motivation vs. Alienation." *Day Care and Early Education* 4.2 (1976): 19-20.

Almy, Millie. *The Early Childhood Educator at Work.* New York: McGraw Hill, Inc., 1975.

Auerbach-Fink, Stevanne. "Mothers' Expectations of Child Care." *Young Children* 32.4 (1977): 12-21.

Bromberg, Susan L. "A Beginning Teacher Works With Parents." *Young Children* 23.3 (1968): 75-80.

Chilman, Catherine S. "Some Angles on Parent-Teacher Learning." *Childhood Education* 51.12 (1974): 119-25.

Croft, Doreen J. *Parents and Teachers: A Resource Book for Home, School and Community Relations.* Belmont, Calif.: Wadsworth Publishing Co. Inc., 1979.

Evans, Judith and Lois Bass. "Parental Involvement: Partnership or Prizefight?" *How To Involve Parents in Early Childhood Education.* Ed. Brigham Young University Press. Provo, Utah: Brigham Young University Press, 1982.

Galinsky, Ellen. "How do Child Care and Maternal Employment Affect Children?" *Child Care Information Exchange.* Issue 48 (1986): 19-23.

Hayman, H.L. "Snap Judgement: A Roadblock to Progress in Parent Involvement." *Young Children* 23.5 (1968): 291-93.

Herwig, Joan. "Parental Involvement: Changing Assumptions About the Educator's Role." *How to Involve Parents in Early Childhood Education.* Ed. Brigham Young University Press. Provo, Utah: Brigham Young University Press, 1982.

Hymes, James. *Effective Home-School Relations.* Sierra Madre: Southern California Assoc. for the Education of Young Children, 1974.

Katz, Lilian. "Mothering and Teaching—Some Significant Distinctions." *Current Topics in Early Childhood Education.* Vol. 3. Ed. Lilian Katz. Norwood, New Jersey: Ablex Publishing Corp., 1980.

Lightfoot, S.L. *Worlds Apart: Relationships Between Families and Schools.* New York: Basic Books Inc. Publ., 1978.

———. "Families and Schools: Creative Conflict or Negative Dissonance." *Journal of Research and Development in Education* 9.1 (1975): 34–44.

Lillie, D.L. and P.L. Trohanis, eds. *Teaching Parents to Teach.* New York: Walker and Co., 1976.

Lombana, Judy H. *Home-School Partnerships: Guidelines and Strategies for Educators.* New York: Greene and Stratton, 1983.

McCandless, Boyd. "The Devil's Advocate Examines Parent Education." *The Family Co-ordinator* 17.3 (1968): 149–54.

Samuels, S.C. "Johnny's Mother Isn't Interested." *Today's Education.* 62.2 (1973): 36-38.

Sarason, S. *The Culture of the School and the Problem of Change.* 2nd Ed. Boston: Allyn and Bacon, 1982.

Swap, Susan McAllister. *Enhancing Parent Involvement in Schools.* Boston: Center for Parenting Studies, Wheelock College, 1984.

Taylor, Katherine. *Parents and Children Learn Together.* New York: Teachers College Press, Columbia University, 1967.

Tizard, Barbara, Jo Mortimer and B. Burchell. *Involving Parents in Nursery and Infant Schools.* Ypsilanti, Mich.: The High/Scope Press, 1981.

Travis, Nancy and Joe Perreault. "Day Care as a Resource for Families." *Current Topics in Early Childhood Education.* Vol. 3. Ed. Lilian Katz. Norwood, New Jersey: ABLEX Publishing Corp., 1980.

Yankelovich, Skelly, White, Inc. *Raising Children in a Changing Society: The General Mills American Family Report.* Minneapolis, Minn.: General Mills, 1977.

Chapter 7 Foundations of a Successful Partnership

Chapter 7 explores some of the attitudes, behaviors and other factors that facilitate the formation of a productive partnership between parents and teachers.

Objectives

After studying this chapter, the student will be able to

1. discuss five attitudes or ideas of teachers that are conducive to forming a partnership with parents
2. discuss concrete actions that are necessary in laying the foundation for a parent-teacher partnership

Teacher Ideas and Attitudes

Jane Briscoe has become convinced that there are enough good reasons to merit really trying to form partnerships with parents. "Where do I start?" she wonders.

Since a teacher acts as initiator in forming the partnership, the starting place lies in an examination of some essential teacher ideas and attitudes.

Concept of Professionalism

Basic to the formation of a parent-teacher partnership is a teacher's concept of the professional teaching role. One traditional characteristic of professionals is to keep a certain distance between themselves and their clients, to allow for more objective professional judgements, emotional protection from too many client demands, and enhanced status. But this separateness precludes an uninhibited social exchange between client and professional (Tizard et al., 1981; Powell, 1978). With the traditional definition of the professional, teachers see their relationships with parents as a one-way process of informing parents and attempting to influence them. In such a relationship, parents are passive clients, receiving services, depending on the experts' opinions, in need of direction, and quite peripheral in the process of decision-making (Wolfendale, 1983). A partnership can develop only when teachers create a different mental concept of their role.

Teachers who can accept the partnership concept consider parents to be active members in making and implementing decisions regarding their children, and capable of making major contributions. These teachers share responsibility, believing that both teachers and parents have strengths and equivalent expertise. Such a belief implies reciprocity in a relationship with parents contributing, as well as receiving, services. Parents are not viewed as a problem, but as part of a solution to common puzzles.

This belief in partnership is a prerequisite to everything else. It requires teachers to define their professionalism in a new way, to see themselves as leaders of an educational team, using their special skills and knowledge to enlist the help of parents, expecting to exchange information with them and consider their opinions (Tizard, et al., 1981). A partnership can be exciting and anxiety-producing, since teachers who function as partners with parents are frequently in a position where so much is untried and without guidelines. But as partners, teachers believe parents are capable of growth, and in demonstrating this belief, they grow themselves. In a partnership, children, parents, and teachers grow and learn as they are drawn together by the same objective: what is best for the children.

Sense of Self

Teachers who are most able to move into a partnership with parents have a strong sense of self. They have learned to be in touch with their feelings and aware of their own strengths, weaknesses, concerns, and values; sure of their positions, they are not easily manipulated, nor do they try to manipulate others (Almy, 1975). Because they respect themselves, they treat others with equal dignity, relate as one individual to another, and avoid stereotyping.

Teachers must consciously clarify their values to understand themselves. Jersild suggests that the crucial question to consider is: "What, in my existence as a person, in my relations with others, in my work as a teacher, is of real concern to me, perhaps of ultimate concern to me?" (Jersild, 1955, p. 4). As teachers identify their values, they also make opportunities for parents to consider and specify their own values.

In a parent-teacher partnership, it is important for both to know themselves and each other, and to know also the areas of agreement and disagreement in their value systems.

Humility

Another attitude of teachers related both to the concept of partnership and to the new definition of professionalism is humility, the ability to wait, be silent, and listen (Jersild, 1955). Teachers who do not make impossible demands on themselves do not expect to understand immediately each question, or to have an instant response. This is not just a pose of hesitancy, but an ability to trust the outcome of the process of communication between individuals that is acquired only when teachers are able to dispense with some professional pretensions. Swick refers to this as approachability (Swick and Duff, 1978). This describes the behaviors that suggest "we're all in this together—help me out—what do you think?" The increased feelings of comfort resulting from continual contact with parents may help a teacher to relax.

Compassion

Teachers who can work in a partnership display compassion for themselves and for others. As they attempt to understand parents, they try to realize not just what they are thinking, but also what they may be feeling. Such sensitivity is a first step towards the development of genuine mutual respect.

There is no question that teachers will encounter parents whose socioeconomic backgrounds, life experiences, and cultural mores are quite removed from theirs. One thing they can do is educate themselves

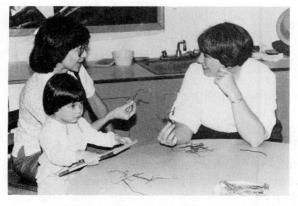

The attitude of "approachability" suggests real partnership.

about some of the general differences they may find in members of a certain class or ethnic group. For example, studies on differing expectations of lower- and middle-class mothers for their children's behavior and educational achievements, or on styles of family interaction in a particular cultural ethos, is helpful in preparing teachers to accept the variations in child-rearing they will encounter. (A useful resource for getting started here is *Cultural Awareness: A Resource Bibliography,* by Velma E. Schmidt and Earldene McNeill, Washington, D.C., NAEYC, 1978.) But, just as they would not depend solely on text book descriptions of typical three-year-old characteristics in teaching their preschoolers, nor will they depend on such general knowledge to guide them in understanding parents. Compassionate teachers attend sensitively to the unique reactions of each parent, no matter what the background.

Respect for Others

Teachers who move into partnerships with parents express a genuine respect for parents, for their position as the most important people in their children's lives and for their accomplishments in child-rearing. They convey this respect by treating them with dignity as individuals. Teachers try to find ways to meet the individual needs of parents. The respect becomes mutual as parents are encouraged to learn more about teachers and a center (Cary, 974).

To summarize, teachers trying to move into a partnership with parents must work towards the following ideas and attitudes:

1. new image of professional role as partnership
2. strong sense of self
3. humility
4. compassion
5. respect for others

External Factors

There are several other concrete, external factors that are important foundations to the successful partnership in addition to the previously discussed attitudes.

Support Systems

Support systems are necessary for teachers striving to work with parents. Administrative support and leadership sets the tone and atmosphere for a parent involvement program. Support may come in the form of a clearly stated philosophy that values and welcomes the contributions of parents in the educational process; assistance, motivation, and appreciation of staff efforts; providing fair compensatory time and staffing arrangements to support efforts; and coordinating plans and strategies that emphasize parent involvement throughout a center. Such support sanctions and gives power to teachers' efforts.

It is still possible for teachers to create an atmosphere for partnership and involvement on their own, but when the administration of a school supports and recognizes those efforts, they are far more productive. There are those instances where the administration actively discourages contact between teachers and parents. If teachers choose to remain in such situations, their only recourse may be to work towards convincing the administration of the need to change this stance, through the positive experiences and proofs offered by research on the effectiveness of parent involvement (see references at end of Chapter 4 for such data), and possibly enlisting the efforts of parents to press for their own involvement.

Even with administrative support, working with a cross-section of parents with individual needs, responses, and demands on teachers' time and energy can be stressful. Teachers can benefit from personal support systems, including colleagues and supervisors, that offer the opportunity to recognize and vent feelings of frustration or strain, and gain new ideas and perspectives.

Communication Time

One of the most crucial components in the foundation of a parent-teacher partnership is time for teachers and parents to communicate freely together. Communication time with parents may be made available by a flexibility in teachers' time options that fit parents' schedules, such

Teachers can gain time to talk with parents when they plan activities the children can involve themselves in without assistance.

as offering evening conferences, prearranged phone conversations, weekend home visits, and early morning coffee discussions. In order to have this flexibility, teachers should have their "after hours" work compensated for in released time. Additional staff members or staggered coverage may be required to cover this released time, as well as to free teachers to talk with parents at the times communication takes place—when children are dropped off and picked up. Since the frequency of casual communication has a direct bearing on the quality of a teacher-parent relationship (Powell, Oct. 1978), it is worthwhile to set up patterns in a classroom and a variety of opportunities that allow teachers the freedom to talk. Time may be an expensive commodity, but worthwhile to the effort of forming parent-teacher partnerships.

Variety in Parent Involvement

Another factor facilitating parent-teacher partnerships is to offer a variety of forms of parent involvement. A program reflects its understanding and responsiveness to the various needs of parents by allowing parents to select when, where, and how to participate. Flexibility in timing increases the variety. A program ready to meet individual needs, concerns, and interests indicates respect for parents and their value within the program. Someone within the program must take the time to find out what parents need and want, what they have to offer and are willing to share, (See Resource Files, Chapter 12 and Surveys, Chapter 13) and evaluate the effectiveness of various methods of involvement. Such variety in parent involvement opportunities allows parents to accept what is useful and reject what does not match their needs.

Information

For a constructive parent-teacher partnership, a clear understanding and knowledge of what is expected or possible in any program is required. Parents who clearly understand their responsibilities and obligations in a school are more comfortable. Routine encounters such as conferences and home visits will lose the apprehension that sometimes accompanies them if parents are familiar with the procedures and their role in them.

Many schools offer this information to parents in the form of a parent handbook, which is discussed as a parent receives orientation information and may be referred to later. A parent handbook should define the general philosophy and services of a program, as well as the specific philosophy concerning parent involvement, so parents understand both the work of a school and how they can be involved (Decker and Decker, 1984). Information is needed regarding a program's policies that concern parents, such as admission requirements, the daily schedule, hours and fees, attendance policies, late pickup policy, health and safety regulations, and children's celebrations. Many handbooks include general information on the developmental characteristics of young children and ways parents can help nurture development. A handbook should also describe the methods that teaching staff use in the classroom and in reporting a child's progress, lists of supplies parents may need, ways parents may be (or are obliged to be) involved in a center's activities. Some well-chosen examples illustrating parent roles can be added.

We welcome parents to enlarge the children's world by sharing an interest (job-related or hobby), ethnc, or religious traditions. Last year two parents helped us learn a Hanukkah song. Another parent helped us prepare a simple Vietnamese dish. A truck driver daddy brought his truck to school, and the mother of a new baby let us look at the baby—toes and all! Please come—what experience can you bring us? At the last parent work night, some of our handy parents fixed three broken tricycles and two limbless dolls. And some of our less handy parents helped us organize the housekeeping area. Please come on the next scheduled night.

Other information to include: dates of scheduled meetings; names and phone numbers of parent advisory committee members; facilities for parents in the school such as bulletin boards or a parent lounge. Clear statements about when the school can be of assistance to parents is helpful. It is important that both limitations and choices for parents are explicit, as well as clear mechanisms that exist for parents who wish to raise concerns (Lurie and Newman, 1982).

In order not to miss important information when developing a parent handbook, it is helpful to ask parents whose children are presently in the school what they would like to have been told before their children started, and to ask teachers what they would like to tell parents (Tizard et al., 1981).

The handbook needs to be concise, attractive, on a basic reading level, and clearly organized, in order to be usable. Much of the information will be reinforced later in newsletters and personal conversation, but it is helpful initially to answer all possible questions for parents, to help them feel comfortable in the new relationship, without the concern that there may be surprises forthcoming. A parent handbook is also a concrete example of administrative support for parent involvement.

Communication Skills

Teachers attempting to create constructive partnerships with parents need to work on developing their communication skills. Many teachers are fortunate to have opportunities to speak with parents frequently. However, frequency of communication does not guarantee increased understanding or improved relationships. Unless teachers are aware of different styles and purposes of communication, of how to communicate verbally and nonverbally, to listen and convey attentive caring, and interpret messages from parents, miscommunication can create real barriers to a partnership.

Some communication styles are almost certain to produce defensiveness: ordering, warning, blaming, advising, and lecturing. Effective teachers learn to avoid these and read the behaviors in others that indicate the communication is causing them discomfort.

Four basic communication styles have been identified, each carrying its own amount of risk and value in sharing information (Flake-Hobson and Swick, 1979).

Style I

The Superficial style ("What a pretty dress you've made"), uses informal small talk to get to know others on an informal basis. There is little risk involved, but little beyond "ice-breaking" is accomplished in a relationship.

Style II

The Command style ("Why are you not firmer about bedtime?"), is riskier, because the authoritative tone that can be used effectively in some group situations often creates defensive reactions in an individual, providing little personal or factual information.

Style III

The Intellectual style ("Research studies indicate that the style of maternal interaction is definitely correlated with cognitive abilities and educational achievement"), is used to convey objective information and is therefore low-risk, though excessive use of this style can create the barrier of too impersonal a relationship.

Style IV

The Caring style ("I am concerned about Ramon. He frequently seems lonely. I wonder if his language understanding is keeping him apart."), openly shares personal information. The caring style requires the use of four sets of skills: listening, sharing self-information, establishing shared meaning through clarifying information received and sent, and a conscious commitment to care for the self and others that requires the individual to risk self in relationships (Flake-Hobson and Swick, 1979).

Teachers will discover that words convey different meanings to everyone. Teachers recognizing the social and cultural experiences of their listeners make adaptations accordingly, and strive for unambiguous, descriptive words with no emotionally loaded connotations. They avoid professional jargon that may alienate or intimidate: words like *cognitive, fine motor, affective*. They reflect tentatively a parent's statements and their own interpretations—"What I hear you saying is:"—to elicit genuine feedback from the parent, to check out their understandings. They use verbal reinforcers—"I see"; "Yes"; the parent's name. They realize that open-ended attempts to obtain more information—"Let's talk about that"; "I'm wondering about. . . ."—are more effective than "who," "what," "how," "when" questions. They summarize for parents the ideas discussed.

Teachers need to remember that the verbal message they send accounts for only a small fraction of communication between people. Mehrabian claims that facial expressions have the greatest impact on the receiver: 55% of the message; that the impact of voice tone is next: 38% of the message, leaving only 7% delivered by words alone. What's more, in situations where the sender's facial expression is inconsistent with the words (such as when a teacher says "I'm glad you could come for this conference," but her face shows apprehension or indifference), the facial expression will prevail and determine the impact of the total message (Mehrabian, 1981).

Eye contact plays an important role in opening or closing channels of communication. Looking at the partner in communication conveys the physical impression of listening, or of seeking feedback, or desire for the other's speech. Looking away may indicate a desire to avoid contact, to hide some aspect of inner feelings, or an attempt to process difficult ideas (Knapp, 1980). Because of the intensity of the emotional bond between parents and their children, teachers may notice that tears are often close to the surface in both fathers and mothers when the conversation touches important issues, including very positive issues. Many parents are uncomfortable with this display of their emotions and look away to hide the tears. Teachers sensitive to the amount of eye contact offered by parents may be able to perceive when their communication is too painful, or too difficult, and can alter the message accordingly. Teachers who realize how closely their own eye contact conveys evidence of listening and acceptance can make conscious attempts to improve this aspect of communication.

Other nonverbal communication for teachers to monitor in themselves and others that may produce effects of distance and discomfort include: leaning towards (or away from) the other person; tone of voice similar to the other person; occasional head-nodding to indicate attention and approval; occasional gestures; smiles; speech errors and higher speech rates that can indicate anxiety and uncertainty; and style of dress.

Such nonverbal cues are sometimes missed if the receiver is inexperienced, temporarily not paying attention, preoccupied with their own internal messages, or from another culture where cues may have different meanings. But a major determinant of communication distortion or failure is a lack of trust (McCroskey, et al., 1971). People are likely to base their response to messages on their perception of the source, rather than on the message content. Therefore, a prerequisite for effective communication is to relate to one another as individuals and avoid stereotyping. (For further exploration of communication techniques the student is encouraged to refer to Knapp, 1980; Mehrabian, 1981; McCroskey et al., 1971.)

Summary

There are concrete steps that can be taken and skills that can be developed to help lay foundations for parent-teacher partnerships. These are:

1. Administrative support to provide corroborative philosophy and tangible assistance with staffing arrangements and time provisions; emotional support systems for teachers.
2. Time, created by allowing teachers to interact with parents at crucial points in the work day and compensating them for offering flexible options for parent involvement beyond normal working hours.
3. A variety of forms of parent involvement allowing parents to select where, when, and how to participate.
4. Clear explanations of policies, expectations, and openness to welcome parents into the educational program.
5. Developing and practicing effective communication skills.

For teachers like Jane Briscoe, who want to create partnerships with parents, these are some starting places. There are a variety of techniques to involve parents that will be explored in Section III.

A word to all teachers who are anxious to start developing parent-teacher relationships. Parent-teacher relationships, as we have seen, are complex things, uniting two sets of internal experiences, needs, and responses with two sets of external circumstances. Teachers who expect total success will be disappointed if they measure complete success as full participation by every parent. Parents have unique responses to parent involvement opportunities; some parents are reached in one way, others in another. And some may be reached at another time, after the seeds of one teacher's efforts have long seemed to bear no result. So the measure of success lies not in the numbers responding to any initiative, but in the quality of interaction; not in total agreement, but in continuing dialogue. Teachers will discover they are in long-term relationships with parents. When children are in a preschool for a number of years, parents and teachers may learn to recognize each other informally before a child is actually in a particular teacher's classroom and maintain ties of friendship after a child moves on to the next classroom. Such an extended period of contact allows for the growth of comfort and communication, as well as the acceptance of ideas. The teacher realizing this is less likely to become frustrated and abandon all attempts.

Student Activities for Further Study

1. Contact several preschools in your community. Ask for copies of handbooks or printed materials they give to parents. Examine the material to discover any stated or implied philosophies of working (or not working) with parents.

2. With your classmates, work on creating a parent handbook that clearly conveys information parents want to know and the attitude of welcoming parents into specific participations. (Each student might take a segment, after the necessary information and format have been decided.)

3. With your classmates, generate a list of words, such as those discussed on p. 117 that might convey different meanings depending on the cultural or environmental experiences of the receiver.

4. Imagine you are a teacher beginning employment at a day-care center. What kinds of guidance, support, and training do you feel you need to become comfortable and capable in areas of working with parents? Devise an appropriate in-service training plan.

5. Observe a teacher you feel works well with parents. What personality characteristics and behaviors do you see? What do you notice regarding the teacher's nonverbal communication?

Review Questions

1. Identify any three out of five attitudes of teachers conducive to forming a partnership with parents.

2. List five external factors important in laying the foundations for partnerships with parents.

References and Related Readings

Almy, Millie. *The Early Childhood Educator at Work.* New York: McGraw Hill, Inc., 1975.

Berns, Roberta M. *Child, Family, Community.* New York: Holt, Rinehart and Winston, 1985.

Cary, S. "Forming a Partnership with Parents." *Day Care and Early Education* 2.1 (1974): 10-14.

Conant, M.M. "Teachers and Parents: Changing Roles and Goals." *Childhood Education* 48.3 (1971): 114-18.

Decker, Celia A. and John R. *Planning and Administering Early Childhood Programs.* 3rd. Ed. Columbus: Charles E. Merrill Publishing Co., 1984.

Dodd, J.H. and N.S. Dodd. "Communicating With Parents." *Academic Therapy* 7.3 (1972): 227-84.

Duggins, Lydia. "Getting It All Together With Parents." *Teacher* 90.4 (1972): 13-16.

Ellenberg, F.C. and Nancy J. Lanier. "Interacting Effectively With Parents." *Childhood Education* 60.5 (1984): 315-20.

Flake-Hobson, Carol and Kevin J. Swick. "Communication Strategies for Parents and Teachers or How to Say What You Mean." *Dimensions* 7.4 (1979): 112-15.

Headley, Neill. "The Impact of Silent Communication." *Parent-Children-Teachers: Communication.* Washington, D.C.: ACEI, 1969.

Herin, Linda R. and Richard E. *Developing Skills for Human Interaction.* 2nd Ed. Columbus: Charles E. Merrill Publishing Co., 1978.

Jersild, Arthur T. *When Teachers Face Themselves.* New York: Bureau of Publications, Teachers College, Columbia University, 1955.

Knapp, Mark L. *Essentials of Nonverbal Communication.* New York: Holt, Rinehart and Winston, 1980.

McCroskey, James C., Carl E. Larson, Mark L. Knapp. *An Introduction to Interpersonal Communication.* Englewood Cliffs, New Jersey: Prentice-Hall, Inc., 1971.

Mehrabian, Albert. *Silent Messages: Implicit Communication of Emotions and Attitudes.* 2nd. Ed. Belmont, Calif.: Wadsworth Publ. Co., 1981.

Powell, Douglas R. "The Interpersonal Relationship Between Parents and Caregivers in Day Care Settings." *American Journal of Orthopsychiatry* 48 (1978): 680-89.

————. "Correlates of Parent-Teacher Communication Frequency and Diversity." *The Journal of Educational Research* 71 (1978): 333-41.

Rutherford, Robert B. and Eugene Edgar. *Teachers and Parents: A Guide to Interaction and Cooperation.* Boston: Allyn and Bacon, 1979.

Schaeffer, Earl S. "Learning From Each Other." *Childhood Education* 48.1 (1971): 2-7.

Swick, Kevin and R. Eleanor Duff. *The Parent-Teacher Bond.* Dubuque, Iowa: Kendall/Hunt Publ. Co., 1978.

Tizard, Barbara, Jo Mortimer, B. Burchell. *Involving Parents in Nursery and Infant School.* Ypsilanti, Mich.: The High/Scope Press, 1981.

Wolfendale, Sheila. *Parental Participation in Children's Development and Education.* New York and London: Gordon and Breach Science Publishers, 1983.

Section III: Techniques for Developing Partnerships

Chapter 8 At the Beginning

Chapter 8 considers initial steps to take in establishing a partnership between home and school, and parent, teacher, and child.

Objectives

After studying this chapter, the student will be able to

1. identify several steps helpful in establishing a relationship prior to the child's entrance into the classroom
2. discuss benefits associated with each step
3. discuss strategies associated with each step
4. describe the separation experience for children and parents, and discuss a teacher's role

Initial Contact Between Teacher, Parent, and Child

First impressions can have a lasting significance. Early attitudes and behavior patterns will determine later limitations on a relationship or what direction it will take. Parents and teachers who begin working together with particular expectations and understandings are likely to continue in that mode. Since it is often difficult to change patterns or behaviors once they have become habitual, it is important to involve teachers, parents, and children in a program of gradual orientation, information exchange, and increasing familiarity. No matter what their age, new school experiences are crucial steps for children. If these steps are facilitated by the adults around them, it is to the children's benefit, and therefore indirectly to the benefit of the adults as well. Between the time when parents first contact a school and the time when their

121

child finally settles in, is an important period when teachers have the opportunity to lay the foundations for successful parent involvement. There are several purposes for an orientation process: to make a child's transition to school as easy and pleasant as possible; to demonstrate to parents that they are welcome in the educational program and can learn to feel comfortable there; to help parents understand the school's goals and practices; and to give teachers a chance to learn from parents about a child and family situation (Tizard, et al., 1981).

The text will consider some ideas to involve parents as Connie Martinez first meets Sylvia Ashley and Ricky. In any situation, time circumstances may dictate modification of these ideas, but teachers striving for effective relationships with parents will see them as a goal to work for.

Choosing a School

The first contact between parents and a school or center is generally initiated by parents in their search for an appropriate facility for their child's care. The school, usually represented by the director, has the dual responsibility of encouraging parents to make the most appropriate educational choices for their children, and sharing information about the school's philosophies and practices, so parents can see if this particular school matches their needs. Information concerning parental responsibilities and opportunities for participation should be included at this time as well.

In selecting a school or center for the early years, parents need to consider more than the usual consumer issues of convenience and cost. If this is their first experience in early childhood education, they may not yet be aware of the variations in educational goals and practices, licensing levels, discipline practices, parental rights and involvement, etc. existing in preschools within any community. Some child advocacy groups and schools offer parents a guide for questions and observations to emphasize their key role in making this decision.

Sample Guide for Parents

THE STAFF   YES   NO

Are staff members friendly and enthusiastic?

Do staff members seem to like and relate well to
    the children and to each other?

Are staff members required to have special
    training in child care?

YES   NO

Is there a staff in-service training program and/or other opportunities for continuous skill development?

Are parent conferences held on a regular basis?

Do staff members welcome questions and inquiry?

THE PROGRAM

Are teachers required to make daily lesson plans?

Is the daily schedule posted?

Is the program schedule balanced between active and quiet periods?

Are there varieties of materials and equipment ready for use and accessible to children, both indoors and out?

Do children have choices about activities?

Do the activities foster the children's physical, social, intellectual, and emotional growth?

Do the children know what to do?

Do the children receive individual attention from caregivers?

Does the center have a policy on discipline?

Do you agree with it?

Are records kept on children and their development?

Are snacks and meals nutritious, well-balanced, and menus posted?

Are the parents linked to the daily life of the program?

THE PHYSICAL SETTING

Are there comfortable, relaxed areas for resting and naps?

Is the center bright, clean, comfortable?

Are the outdoor and indoor areas safe and free from hazards?

YES NO

Is there enough space for free, easy movement?

Does it allow for both group and individual activities?

Does it provide possibilities for privacy?

Is there appropriate, clean equipment for different age groups?

Quality care provides:

- a caring, pleasant atmosphere
- care by an adequate number of well-trained, nurturing and affectionate caregivers
- a program that responds to each child as an individual
- experiences that facilitate exploring, skill development, and learning
- support for, communication with, and involvement of parents

Consider what is best for your child. If you are not satisfied with the care found, continue your search. You are the parent: the choice is up to you. (Adapted from Child Care Resources Inc., Charlotte, N.C.)

In many centers, parents are invited to observe a teacher in action with her present class before deciding whether to enroll their children. Such a practice sends two clear messages to parents: (1) the center respects their judgement and obligation to know exactly what arrangements they are making for their children; and (2) the center is proud of what it does, and wants parents to see it for themselves (Balabian, 1985). Parents are quite justified in being suspicious of a center where such visiting is not encouraged or allowed.

It is preferable to enroll a child whose parents have carefully considered the issues important to them and their child, matched them with all the available options, and chosen a particular school on the basis of meeting needs, rather than parents who made a hasty decision based on whether or not they have to cross the line of traffic to reach the parking lot! Schools for young children have a responsibility to help parents realize the full extent of their decision-making role. Once parents choose a school, their next contact moves beyond the director as general spokesperson to meeting the specific teacher(s) where their child will begin.

Let's look at the beginning for Sylvia Ashley and Ricky.

In Sylvia Ashley's case, social services had selected the center for Ricky, and Sylvia went to look it over and talk to the director. As always, she had Ricky with her. "We're delighted that Ricky will be entering our school, Mrs. Ashley. Since he'll be entering our group of three's, let me take you down to meet Connie Martinez, our lead teacher in that class. Then you two can find a convenient time to get acquainted further."

First Encounter—Teachers and Parents

The first conversation between parents and a teacher is best scheduled for a time when parents can come without their child. At that time, parents are free to talk without concern for their child's response in a new situation, and a teacher can concentrate her efforts on helping parents become comfortable without her attention divided between adults and child.

Sylvia had told Connie Martinez that she had no one to leave Ricky with, so Connie was not surprised when Ricky walked in with his mother. Connie got two puzzles, a book, crayons and blank paper, and helped him settle in a corner distant enough that he could see his mother but not overhear the conversation. As Connie thought about it later, she realized that was the first time she'd ever conducted that first conversation with the child present. It certainly was far from ideal, but she'd at least had some time to talk freely with this new mother.

This meeting has several purposes. One is to permit a parent to share initial information about an entering child. Many schools ask parents to fill in a questionnaire about their child's personal and social history. Parents may fill this out at home and bring it to the meeting. In practice, if teachers and parents talk their way through a completed questionnaire, parents often supply additional information in a more easily remembered way. As parents talk, teachers can gain an impression of the relationship between parent and child, of how a child has reacted to other new situations, and of how parents feel about enrolling their child in the program. This also establishes a precedent of cooperation, of sharing information, with parents making important contributions and teachers listening. Teachers can also use this opportunity to acquire parent history and resource information. When asking questions, teachers must let parents know how this information will be used.

Selection of Sample Questions

Information on Routines

Eating

As a rule, is your child's appetite:

excellent   good   fair   poor_____

Does child eat alone or with family?_____

List favorite foods_____

List foods especially disliked_____

Sleeping

Approximate time child goes to bed_____

Approximate time wakes in morning_____

Attitude at bedtime_____

Usual activities before going to bed_____

Elimination

At what age was training started for:

Bowel control_____ Response to training_____

Bladder control_____ Response to training_____

What words does child use when stating need for
elimination? _____

Other Information

What do you enjoy most about your child?_____

_____

_____

How does your child usually react to new situations?

_____

_____

Pleasures your family enjoys most?_____

_____

_____

Has child been separated from either parent for a long period of time? If so, how did child react?_____

_____

What things repeatedly cause conflict between parent and child?_____

Is child happy playing alone?_____

List age and sex of child's most frequent playmates

_____

Favorite activities_____

Many of the ideas discussed may be helpful in increasing a new child's comfort in the first days in school.

"I see here that you mentioned Ricky likes to sleep with a favorite teddy bear. Do you suppose you could bring that along to leave in his cubby for nap time? It might feel good to have something so familiar."

This first meeting allows parents to ask specific questions about the classroom.

"Yes, there are four other boys who have entered the classroom quite recently, so he won't be the only really new one."

It also allows parents and teachers an early chance to know each other on a one-to-one basis.

"You're going back to school—good for you! That's great. You'll certainly be busy, but I'll bet you'll find it's worth it, when it's all over. I'm taking some classes at night too, so we can complain about it together."

This is a good time to establish clearly what teacher and parents will call each other. If this subject is never discussed forthrightly, there is often an awkwardness, with the result that neither calls the other anything.

> "I prefer that parents call me Connie, though the children call me Miss Martinez. Then may I also call you Sylvia? Are you comfortable with that? I'm just more comfortable with first names."

During this time a teacher can inform parents of the rest of the orientation schedule, fix a time for the next visit, and discuss separation patterns that children and parents frequently experience. This establishes the precedent of a teacher casually informing and educating, as well as empathizing, with parents.

> "It's a good idea to get Ricky started the week or so before you have to start your classes. You know, we find a lot of our three-year-olds take a couple of weeks or more to feel comfortable letting mother leave. Please feel free to stay in the mornings as long as you can, but if he's upset when you leave, don't worry, we'll give him lots of special attention. I know it's hard for mothers too, but we'll help each other along."

By raising the issue of separation in advance, a teacher gives parents the opportunity to prepare themselves and their children for the transition.

In situations where a school begins an entire new class of children at the same time, it works well to have an orientation meeting for all new parents covering the information they need. This enables a teacher to offer information to the entire group and enables parents to meet each other right from the beginning. Still, individual meetings between parent and teacher offer opportunities to gain specific information on a child, answer personal questions a parent might not raise in a group, and establish the parent-teacher relationship.

So this first brief meeting of parent and teacher establishes the patterns of relaxed communication, of mutual informing and asking that are important for the working relationship to grow.

First Encounter—Teachers and Children

For the first meeting between child and teacher, it is preferable to have it where a child is most comfortable—at his home (Hildebrand, 1985). Whenever a child has to get used to a new concept, such as school and new adults caring for him, he can best adjust when fortified by the security of familiar people and surroundings (Cox and Fleming, 1968). This first visit, scheduled at a family's convenience, may be very brief—fifteen minutes or so—but a child will have a chance to briefly socialize and observe his parents doing so. Any teacher who has experienced such an initial home visit will remember the comfort this gives children timidly entering a new classroom. "You've been to *my* house." (Home visits are discussed further in Chapter 11.)

The brief visit also offers a teacher a glimpse of the parent-child relationship and a child's home learning environment.

Sylvia had been reluctant to have the teacher make a visit to their apartment, but when Connie Martinez explained it might help Ricky feel more comfortable with her (so far he wouldn't speak to this stranger), she agreed. Connie scheduled the brief visit for late afternoon, after learning Ricky's big brother would be home. And that did help. Terrence talked to the teacher and encouraged Ricky to show her their bedroom. Ricky smiled and waved good-bye when she left.

First Visit to a Classroom

During a home visit, a teacher can arrange a time for a parent and child to visit the classroom. It is most desirable that a child have a chance to visit before the first time of coming to the classroom to stay. This visit also will be brief, a chance for a child to see and become interested in a new environment.

Ricky and his mother came in mid-morning, two days after the home visit. He said hello to Connie and let her show him around the room. He especially liked the big fire truck. When the other children came in from the playground, he clung to his mother, but watched intently. He turned down the invitation to come to the table for juice, but joined his mother when she sat near Connie and drank juice. He nodded when Connie told him that next time he could stay longer and play with the fire truck.

It is often overwhelming for a young child to enter a classroom full of other children busy with activities. For this reason, it is a good idea to schedule this visit for a time when children from the classroom are outside playing, in a gym or other area with another teacher, or at the end of the day when fewer children are present. Then a child is free to be welcomed by the teacher he's met, shown that he will be a part of this classroom (having a cubby with his name and picture

**A cubby with a child's name and picture
gives a sense of belonging.**

on is a good idea), and given a chance to investigate the toys and
equipment on his own. It works well to have a visiting child join the
group briefly for a snack or cup of juice. He can then enjoy the eating
experience and have a chance to see other children, without being
called upon to participate. The parent stays in the classroom during
this visit, offering his child a secure base from which to move and
sharing his pleasure in new discoveries. Parental concerns may be allayed
by observing the teacher and child interact and seeing how the classroom functions. This visit gives the parent specifics to discuss at home
to continue to prepare his child for this new experience.

If an entire class of entering children is new, teachers may schedule
brief opportunities for a group of five or six children to come in for
"tea parties" and a chance to look about the classroom. Breaking a
class down offers teachers a chance to interact with each child while
saving teacher time.

Child's Entry into a Classroom

The groundwork is laid for a child's entry into a classroom. Teachers
and parents need to remind themselves of how much there is for a

child to become accustomed to in a school experience: the "how's" of interacting with a large group of children; the new rules and practices of a classroom; the leaving of parent and becoming comfortable with another adult. (It is also important that teachers let parents know that children faced with all this may act out afterward, in the secure environment of home.)

Since these adjustments can be exhausting for a young child, his first days in a classroom need to be as abbreviated as possible. For example, if a child is beginning a full day-care program, it is helpful if he is picked up at the end of the morning for several days, then slowly extend the day to include lunch, nap, and then the afternoon. Children entering a half-day program will benefit from attending for half the morning at first. A school that enters its whole class at one time can shorten the entire schedule for the first week or so, gradually extending from one hour to three. The people most inconvenienced during this easing-in period are parents, so it is important they understand the rationale for this approach and its benefit for their children in building feelings of comfort and security. Some centers offer a place where parents can have a cup of coffee during these shortened days, as a place to wait and converse with other parents.

> After the teacher suggested it, Sylvia had decided to let Ricky stay for two mornings before she left him for the whole day. The first morning he cried hard as she left; Connie encouraged her to stay a little longer if she wanted, but she just hurried away, feeling a little sick herself. He was very quiet when she went back to get him before lunch, but after his nap he told her and Terrence a little about playing with the fire engine. The next morning he cried for about ten minutes, but as she stood in the hall, she heard him stop. The third day she and Terrence went together to get him after his nap. Connie said he'd had a hard time falling asleep, but she'd rubbed his back until he drifted off. Sylvia was starting to think Ricky might be all right.

Parents as well as children need special attention during this transition time. A teacher's evident concern and specific comments do much to further a sense of partnership, as she takes the time to communicate with parents before and after school.

> Every day when Sylvia came back to get Ricky, she looked eagerly for the teacher. Connie always tried to leave the children with her assistant briefly and come to tell her what Ricky had played with and how he seemed to feel.

Parents and children both need special attention during beginning times.

Through the orientation process, no large amount of parent time is spent; most of the visits are one-half hour or less, and can be worked into a parent's employment schedule. For a teacher, the time can be scheduled into a normal teaching day with coverage from an assistant. Both adults need to realize the priority of a child's growing security and try to fit in as many of the steps as practicable. In addition to a child's security, it is important to set patterns of teachers and parents working together in home-school transitions and discussing a child's needs. As they work together, parents and teachers will get to know each other and start to build a trust that will help in the future. A good beginning for all.

"You know," says Sylvia, "Ricky is going to get along all right in the school. I really like the teacher; she's helped me a lot to get used to things. I won't have to worry so much."

(For further discussions of easing-in patterns and suggestions for specialized school settings, see Hildebrand, 1985; Balabian, 1985; and Frederick, 1969.)

Dealing with Separation Experiences

The emotional responses to a new school experience may be heightened by the separation anxiety experienced by most children and parents. The mutual parent-child attachment, developed during the early years of a child's life, means that both adult and child feel more secure in each other's presence. A removal from each other's presence causes concern and changes in behavior for both (Cox and Fleming, 1968).

What behaviors are expected of children experiencing separation? Many children up to age three or so will cry and be sad when a parent leaves. But even older children may find the initial leaving difficult. Sometimes this sadness continues off and on for a good part of the day; some children continue this pattern of crying for weeks. A child may come in quietly in the morning, and then begin to cry later. Such delayed reactions may occur days, or even weeks, later. Some children

Saying good-by may be very hard.

find times like mealtime or naptime particularly hard as they are reminded of home routines. Many children experiencing separation difficulties cling to a teacher and participate very little. Separation problems are also demonstrated by an increase in dependence or disruptions and changed behavior patterns at home, such as resisting bedtime, out-of-bounds talk with parents, new and assertive ways of behaving, and "games" that play on parents' guilt. Some children demonstrate regressive behaviors, reverting to thumbsucking, wetting, or other behaviors from an earlier time. And some children exhibit "very good" behaviors, no signs of upset, just controlled passivity. These behaviors are considered usual for a child experiencing separation (Balabian, 1985) and the duration of the behaviors varies with each child. While they require special consideration, the behaviors are not cause for alarm. Teachers need to be matter-of-fact in their expectation of these behaviors so they reassure parents of both their normalcy and temporary nature. Most young children have this period of stressful adaptation to supplemental child care away from their parents. But once they understand that regular separation from parents does not imply their loss, the problematic behaviors subside.

Parents often have a difficult time with separation too. This is a time of ambivalent feelings: satisfaction that their child is more independent; fear of becoming displaced in their child's affections; and sadness at the changing status in their relationship. Parents may feel concern that their child no longer needs them and jealous of the person he appears to need. They may be concerned about how their child is cared for in their absence and that this change is too disruptive to their child's life and their own, as evidenced by the upset behaviors.

"Look, I thought it was going to work out fine at this center, but now I'm not so sure. Janie screams every morning when I leave and clings to my neck. I can hear those screams all day. I'm afraid of her changing; she's always been such a happy child. And I worry—wonder whether anybody's looking after her when she's so upset. I miss her too. But I'd hate to think I was one of those clinging mothers who can't let their kids go."

A parent may be struggling with more than her own separation feelings. If she's beginning a working situation, she may be feeling great pressure for her child to adjust to the care situation as quickly as possible. Getting her child adjusted is not an option; it has to work!

A teacher is in an important position to help parent and child deal with separation emotions and behaviors. The basic aim for a teacher to remember is that she is doing not just what works best, but what best strengthens a child (Gross, 1970). Teachers' attentions need to be directed to both parent and child, "for the way you treat the child affects the parents, and the way you treat the parents affects the child" (Balabian, 1985, p. 71). Some basic strategies follow.

Prepare Parents for Separation Behaviors

Prepare parents in advance to accept separation behaviors and emotions as normal. Parents are more open about their concerns if they realize that a teacher is not judging their child or themselves negatively for experiencing separation anxieties.

> "Most children Janie's age have a pretty hard time at first saying good-bye to parents. In fact, though they don't show it as freely as children, most parents find this a pretty major adjustment too. I'll be here to help you both however I can."

Welcome Parents Into a Classroom

Help parents feel welcome to stay in a classroom as long as is helpful to a child. Both parents and children may benefit from not having a rushed good-bye in the morning, by slowly helping a child get interested in the classroom activities, and by having a parent see her child receive a teacher's attention. This approach will help a parent feel a part of her child's school world.

> "Janie, maybe you'd like to show your mommy the puzzle you did yesterday" conveys such a welcome.

Allowing a child to decide when parents should leave the room— "Shall Mom go now, or after our story time?"—may help a child experience self-confidence (Balabian, 1985).

Teachers can help parents and children plan together for the next day's parting and move toward establishing a regular morning routine.

> "The two of you might like to decide before you come tomorrow whether she'll give you a hug at the door, or after she's put her things in her cubby."

In general, teachers must let parents know they will follow their cues concerning their desire or ability to stay. But, an alert teacher picks up on the times a child is ready to move away from his parent

| Coming in may get a little easier— | —when parents have a few extra minutes to help their child slowly become involved and comfortable with the teacher. |

who is lingering on, perhaps due to her own needs. Here a teacher can help a parent leave.

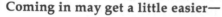

"Mrs. Smith, since Janie's started to play, it might be a good time to tell her good-bye. You and I can watch her from outside, if you'd like."

It is important that teachers make decisions regarding the timing of actual separation in such cases where a child's readiness precedes a parent's. When parents are feeling ambiguous and shaky, they may need or appreciate such help. However, when a parent is unable to respond to such a direct approach, it is probably an indication that the point of personal readiness for separation has not yet arrived, and teacher patience and support is necessary.

An important concept for teachers and parents to realize is that parents must consider their own anxiety separately from that of their child's; in other words, the reactions of a parent may not be identical to a child's feelings, and it is important not to project those feelings onto a child. It can set up long-lasting problem patterns if a child learns to give a parent a demonstration of his reluctance to be left before a parent feels satisfied that he will be truly missed. A parent may be more able to deal with personal emotions with an awareness of whose problem it is.

Develop Children's Trust in Parents

An important step in a child's working through the separation process is to learn to trust that parents will reliably leave and then return. Teachers may need to help parents become aware of behaviors that can foster this sense of certainty.

Though less painful at the time, it is not a good idea for parents to slip away unnoticed while a child is distracted. A child can't help but become a little dubious of a parent's trustworthiness (Balabian, 1985). Teachers can help parents realize the need for a definite leave-taking.

"I know it bothers you when she cries as you leave, but it's really better for her in the long run to know she can rely on you to go and come just as you say you will. I'll help her say a quick good-bye to you."

It is important to a child's sense of security to be picked up on a predictable schedule.

In the same way, parents may not realize the importance of picking up a child at a predictable time. Clock time means very little to children, and even a short time elapsing after a parent's expected arrival will seem like a very long time. It is best for parents to equate their return with a scheduled event and absolutely keep to it, especially during this transition time.

> "After you eat your snack, I'll be back to get you."

Discuss Separation Experiences

It is helpful to discuss the emotional responses of separation openly, with empathy. Such an approach frees both child and parent to realize their feelings are recognized, accepted, and can continue to be communicated. Keeping "stiff upper lips" is too costly in terms of emotional health.

> "I know you're sad when your Mom leaves, Janie. It's a little scary too. But I'll be here to look after you until she gets back, and we can have a good time too."
>
> "Most parents have some pretty mixed feelings about their child starting off in school. It can be kind of sad and scary, I'm sure."

Small touches can demonstrate to parents and children a teacher's empathy: a phone call in mid-morning to let a parent know that her child who was screaming when she left is now happily playing with play dough; an extra minute to share the day's events fully with a returning parent; talking with a child throughout the day about what they'll have to show Daddy when he returns.

Special Attention to Parents and Children

Special attention to both parents and children is warranted at this time. Teachers may choose special children's books about separation and new experiences to read to children (Fassler, 1978). They may stay close to children, holding their hands at transition times, holding them on their laps when they are sad, talking with them often (Balabian, 1985). Some teachers find that in order not to foster dependency, some of this special attention and support can be supplied by pairing a new child with a "special friend," someone already adapted to the classroom with a personality that would enjoy helping to nurture a new child. A new parent can be introduced and provided opportunities to converse with a parent who has weathered the stress of separation. But dependency is less of a concern than fostering feelings of comfort and confidence.

All beginnings are important. The long-term effects of establishing parent-teacher relationships with clear patterns of empathetic communication, as well as a child's successful adaptation, justify taking these additional steps.

Summary

Good beginnings include the following:

1. A meeting with a school's director to consider what a parent is looking for in a preschool and how this matches with a school's philosophy and practices.

2. An introductory conversation between a parent and individual classroom teacher. Specific information on a child and classroom is exchanged. Further orientation plans are formed.

3. A brief home visit so a teacher and child can meet on a child's secure home base.

4. A brief visit of parent and child to a classroom, specfically planned for a time when a teacher is free to interact with the child.

5. An easing-in schedule, so a child can slowly adjust to classroom life on less than a full-time basis.

6. Teacher assistance to parent and child during peak separation stress.

Student Activities for Further Study

1. With your classmates, role-play the following situations, with one of you being a teacher who is trying to get to know, support, and establish a relationship with a parent who is enrolling a preschool child in your center.

   a. Parent says the child has never been left with anyone else in three years.

   b. Parent seems very reluctant to answer any questions about the child.

   c. Parent asks if she can stay until child stops crying—"It may take a while"—parent seems very tense.

   d. Parent says she really doesn't have time for the teacher to visit or have an extended conversation with the teacher, or allow the child to visit or "ease-in."

    e. Parent seems very frightened of the teacher.

2. Role-play the following situations and have your "audience" discuss a teacher's role in helping both parent and child during separation stress.

    a. Teacher with a parent whose child is screaming and clinging to the parent's neck—parent started a new job two days ago.

    b. Teacher with a parent whose child is screaming and clinging to the parent's neck—parent starts new job next week.

    c. Child says good-bye happily; mother stands at door looking very sad.

    d. Two hours after parent left, child begins to cry and says, "I want my Daddy."

    e. Parent begins to sneak out while child is distracted with a toy.

3. Ask several parents how they chose their preschool center: did they visit; were there particular things they were looking for; what convinced them this was the place for their child?

4. Look at the information forms that parents fill in at your center and several others. Do the forms really allow the parents to begin to share their particular knowledge of their child? What additional questions might be helpful?

Review Questions

1. Describe an ideal process of orientation to a center for a child and his parents.

2. Discuss why each step of the orientation process is beneficial and what strategies a teacher may consider with each step.

3. Identify several behaviors typically associated with separation problems in preschool children.

4. Discuss several teacher behaviors that are helpful in assisting parents and children in adjusting to separation.

References and Related Readings

Anderson, L.S. "When A Child Begins School." *Children Today* 5.4 (1976): 16-19.

Balabian, Nancy. *Starting School: From Separation to Independence (A Guide for Early Childhood Teachers.)* New York: Teachers College Press, 1985.

———. "The Name of the Game is Confidence: How to Help Kids Recoup from Separation Anxiety." *Instructor* 95.2 (1985): 108-12.

Cox, F.N. and E.S. Fleming. "Young Children in a New Situation With and Without Their Mothers." *Child Development* 39 (1968): 123-31.

Duggins, Lydia. "Start From a Safe Place." *First Teacher* 6.9 (1985): 2.

Fassler, J. *Helping Children Cope: Mastering Stress Through Books and Stories.* New York: Free Press, 1978.

———. "Children's Literature and Early Childhood Separation Experiences." *Young Children* 29.5 (1974): 311-23.

Frederick, Lucille W. "The Orientation of Children to School." *Parents-Children-Teachers: Communication.* Washington, D.C.: ACEI, 1969.

Gotkin, J. "Coping With Separation Anxiety: A New Way to Cut the Apron Strings." *Parents* 52.1 (1977): 35, 37, 60, 64.

Gross, Dorothy W. "On Separation and School Entrance." *Childhood Education* 46.5 (1970): 250-53.

Hildebrand, Verna. "Introducing a Child to a New Group of Children." *Guiding Young Children.* 3rd Ed. New York: Macmillan Publ. Co., 1985.

Hock E, et al. "Child's School Entry: A Stressful Event in the Lives of Fathers." *Family Relations* 29 (1980): 467-72.

Janis, M.G. *A Two Year Old Goes to Nursery School: A Case Study of Separation Reactions.* New York: NAEYC, 1965.

Provence, S. et al. *The Challenge of Day Care.* New Haven: Yale University Press, 1977.

Schwartz, Conrad. *The Effects of Mothers' Presence and Previsits on Children's Emotional Reactions to Starting Nursery School.* Eric Document ED 034 596 Washington D.C.: Office of Education, 1969.

Spock, B. "When Children Are Afraid to Start School." *Redbook* 145.4 (1975): 22, 24, 27, 29.

Tizard, Barbara, Jo Mortimer, B. Burchell. *Involving Parents in Nursery and Infant Schools.* Ypsilanti, Mich.: The High/Scope Press, 1981.

Twining, Geraldine. " Parent-Readiness for Kindergarten." *Parents-Children-Teachers: Communication.* Washington D.C.: ACEI, 1969.

Chapter 9 Informal Communication with Parents

Chapter 9 examines a variety of methods of informal communication that teachers can utilize to build relationships with parents.

Objectives

After studying this chapter, the student will be able to

1. identify seven techniques a teacher uses to convey information, interest, and support to parents
2. discuss details for implementing each communication technique

Communication Techniques

As teachers begin to work with parents and children, it is important to open and keep open the lines of communication. As previously discussed, the initiative for opening a dialogue should come from teachers. By approaching parents, teachers demonstrate their willingness to adapt to individual differences in personality, preferences, and time constraints that may result in different responses to the same method. For example, a busy parent may barely glance at the parents' bulletin board while rushing by, but enjoy reading a newsletter at home, while a quiet parent who does not usually talk much to teachers may eagerly read everything offered on the bulletin board. For this reason, teachers should utilize as many of the communication techniques as they can. Most techniques are not time-consuming; a few minutes a day to work on ideas for the next newsletter or bulletin board, or for writing several individual notes may be sufficient.

Communication techniques can be a one-way or two-way endeavor (Berger, 1981). One-way communication from a class or school can inform parents about events or plans, or attempt to educate parents. While this is important, since parents have a need and desire to know what is going on, a real sense of partnership grows through two-way communication that encourages and facilitates true dialogue with parents actively reacting and responding. Devices can be incorporated into many communication methods that are normally one-way communication, to expand them to two-way communication.

No matter what other informal techniques teachers use as alternatives for establishing communication with parents, it must be remembered that these techniques should not replace personal contact. Nothing is as important as personal, face-to-face conversation for building relationships.

Daily Conversations

Connie Martinez says, "I don't have time for too much else, but I do a lot of talking to parents every day."

Frequent daily conversations when parents drop off and pick up their children are extremely important in building trust by fostering a sense of familiarity. (There is an obvious problem when children are brought by car-pool drop-off or bus; teachers in these situations have to work harder to maintain regular contact by telephone calls or notes.)

Important things happen during these brief exchanges. Parents want to know that their child is known and recognized as a person. To see a teacher greet their child personally by name is reassuring. Parents also want to be greeted by name themselves (Croft, 1979).

When children are dropped off by car-pool, teachers have to work hard to maintain regular contact with parents.

"Good morning, Pete. You look ready to play today. I've put some of those new little cars that you like in the block corner. How are you this morning, Mrs. Lawrence? Pete's been telling me about his new bedroom—you must be pretty busy at home these days."

This can be a time for brief but substantive exchanges on child- and family-related issues. Studies indicate that these conversations may be the most frequent form of parent involvement, although the substance of the conversations may not progress beyond social niceties (Powell, 1978). In defining "quality day care," Endsley suggests that the home–center coordination needs for children necessitate extensive dialogue between parents and teachers, and points out that in good centers, "not only do they talk to one another, they seem to talk about substantive issues" (Endsley, 1981, p. 128).

The frequency and quality of these daily contacts depends primarily on the classroom routine (Tizard, et al., 1981). Teachers can plan to be available to talk at specific times. Preparing materials before parents arrive or saving cleanup for after parents depart, keeps a teacher's attention from being diverted. Having adequate staff during these transition times and making definite assignments for either child care or adult conversations clarifies expected behaviors for both teachers and parents.

The atmosphere created by teachers and staff can either open or close the opportunities for informal chats. The teacher who says, "Hello, how are you?" and turns to busy herself elsewhere indicates her unwillingness to prolong the contact. A teacher who asks a broad question

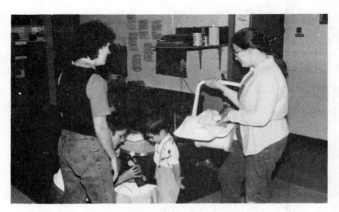

When teachers create the expectancy for conversation, parents usually respond.

that invites response—"Looks like you've had a busy day"—and stands by the parent obviously ready to continue, creates an expectation of conversation.

Some teachers complain they can never think of anything to say when a parent comes in. For these teachers, it might be helpful to consider what they most enjoy about a child and share these observations. It is difficult for most parents to resist a conversation that begins by focusing personally on their child.

Teachers striving for daily contact with all parents are helped to perceive their own patterns by keeping an informal tally (on a file card in the pocket or on a paper taped to the wall) briefly recording who was spoken to, for how long, and the topic of the conversation (Herwig, 1982). This often identifies a parent who was slipping in and out unnoticed or with whom a teacher never felt comfortable enough to progress beyond the "How are you" stage.

One study indicates that almost 30% of day-care parents do not enter a center when leaving their children for the day (Powell, 1978).

A school policy stating that parents accompany their children to the classroom facilitates daily contact with teachers.

A clear and firm center policy about parents accompanying their children to a classroom is needed, stressing to parents both the need for safety and a child's emotional security, as well as the importance of making daily contact with a teacher. The same study showed that as the frequency of communication between parents and teachers rises, the number of parent and family related topics that are discussed increases, and communication attitudes become more positive. A policy that facilitates and supports this contact is beneficial.

Teachers may need to help sensitize parents to the concept that conversations about children do not take place over children's heads, as if they cannot understand the meaning, or the fact they are being discussed. By modeling such respect for children's feelings, teachers help parents grow in their understanding of children's needs and emotions. It is appropriate to direct conversations that turn to specifics involving children or families to another time or place.

> "I'd like to talk more about this with you—could we step outside for a minute?"
>
> "This is important information that I'm not comfortable talking about right here—can we find a few minutes when you come back this afternoon to talk more privately?"

Some teachers are afraid that by encouraging parents to talk, they will begin a flow of conversation that they will be unable to cut off, and that the conversation will interfere with a teacher's accomplishing certain tasks and operating the classroom smoothly. In most situations, this is not the case, as parents' own pressing demands limit their available time. In those situations where parents completely accept an invitation to talk and spend long periods of time in a classroom, teachers should realize these parents are showing a need for companionship and feelings of belonging, and try to find ways to meet this need. Teachers may suggest that parents join in an activity or find a way of linking one parent with another.

> "I've enjoyed talking with you, and I must get busy mixing the paint now. If you can spend a little more time with us, I know the children in the block corner would enjoy having you be with them."
>
> "Mrs. Jones, let me introduce Mrs. Brown. Your boys have been very busy building together this week; have you been hearing about these adventures at home?"

If a teacher realizes that daily conversations are valuable, she is more likely to find creative ways of dealing with potential problems like this, rather than cut off all forms of communication.

Occasionally, teachers can encourage parents to spend a few extra minutes in the classroom with their children and teachers by making a cup of coffee available. No elaborate preparation is necessary for teachers or parents. Usually a day or two advanced notice helps parents keep a little time free. Children can show things to parents or play as parents chat with each other. Such an occasion offers a brief chance for everyone to relax together and is supportive for both parents and teachers. Chapter 12 examines ways that parents' casual visits to the classroom for lunch or celebrations help to involve them more deeply in classroom life, as well as being pleasant opportunities for further communication.

Although daily conversations are probably most important in the context of other plans for parent involvement, they should not be seen as an end in themselves; other arrangements are needed to ensure the development of trust and full communication. In studies of groups of parents, it is uncertain whether trust develops solely on the basis of informal conversations, or is instead a by-product of parents being impressed by the many efforts of teachers to be open to them (Tizard, et al., 1981). Nevertheless, beginning steps towards openness are perceived in daily interactions.

Bulletin Boards

Bulletin boards offer another form of reaching out to parents. Powell found in his study of day-care parents that those he characterized as "independent" had a low frequency of communication with staff and used non-staff sources of information, such as bulletin boards (Powell, 1978).

A bulletin board needs to be clearly visible, in an area well traveled by parents, preferably just outside a classroom so parents make a clear connection between the information offered and the teacher as the source. It needs to be labeled for "Parents," so parents realize this information is meant for them. Eye-catching materials, such as snapshots of children, classroom activities, and samples of work invite closer attention. Using different colors of paper or fabric as backgrounds is a visual indication to parents that there is a change in bulletin board offerings.

The information offered by a bulletin board will be decided upon by a teacher as she listens to parents' questions and comments, or finds areas where they need resources or help (Marion, 1973). Occasionally, bulletin boards may offer guidelines in choosing books or toys, on childhood diseases and immunization needs, nutritious menus appealing to children, suggestions for movies, television, or local events, articles

Bulletin boards can help parents learn about community resources.

that prepare or follow up on a topic under discussion at a parents' meeting. Sometimes a sequence of bulletin boards can be planned. For example, one on how to choose good books for children, followed by one on library resources for parents and children. A third board on using books to help deal with childhood problems can be planned. Longer articles, recipes, or directions for making things can be mimeographed and offered in a folder of "take-aways." (The empty folder offers proof to a teacher that a bulletin board is used.)

A bulletin board, or part of one, can be provided for parent contributions such as offers to babysit, exchange outgrown snowsuits, or requests for car-pool drivers.

If a teacher wants to have a bulletin board used, it is necessary to change it frequently; a board that stays the same for weeks on end teaches parents not to look at it. When a teacher does put new material out, it helps to emphasize it by a visual change—new pictures or background colors. (If a teacher has the dilemma of choosing to spend time on elaborate changes or new information, it is preferable to pick the latter and keep it neat, simple, but above all, new.) Material too long to be read in a few minutes needs to be offered as a "take-away" or it won't be used. Keep a board's appearance simple and uncluttered; it is better to offer one important point than so many that a busy parent feels it will take too much time to absorb the information.

Bulletin boards can offer support to parents in the form of a wry cartoon reminding parents that a teacher understands the childhood foibles confronting them.

If a center has enough room, a separate area for parents close to the main reception area can be provided, with comfortable chairs, a coffee pot and interesting periodicals (Marion, 1973).

Having a space for parents is a concrete reminder that parents are welcome to stop, relax, and enjoy what a school has to offer.

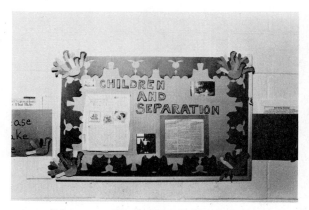

Longer articles can be offered in a folder of "take-aways."

Daily News Flash

"What about the parents I can't see or talk to every day?" wonders Dorothy Scott. "Is there any way of making contact with them?"

There are a number of ways of connecting with parents who are too busy for conversation. A daily news flash is one method of letting parents know what's going on and that teachers want parents to know. In a prominent place outside a classroom door or near the main entrance for parents waiting in the car-pool line, is a large board—perhaps a chalk board, a bulletin board, or a corner of one—that briefly describes one thing the children have done or talked about that day.

This morning we blew bubbles outside.

We learned a new song today about squirrels.

Tommy's mother had a new baby boy last night, so we talked a lot about babies.

A daily flash may be a part of a bulletin board.

Classroom daily news flashes are not earth-shaking, but offer something tangible that parents can pursue with their children. Most parents are grateful for these bits of news that make them feel a part of the day.

Telephone Calls

For teachers who cannot be in daily contact with parents, the telephone offers an opportunity for personal conversation. Sometimes teachers use phone calls to express concern if a child is absent for several days.

> "Hello, Mrs. Rodriguez. I just wanted to let you know we've missed Tony at school. Has he been sick?"

Another important use of the phone call is to share personal observations about a child (Gotkin, 1972; Wenig, 1975).

> "I thought you'd like to know. Lisa has been working so hard on the new climbing apparatus, and today she got to the top with no help at all! Was she pleased!"
>
> "I know you've been worried about Ricky's appetite, so I wanted to let you know I've been noticing him doing much better at lunch lately."

Such phone calls take only a few minutes each, but they let parents know of a teacher's interest and knowledge of their child. And the telephone facilitates two-way communication.

Communication opportunities can be further increased by the establishment of a telephone hour when parents can feel comfortable calling a teacher. One teacher chose an evening hour once a week; another chose a nap-time hour when other staff were available to supervise her children (Swap, 1984).

Personal Notes

Sharing positive, personal observations or anecdotes can also be accomplished by a teacher sending a personal note home with a child. Notes tend to be perceived as one-way communication, but a teacher may design them to invite a response.

> "I wanted to let you know I've noticed Ricky is eating more at lunch lately. Have you also noticed an increase at home?"

Some teachers use pre–printed "Happy-Grams," filling in the blanks:

> " ___Pete___ has been doing a good job at ___cleanup___"

However, this lacks a personal tone. Personal notes take only one or two minutes to write. If a teacher sends out two or three notes a day, each child in a classroom might take one home within a week or two.

Personal notes of appreciation to parents who have shared materials, time, or ideas reinforce a teacher's expression of pleasure (Wenig, 1975). Notebooks can be sent back and forth between teacher and parent with the expectation that both will contribute comments regularly (Moses, 1967). A tape recording of a child talking about a new experience or with a friend at snack time can be sent to parents, along with the tape recorder if necessary (Coletta, 1977).

Newsletters

Another communication technique involves sending regular newsletters to all parents. Newsletters have four main objectives: (1) to keep parents informed of classroom activities and plans; (2) to give parents insight into the educational purposes underlying classroom activities; (3) to enhance children's and parents' abilities to communicate with each other; and (4) to reinforce and extend learning from school into the home (Harms and Cryer, 1978).

Parents are often frustrated when attempting to learn directly from their children what has gone on in school (Andrews, 1976), and newsletters will solve this problem.

> With the holiday season approaching, we will be discussing families—how many people in our families and the things families do together. If you have an old family snapshot we could use for making a book together, we'd be grateful for you to share it.

> We had an exciting snack time last Thursday. The children watched in amazement while the popcorn popped—right out of the popper, on to a clean sheet spread on the floor. The children enjoyed their snack of popcorn and milk. We are trying to emphasize healthy snacks now. If you would like to join us for snack or have an idea which would be fun and healthy for snack, please share with us.

> I know some of you have been frustrated in trying to understand the newest songs your children have been singing this fall. Enclosed are some words so you can sing along. (Words added)

> Dear Parents,
>
> Here are some things we have done in the last two weeks to introduce the sense of smell to the children.
> 1. We made smell vials using cloves, peppermint, coffee, cinnamon, garlic, chili powder, vanilla, and perfume. We put each ingredient in a vial, poked holes in the lid, and covered them with nylon to keep the ingredients inside.
> 2. We roasted peanuts and used them in making peanut butter.
>   2 cups roasted shelled peanuts
>   2 tablespoons salad oil
>   Salt

First we shelled the peanuts and put them in a meat grinder. This is much more fun for the children than a blender. Then we added the oil and salt.

3. One day we made collages of magazine pictures of things that smell.
4. Another day we cooked play dough using oil of wintergreen. It sure smelled good!
5. We also learned "The Smelling Song." Tune: "Did You Ever See a Lassie?"

Have you ever smelled a rosebud, a rosebud, a rosebud?
Have you ever smelled a rosebud?
Oh, how does it smell?

The children suggested substitutes by themselves, and responded verbally after each verse.

These are some basic understandings we were trying to teach:

1. We smell through our noses.
2. We learn about things by the way they smell.
3. Some things smell good; some things smell bad.
4. Animals find things by smelling.
5. Smelling some things warn us of danger.

This might be fun to carry on at home. Ask your child if he can close his eyes and identify foods in your kitchen, or on the dinner table. Let us know how the game went.

Newsletters need to be fairly short—one printed page is about enough—so that parents do not set them aside, unread, thinking they are too time-consuming. Newsletters sent regularly, monthly or biweekly, will not get too far behind on current activities. They need to be neat, attractive, and display care for grammar and spelling. Care with details indicates planning and effort on a teacher's part, further evidence of a teacher's concern.

Sometimes anecdotes from children or use of children's names capture parent interest.

We have some new toys we're enjoying. Maria and Lisa have been busy mothering the new dolls. Seth, Tony, and Mathew have been fighting fires with the new fire truck, and Justin and Isaac enjoy outside time when they can ride the new hot wheels.

Parents enjoy reading news of classroom activities.

Recognition of special parent involvement and announcements of family events may build feelings that the classroom sees itself as a link for connecting parents.

> We especially enjoyed Mrs. Rodriguez helping us build a pinata for the Christmas party.
> We're all waiting, along with Pete, for the arrival of his new baby. Fannie Lawrence will be taking a few months off from her teaching job after the baby arrives.

To elicit two-way communication, teachers sometimes add a question for parent response and include the responses in the next newsletter.

> Would you please share ideas with other parents of activities and places you and your child have recently enjoyed in the community on weekends? We'll include these suggestions in our next letter.

Some teachers find that newsletters offer an opportunity for self-evaluation as they answer the questions asked by parents concerning what they have been doing and why. Others use a collection of the newsletters for the orientation of new parents, since the pages present a summary of classroom activities throughout the year (Harms and Cryer, 1978).

Traveling Suitcase and Libraries

Teachers can make contact with parents by sending home with a child a "traveling suitcase." On a rotating basis, each child has the privilege of overnight or weekend use of several items selected from the classroom. A child may choose a favorite book to have her parent read or a puzzle he has just mastered to show. Depending on a teacher's knowledge of the socioeconomic background of the families involved, one or more of the items might be to keep—a lump of cooked playdough, with a recipe for making more later, construction paper for using at home, or a teacher–made matching game. Some teachers include a class-made book with pictures and names of each child in the class; parents enjoy associating faces with the names they hear from their children.

Most children are very pleased to show their parents something that has been enjoyed at school, and a child's enthusiasm often guarantees that the materials will be used and discussed. Children who have been taught that the "traveling suitcase" is a special privilege are usually very responsible about the care of these "school things."

The bag can be used to exchange teacher and parent notes as well. A teacher may suggest "homework assignments" that parent and child can enjoy together. "Help your child find a picture of something big and of something little." "Help your child count out two crackers to bring—one for him and one to share with a friend" (Moses, 1967).

Offering parents the opportunity to borrow materials they can use with their children is further evidence of caring. A stock of paperback children's books, perhaps those no longer used in classrooms or homes, may be borrowed for use at home. Parenting books can also be available on loan (Edmister, 1977). In the same way, children's toys can be available to parents and children (Nimnicht and Brown, 1972; Duff et al., 1978; Faygella, 1985).

Summary

The ideas discussed in this chapter are not time-consuming and most don't require a great deal of formal planning. However, these efforts convey to parents that teachers are paying personal attention to their children and are really trying to keep in touch. Teachers who use newsletters and bulletin boards often keep a file of ideas, articles, and clippings for future use, and save things from year to year. What is important for teachers to realize is that these contacts provide vital on-going links between parent and teacher that are irreplaceable for building knowledge of and comfort with one another, and evidence for parents that their involvement is welcome.

To summarize, a parent-teacher partnership is strengthened as teachers utilize the following informal communication methods with parents:

1. Daily conversations
2. Bulletin boards
3. Daily News Flash
4. Telephone calls
5. Personal notes
6. Newsletters
7. Traveling suitcases and library

Student Activities for Further Study

1. If you are in a classroom situation, keep a tally of the parents you speak to at drop-off and pick-up times each day for a week. (A file card in your pocket can be used conveniently to jot down names.) Are there any parents you are missing contact with? Do you know why? Are there any parents you have little conversation with, beyond "hello" and "good-bye?" Do you know why? What circumstances create difficulties in finding time to talk in this particular classroom situation? Are there any alternatives that could help solve the problem?

2. Observe the encounters as teachers and parents meet each other at drop-off and pick-up times. What nonverbal clues of comfort or discomfort do you note? How do teachers use space to convey messages of welcome or distance? Are names used? What topics are discussed? What are children doing as parents and teachers talk?

3. Write and distribute a newsletter for your classroom. (Let parents know what has happened recently and why it happened, or how the children reacted to it.)

4. Design a bulletin board with a theme that you feel would be helpful to a group of parents.

5. Plan a brief, personal note that you could write to each parent, sharing something positive about their child.

Review Questions

1. Identify seven techniques teachers may use to convey information, interest, and support to parents.

2. For each technique discuss two ways to implement it.

References and Related Readings

Andrews, Palmyra. "What Every Parent Wants to Know." *Childhood Education* 52.6 (1976): 304-5.

Bell, Ruth Ann. "Parent Involvement: How and Why." *Dimensions* 14.1 (1985): 15-18.

Berger, E.H. *Parents as Partners in Education.* St. Louis: C.V. Mosby Co., 1981.

Coletta, Anthony. *Working Together: A Guide to Parent Involvement.* Atlanta: Humanics Press, 1977.

Croft, Doreen J. *Parents and Teachers: A Resource Book for Home, School and Community Relations.* Belmont, Calif.: Wadsworth Publ. Co. Inc., 1979.

Duff, R. Eleanor, M.C. Heinz and C.L. Husband. "Toy Lending Library: Linking Home and School." *Young Children* 33.4 (1978): 16-24.

Edmister, Patricia. "Establishing a Parent Education Resource Center." *Childhood Education.* 57.2 (1977): 62-66.

Fedderson, J. "Establishing an Effective Parent-Teacher Communication System." *Childhood Education* 49.2 (1972): 75-79.

Gotkin, L.G. "The Telephone Call: The Direct Line from Teacher to Family." *Ideas That Work with Young Children.* Ed. K.R. Baker. Washington, D.C.: NAEYC, 1972.

Harms, Thelma and Deborah Cryer. "Parent Newsletters: A New Format." *Young Children* 33.5 (1978): 28-32.

"Hello Out There: Two Ways for Getting in Touch With Parents." *Learning* 7.1 (1978): 156-57.

Herwig, Joan E. "Parental Involvement: Changing Assumptions About the Educator's Role." *How to Involve Parents in Early Childhood Education.* Ed. Brigham Young University Press. Provo, Utah: Brigham Young University Press, 1982.

Marion, M.C. "Create a Parent Space—a Place to Stop, Look, and Read." *Young Children* 28.4 (1973): 221-24.

Moses, Lois. "Homework for Preschoolers." *Young Children* 23.1 (1967): 19-21.

Nimnicht, Glen P. and Edna Brown. "The Toy Lending Library: Parents and Children Learning With Toys." *Young Children* 28.2 (1972): 110-16.

Nedler, S. "Working with Parents on the Run." *Childhood Education* 53.3 (1977): 129-32.

Powell, Douglas R. *The Interface Between Families and Child Care Programs: A Study of Parent-Caregiver Relationships.* Detroit: The Merrill-Palmer Institute, 1977.

———. "The Interpersonal Relationship Between Parents and Caregivers in Day Care Settings." *American Journal of Orthopsychiatry* 48.4 (1978): 680-89.

———. *The Coordination of Preschool Socialization: Parent-Caregiver Relationships in Day Care Settings.* New York: Ford Foundation, 1977 (Eric document ED 136 939).

Stein, L.S. "Techniques for Parent Discussion in Disadvantaged Areas." *Young Children* 22.3 (1967): 210-17.

Swap, Susan McAllister. *Enhancing Parent Involvement in Schools.* Boston: Center for Parenting Studies, Wheelock College, 1984.

Swick, Kevin J., C. Hobson, and R.E. Duff. *Building Successful Parent-Teacher Partnerships.* Atlanta: Humanics Press, 1979.

Tizard, Barbara, Jo Mortimer and B. Burchell. *Involving Parents in Nursery and Infant Schools.* Ypsilanti, Michigan: The High/Scope Press, 1981.

Wenig, M. and M.L. Brown. "School Efforts and Parent/Teacher Communication=Happy Young Children." *Young Children* 30.5 (1975): 373-76.

Chapter 10 **Parent-Teacher Conferences**

Chapter 10 discusses techniques that can be part of a teacher's attempt to structure productive situations for the exchange of information and plans.

Objectives

After studying this chapter, the student will be able to

1. identify four reasons for holding regular parent-teacher conferences
2. list eight factors that facilitate productive parent-teacher conferences
3. list six pitfalls to avoid in parent-teacher conferences

Regular Conferences are Important

Casual conversations are extremely important, but the more formal arrangement of parent-teacher conferences offer additional opportunities for parents and teachers to work as partners. Yet conferences are often not used by many teachers or centers unless there are problems. The reasons for this include both fear and misunderstanding of the purposes of conferences.

The hearts of many parents and teachers may be filled with anxiety when it is time to schedule conferences. Part of this negative feeling may come from the fact that an infrequent parent-teacher conference may be virtually the only contact between them. Ideally, a parent-teacher conference offers an opportunity for the free exchange of information, questions, and ideas, and can be accomplished best after a relationship is already established. Conferences can help a relationship to grow, but cannot function optimally if participants are not already comfortable with each other. All of the earlier contacts and communications are helpful prerequisites for a successful conference. In some cases, circumstances may prevent the formation of a prior relationship;

this is no reason to avoid scheduling a conference and begin the communication process.

Unfortunately, many parents and teachers view conferences as a last step in dealing with negative behavior (Flake-Hobson and Swick, 1979). If it is assumed that parents and teachers meet only when behavior is a problem, no one can anticipate such a meeting with pleasure. Parents' history of conflict or success in their own early school situations may lay the ground for this assumption. Some will recall negative experiences when their own parents were called in for conferences. In fact, most of this reluctance probably comes from the fact that for many years, in the school systems for elementary-aged children and beyond, the only parent-teacher contacts were infrequent conferences where virtual strangers came together rather defensively to clear up some difficulty. As early childhood education programs and day-care centers began to work with parents, teachers had little except these negative conference models to work from.

To be productive, it is important that conferences be seen as a routine and necessary component of the on-going coordination of information and efforts in a teacher-parent partnership.

> "Oh sure, I understand how important it is for parents and teachers to talk," says Connie Martinez, "but I don't really see the need to get so formal as to have a conference. I talk to most of my parents every day. And these are, after all, pre-schoolers. It's not like we have to talk about reading and math test scores or anything. So why should I have conferences?"

There are several reasons why holding regular parent-teacher conferences is important, regardless of a child's age.

To Provide Developmental Overview

Conferences provide an opportunity to examine the overall progress of a child in a detailed and organized way. In daily conversations, particular accomplishments or aspects of development may be discussed. This may be a new ability—such as climbing up the slide—or a different behavior—such as a decrease in appetite at lunchtime. Particular problems may catch the attention of a teacher or parent—a new tendency to cry when mother leaves or an increase in toileting accidents; such matters are frequently discussed in daily exchanges. But a complete look at a child's development is not possible in these brief encounters. Conferences provide opportunities for both parents and teachers to move beyond the daily specifics to an objective examination of total development (Tizard et al., 1981).

To Provide Time and Privacy

Conferences provide uninterrupted blocks of time and an atmosphere of privacy, two essentials for facilitating the sharing of information and the formulating of questions and plans. Regardless of a preschool teacher's commitment to talk with parents, the demands of caring for a group of young children may emphatically pull a teacher away from a conversation. She can't stand and discuss toilet training techniques at length while two children in the block corner are boisterously trying to knock down the tower of a third.

Parents often postpone talking about their concerns because of their awareness of the demands for a teacher's time.

> "I've been wanting to talk to Miss Briscoe about helping Pete get ready for this new baby," sighs Pete's mother. "But I hate to interrupt her—she's always got so much to do. I thought I'd go in a few minutes early this afternoon, but then a child upset some paint and another was crying when she got up from her nap, so it just didn't seem like a good time again."

Knowing they have time for just talking is important for both parents and teachers.

Privacy is also needed to facilitate comfort in talking. Teachers who are trying to model sensitivity and respect for children's feelings often prefer not to discuss them within their hearing or the hearing of other children. While there are occasions when teachers feel it is appropriate to include a child in a parent-teacher conference, every conference would have to be considered separately, thinking of the individual child and the material for discussion (Hogan, 1975; Readdick, 1984; Freeman, 1986). Some feel that a child's presence can seriously inhibit parents' willingness to discuss family matters (Losen and Diamant, 1978).

Parents are often understandably reluctant to ask for help in parenting skills or to discuss relationships where they might be interrupted by other adults. The privacy of a conference situation makes important discussion easier.

To Increase Mutual Knowledge

The unhurried flow of conversation in a conference setting allows for an exchange of questions and information that brief contacts at the beginning or end of a classroom day simply cannot.

> "You know, it wasn't until after we'd gone through the developmental check list and Mrs. Butler saw how well Sam

compares with the average for four-year-olds that she told me how worried she's always been that he'd be slow. Seems he resembles a cousin in her family who has a learning disability, and she was afraid Sam might have inherited the same problem. It really helped me understand why she's been asking so many questions about getting early academics started in the classroom, and doing so much at home. It was a relief for both of us to be able to talk about how really well Sam does, and to know what she really wanted to talk about was the best ways to stimulate learning in the preschool years."

Misunderstandings and concerns can only surface in longer conference conversations, with time to reflect on what each other is saying. Conferences offer opportunities for clarification and deeper explanations of many issues.

To Formulate Goals

Conferences can provide an important basis for formulating future goals and working plans.

"She decided, during our conversation, that maybe her teaching sessions with Sam at home weren't the best idea. I said that in the classroom I was trying to provide lots of books about dinosaurs, his current interest, and was trying to be available to read one to him each day. She thought she'd try something like that at home. We decided to get back together in three months and see whether this method was helping him enjoy books more."

Conference situations contribute to a sense of mutual knowledge and respect, and to the enhancement of a parent-teacher partnership to a child's benefit.

FOUR REASONS FOR REGULAR CONFERENCES

1. To facilitate a balanced examination of all aspects of development

2. To provide uninterrupted time and privacy for conversation

3. To facilitate a free-flowing exchange of questions and information, to increase mutual knowledge and respect

4. To provide the opportunity to formulate and coordinate goals and plans

Groundwork for a Successful Conference

Such goals are not met without effort. There are important components to successful parent-teacher conferences.

Explain the Purpose of a Conference

Administrative policies and explanations help clarify the routine nature of parent-teacher conferences and the responsibilities of the participants. In both teacher job descriptions and parent handbooks, a statement about the purpose of regular conferences, an indication of when they will occur, such as November and May, and a description of probable content will make this a better understood procedure. Offering examples of the topics that will be discussed and questions parents may want to ask helps to destroy any misconceptions about conferences. Parents who are informed during orientation when they enroll their children that conferences are part of a program, do not immediately assume there is something wrong when asked to a conference, nor are they afraid to take the initiative when they want a conference.

> Parent conferences are a routine part of our center life. A parent conference does not mean that your child is having a problem in the classroom. A parent conference is a time for parents and teachers to exchange thoughts and ideas, as well as a progress report from the team of teachers on all aspects of your child's development. The teachers may ask you questions about how your child plays at home, any special friends, etc. You will be able to ask the teachers about any aspect of his care or development in or out of the center, and share any information that would help the teachers. (Sample from hypothetical parent handbook.)

Plan for Uninterrupted Time

Carefully selecting conference times is important, as parents and teachers both have needs to be considered and must have a voice in choosing the time.

Teachers should first decide when they are most free to leave a classroom under the care of another teacher or aide. Naptime is often a convenient time. Other possibilities may be early morning, when children filter in slowly at different times, or late afternoon, as children's departure times are staggered and there are fewer for whom to care. Some teachers find they are available during outdoor play time, when other adults can supervise on the playground. With families where both parents work, it may be necessary to offer the option of evening or weekend hours. This may sound like a great inconvenience for a teacher, but being flexible enough to meet parents' needs indicates a real commitment to the idea of parent involvement. It is desirable to have both parents present from a two-parent family, so that questions and information are not dealt with secondhand. In too many cases, mothers come for conferences alone. Specific invitations to fathers and accommodations to their schedules, demonstrate that teachers value the participation of fathers (Manning, 1983), and increase the probability that a conference will be fruitful.

Having decided upon available conference times, teachers may then suggest to parents that they find a specific time convenient to

The presence of both parents at a conference is extremely valuable.

their own schedule. These invitations can be made in person or by telephone. Merely posting a sign-up sheet eliminates the personal touch and tends to de-emphasize the importance of a conference, as well as missing car-pool parents. Personal contact also helps teachers find out if there are scheduling problems (Goetz, 1975). When a sheet is posted, after a spoken invitation, it should make obvious the abundant choices of days and times, allowing for different working schedules, days off, and giving employers advance warning for a long lunch hour, etc. Teachers need to make it very clear, from conversation as well as a sign-up sheet, that they are anxious to be as flexible as possible in accommodating the needs of parents. If teachers are clearly willing to adapt a schedule to parents' needs, they will find responsive parents.

A sign-up sheet might look like this:

NOTICE

It's time to get together to discuss your child's development. Please sign up for a time convenient to you. If you can't find one here, let's find one together.

Nap-time 12:30–2:30 P.M.
Arrival time 8:00–9:00 A.M.
Departure time 3:30–5:00 P.M.

I can also arrange to be available from 6:00–7:30 P.M. on the following days:
M–13, T–14, W–15, Th–16, M–20, T–21, W–22, Th–23

Tommy

Lisa

Seth

Jenny

Isaac

Akwanza

Pete

Let's look at a sign-up sheet that is less of an invitation to a parent.

Time to Sign up for Conferences

Any Monday, Wednesday or Thursday between 4:00–5:00 P.M.

Do you see the problems here?

For parents who cannot be off work between 4:00 to 5:00 p.m., it looks as if they have no other possibility, and the teacher doesn't much care to be either understanding or helpful.

For busy parents, it looks as if this conference may be scheduled almost any time, so there's no motivation to set an appointment now.

It's too easy to walk by and leave blank a sheet of paper that doesn't seem specifically meant for you. It's much harder to ignore a message when your child's name is there with a space beside it.

As stated earlier, teachers certainly should not depend on words on a sheet to make an invitation clear. When frustrated by parents' seeming indifference, teachers might well consider these details.

Teachers and parents must remember that young children are sometimes upset by a change in the routine. Especially for young children, it is valuable to schedule conferences for times when children can leave with their parents, rather than see their parents leave again without them.

Plan for a Private Location

Planning for a quiet, private location is important. In a center or school, this may mean coordination among staff members for use of available space—staff room, conference room, empty classroom, or other. All that's really needed is two or three comfortable, adult-sized chairs, perhaps a table on which to spread papers or coffee cups, and a door that can be closed and posted with a sign—"Conference in Progress. Do Not Disturb." The physical environment probably least helpful to the conference goals is a formal office, with a teacher sitting behind a desk; the separation of one participant from the other by a desk conveys avoidance. A desk acts as a barricade between parent and teacher; it implies that the person seated behind it is dominant (Mehrabian, 1981). These are not the nonverbal messages teachers want to send as they try to establish a partnership with parents.

Plan Goals to be Discussed

In preparation for a conference teachers must set their goals and devise plans for meeting each goal.

Since one goal for every conference is undoubtedly to share information for a developmental overview, teachers need to accumulate the resources they will use to guide this discussion. A simple developmental evaluation tool, such as the LAP or DIAL, or one that has been devised for a center's needs, is useful here. The use of a developmental assessment tool in a conference with parents ensures that the conversation covers all aspects of development: physical (including self-help skills), cognitive, language, social, and emotional development. The checklist also offers concrete examples of what is usually expected at a particular stage of development, therefore educating parents as

Samples of art may be used to illustrate a child's development.

well as helping them to consider their child's behavior in an objective way.

Other materials may be used to reinforce this developmental information visually and concretely for parents. Samples of art, collected over a period of time, illustrate the refinement of small muscle skills, new concepts, or a new stage in a child's art. Snapshots of classroom activities indicate children's interests or interaction. Sharing of brief anecdotal records also helps to make the discussion of a changing child more vivid (Anselmo, 1977).

To say simply, "Tony is doing well with the other children" conveys little a parent can learn from. Vague statements are not helpful to a parent and give the impression that a teacher has learned little specific information about a child.

To check "Yes" to three questions about social development on an evaluation scale offers more.

	YES	NO
A. Takes turns without objection		
B. Can begin playing with other children without adult initiation		
C. Plays with other children often		

Sharing reports of actual incidents that reflect social growth is probably most meaningful.

You know, each day I try to jot down things that may be interesting to look back on. Let me show you some notes about Tony which show how he's progressed this year in his relationships with other children. Here's one—Sept. 30th—the beginning of the year.

Tony was playing by himself in the block corner, pushing two trucks down a ramp he'd made. When David came over and wanted to play too, Tony grabbed the cars and held them tightly. When I went over and suggested they both could play, Tony lost interest and wandered over to the puzzle table.

Playing with other children and taking turns was pretty new and hard for all our children then. For some it's still pretty hard. But let me read you a later note which suggests how Tony's doing in this area now.

> Feb. 15th. Tony began to build a gas station. He looked around, saw David, called him to come over. Said: You can help me build this gas station. David said: I know, let's build a fire station and I'll be the fire chief. Tony said: OK, and I'll drive the fire truck and make the siren go.

Teachers should present impressions from observations in such a way that parents feel encouraged to comment on or react to them. Parents are not told precisely what an observation might imply about a child, but the data is presented for mutual discussion and consideration (Losen and Diamant, 1978).

Anecdotal records are also useful in describing to parents, and not evaluating, aspects of behavior that are of concern. One of the best reasons for using such records in a conference is that they offer tangible evidence of how well teachers have paid attention to a particular child—important to every parent.

In addition to planning what to share, teachers should prepare a list of the questions to ask, so they will be sure to learn from a conference.

Making a brief outline of the topics to be discussed is helpful to both teachers and parents. A teacher will not forget items of importance as the conversation continues. An initial sharing of the list of topics with parents and asking for their additions, indicates to parents that they have more than a passive listening role to play, and may prevent them from beginning too quickly to discuss problems, before a balanced overview is achieved.

The organization of anecdotal records and developmental assessments in preparation for a conference should take a small amount of time. Being confident in their preparation leaves teachers free to initiate the social interaction of a conference.

Teachers may also suggest ways parents can set goals and prepare for a conference. This can be accomplished in two ways.

A handout to stimulate parents' questions may be displayed near the conference sign-up sheet or mailed to car-pooling parents (Coletta, 1977). A suitable handout may resemble the following:

> Parents usually have lots of questions about their children and school. Why not consider which of these might be helpful for us to discuss at our conference?
>
> —why we do what we do in the classroom?
> —your child's interests?

> —reactions to others?
> —sleeping patterns?
> —eating patterns?
> —your concerns about discipline?
> —what else have you been wondering lately?

Whatever form it takes, the clear message is that parents can expect to talk about any issue or concern.

Another idea is to suggest that parents spend a brief period observing in a classroom before a conference—perhaps joining a group for lunch before a naptime conference or coming in earlier for a late afternoon appointment. Here again, a simple list with a few questions can guide parents in watching their child, the activities in which he's involved, his interaction with others, a teacher's methods, etc. Such observation often stimulates immediate responses or questions (Hatoff, 1981).

GROUNDWORK FOR A SUCCESSFUL CONFERENCE

1. Teacher and parent understanding of the purpose and their roles
2. Planning for uninterrupted time, agreeable to teacher and parent
3. A relaxed and private physical environment
4. Planning of goals and organization of materials

Strategies for a Successful Conference

Preparation for conferences has been discussed at length because setting attitudes and atmosphere conducive to full partner participation is vital. Now let's consider the conference itself.

Help Parents Feel at Ease

It is teachers' responsibility to help parents become comfortable and at ease. Teachers are on familiar territory; parents are not. Unless parents are made to feel comfortable, their discomfort may be such a distraction that communication is hindered (Goetz, 1975). A few minutes spent in casual conversation is time well spent. An offer of juice or coffee may be appreciated by a tired parent, as well as creating more social ease.

It may be valuable for parents to observe before the conference.

"I appreciate your taking the time to come in today. Pete's been telling me about your camping trip plans. Sounds like you're going to cover a lot of territory!"

Begin With a Positive Attitude

As teachers turn the conversation towards the child, they begin with a positive comment about the child. It is important to indicate to parents at the outset that you like and appreciate their child. Parents are more likely to accept later comments, even constructive criticism (McCroskey, 1971), if a conference begins with both adults clearly on the same side and with a teacher's clear indication that she has paid specific attention to a child and knows him well. A positive opening comment also removes any lingering concern a parent may have about the purpose of a conference.

I'm enjoying having Pete in my classroom. I think one of the things I most enjoy is his enthusiasm about everything! I wish you could have seen him this morning when he was talking about the plans for your trip—eyes sparkling and words just tumbling out!"

Encourage Parent Participation

Although teachers clearly guide the conversation through the planned topics, they should be continually aware of the principle of partnership and try to draw a parent into participation at all times by frequently asking open-ended questions.

> "So he's achieved all of these self-help skills except for shoe tying, and we're working on that. What kinds of things do you see him doing for himself at home now?"

The use of questions will help a parent expand on a statement, so they can both get a clearer picture.

> "When you say you're having problems with him at mealtime, could you tell me a bit more about some things that have been particularly troublesome at dinner recently?"

Teachers who want to help parents assume the role of "expert" on their child use questions to guide parents towards thinking about possible courses of action, instead of telling them what to do.

> "What are some of the things you've tried when he's begun playing with his food?"

They encourage parents to continue talking by *active listening.* Active listening refers to the technique of giving sensitive attention and picking up a speaker's verbal and nonverbal messages, then reflecting back the total message empathetically, for a speaker's verification. (See Gordon, 1970 and Briggs, 1975, for a full study of active listening concepts.) It is necessary for teachers to put themselves into the position of the other person, to be able to feel as he does, and to see the world as he is now seeing it. This involves accepting the feelings of a parent without judgement and reflecting the feelings back to him in a way that lets him know that the teacher understands. When a teacher is not just quietly attentive, but is responsive to the feelings behind the other person's words, active listening encourages fuller communication. As a teacher reflects her understanding of a parent's message back, the parent is often stimulated to continue talking about a situation, allowing for a deeper understanding into his own feelings.

> Teacher: "It really seems to concern you that he's not developing good mealtime habits."
>
> Parent: "Well, you know, it does bother me. I guess because I used to be something of a food fusser and I remember some very unpleasant mealtimes as a child. I want to avoid it developing into a real problem with Pete, if I can."

Active listening has the advantage of sending a message of clear acceptance, defusing hostile behavior, and assisting in identifying the real problems (Berger, 1981; Coletta, 1977).

> "It sounds to me like mealtime has become a time of day you really don't look forward to."

Throughout a conference, teachers depend heavily on questions and reflective statements to indicate they have much to learn from a parent. Asking, not telling, and respect for a parent's opinion, are important aspects of a partnership, as well as a good way to obtain information. Parents who sit through a conference and listen to a teacher talk are less likely to think about ideas that come through a one-way flow—or come back for another conference (VanderVan, 1977).

Summarize for Parents

There is much to talk about when parents and teachers get together. But teachers must be mindful of the time pressures on busy parents and keep a conference to the scheduled time. If more areas arise that need to be discussed, it is preferable to make a second appointment. Too much information at any one time may be burdensome and not fully absorbed.

As a conference ends, it is again a teacher's responsibility to summarize the main points discussed, as well as any projected plans. Parents need to leave a conference feeling their time was well spent; a summary to reinforce the discussion is useful. Once again, it is especially appropriate to be positive about a parent's efforts and contributions.

> "Thank you for coming in today. I've certainly appreciated your sharing so much helpful information about Pete. As you've seen from our assessment, he's doing very well in every area.

I'm particularly glad to know of your concern about meal-time so I can support your efforts here. Your plan of trying a time limit sounds good—do let me know how it goes."

These general strategies can help to achieve a successful conference.

STRATEGIES FOR A SUCCESSFUL CONFERENCE

1. Teacher taking initiative in putting parent at ease
2. A positive beginning and ending
3. Give and take in conversation, facilitated by a teacher's questions and reflective listening
4. A summarizing of areas discussed and action to be taken

Ending with a conference on a positive note and with a summary of the discussion helps parents feel their time has been well spent.

Pitfalls to Avoid for a Successful Conference

In addition to paying attention to these strategies, there are specific pitfalls that teachers need to be aware of and avoid.

Avoid Using Technical Terminology

When teachers explain developmental progress to parents, they must be careful not to use jargon or technical terms that are not easily understood and can create distance between the adults. Parents are not likely to listen to someone talking over their heads and are understandably reluctant to ask for clarification of terms (Nedler, 1979).

NOT: "He functions well in the Piagetian sensorimotor stage!"

RATHER: "He is a very active explorer. Every time we offer him a new material, he examines it very carefully, from every angle."

Avoid Role of "Expert"

Teachers should be careful not to set themselves up as experts on any child. Such a stance prevents the growth of a working partnership; many parents feel shaky enough at the business of parenting without being faced with a teacher who seems to "know it all." Rather than peppering their comments with advice that focuses on "shoulds" and "musts," teachers need to avoid such authoritarian dogmatism. The implication that if one disagrees, one is wrong, will inhibit discussion (Losen and Diamant, 1978).

To avoid the appearance of being a dogmatic expert, teachers need to be cautious about the phrases they use as they share knowledge. Many teachers say—"lots of parents find" or "some of my parents have told me"—they find these phrases more easily accepted than "*I* think," which sounds too authoritative.

Certain areas of concern to a parent may be far beyond a teacher's scope of knowledge and competence. It is necessary for teachers to be straightforward in admitting this (Bradley, 1971) and know when to refer a parent to an expert.

> "I appreciate your concern about Billy's language. Let me give you the number of the people at Speech and Hearing. They can answer your questions far better than I."

If teachers feel questions could be answered better by another, they may invite the director, social worker, or co-teacher to join a discussion.

Contrary to what some teachers believe, when they confess their limitations it tends not to demean them, but earns them respect in parents' eyes for their honesty.

Avoid Negative Evaluations

Knowing how closely parental self-esteem is tied to others' perceptions of their child, teachers must be sensitive to avoid the appearance of being critical or negative about a child's capabilities. Certain key words trigger defensive feelings in parents, and parents who feel defensive are unable to communicate and cooperate fully. Some words to avoid are:

> problem—"I'm having a *problem* with Jimmy."
> behind—"Jimmy is *behind* in language."
> immature—"Jimmy is more *immature* than the rest of the class."
> never, can't—"Jimmy *never* finishes lunch with the others; Jimmy *can't* do most of our puzzles."

Any labels such as hyperactive, learning disability, etc. should also be avoided

> labels—"Sometimes I wonder if Jimmy isn't *hyperactive.*"

Comments that are objective observations rather than subjective characterizations are more helpful and more easily received (Goetz, 1975).

NOT: "Jimmy doesn't like art." (Subjective)
RATHER: "Jimmy rarely participates in art activities." (Objective)

When teachers merely describe behavior, parents are left to draw their own conclusions. This offers information in a neutral way, without implying evaluation or criticism. Teachers have a responsibility to help parents think positively about their children and negative judgements are simply not helpful. Any parent would react emotionally to hearing these. Parents need teachers who can help with realistic and constructive, not destructive, comments. Because behavior is complex, it would be impossible, as well as unproductive, to assign reasons or blame for a particular behavior.

NOT: "Jimmy's having so many temper tantrums because your husband has been out of town so much lately."
RATHER: "One of the things we're working on with Jimmy is . . ."

The first statement if not necessarily true, is certainly not helpful, and likely to alienate a parent from a partnership. The second comment does not imply negative evaluation, but action that can be taken. An observant teacher watches parents' body language to notice if there is emotional reaction to what she has said.

Avoid Unprofessional Conversation

Teachers need to be sure a conversation remains professional, though warm, and centered on the adults' common concerns related to a child.

Teachers never discuss other children and parents in a conference with another; to do so would make parents question how confidential their own conversation is.

NOT: "You know, Mrs. Smith has been having an even worse time with Janie—she had a terrible tantrum the other day."

RATHER: "Many parents find that four-year-olds can get quite out of bounds."

This might have been intended as a reassurance, but is probably unsettling to the other parent who hears it!

Teachers should not ask personal questions except when they are absolutely related to a concern being discussed about a child.

NOT: "How do you spend your spare time on the weekends?"

RATHER: "I've been wondering what time Jimmy goes to bed—he's been very sleepy in the mid-morning."

When parents turn a conversation to personal matters not directly related to their child, teachers need to make it clear that their only role is to listen supportively if a parent needs to talk—of course assuring confidentiality—and to refer to more expert community resources if a parent seems interested (Hauser-Cram, 1986).

> "I'm sorry to hear that you and Jimmy's father have been having some difficulties. If it helps you to talk about it, I'll be glad to listen. I can also suggest a couple of agencies that could be really helpful during a difficult time."

It is inappropriate to cut this parent off completely; teachers are sometimes so oriented to children's problems that they do not realize that parents have their own exhausting problems.

Sometimes, especially in a conference with two parents present, teachers can get caught in the middle of a family disagreement (Hauser-Cram, 1986).

> "Mr. Jones, my husband and I just don't agree about disciplining Bobby. He spanks him whenever he misbehaves but I just don't believe in spanking kids. What would you say?"

There could only be future difficulty in working with this family if the teacher were to take sides. His answer needs to be helpful and neutral.

> "Discipline's a broad subject, and even many experts don't agree. I think families have to make up their minds and do what's right for them. If it would help, I can tell you some of the things we do in the classroom and why."

Teachers' awareness of their roles as professionals will help them avoid these pitfalls. Professional ethics also require that teachers do not share personal family issues with other teachers except when necessary to understand children's behavior or situation.

Avoid Giving Advice

It is easy for teachers to make the error of giving unasked-for advice to parents, since teachers may see a need and have a fairly good idea what can help. But advice from others is seldom effective; it is only when parents reach a personal conclusion that they become committed to a course of action. Just because a parent mentions a problem, a teacher should not conclude that the parent is asking for a solution to that problem. A teacher is likely not to know the full complexity of the situation and may give inappropriate suggestions. Giving advice tends to distance a teacher from parents. Parents might quietly listen to this advice while inwardly fuming:

> "Who does he think he is? A lot he knows about it anyway—this is my child, not his."

Giving advice may usurp a parent's right to decide. Giving advice may also be dangerous; when the "expert's" suggestions don't work, the expert gets the blame and future mistrust.

It's easy to fall into the trap of giving advice to parents when they do ask for it—probably because it's a good feeling to know you have the answer someone else needs! The best way to avoid such a pitfall is to make several suggestions, and turn the thinking process back to parents.

> "Some of the things we've tried in the classroom for that are: . . ."
> "Let me pass along some ideas on that that have worked for other parents: . . ."
> "Do any of those sound like something that could work for you?"

It's very appropriate to help parents understand that, in guidance, there is seldom one right answer. Parents should be encouraged to come up with their own plans, which they are more likely to carry out than a plan handed to them. If teachers remember that one of their goals is to enhance not only parenting skills but also parental self-esteem, they will realize how important it is to be speculative in offering suggestions, not dogmatic in giving advice. "If I were you, I'd . . ." is definitely not the most helpful phrase, since it implies an absolute and sure position.

Avoid Rushing into Solutions

Another easy error for either parent or teacher is to feel that all problems must be solved and conclusions reached during a designated conference period. Changing behaviors and understanding is a process that takes time and cannot be artificially rushed to fit into a brief conference. It is better to suggest the need for time:

> "All right, then both of us will try to watch and see when these outbursts occur. Maybe then we can work out some appropriate response. Let's plan to get back together and talk again next month."

It is also a mistake to assume that parents and teachers will always be able to agree and work together, and that a conference is a failure if a teacher is unable to "convert" a parent to her understanding. Different experiences, personalities, value systems, and needs influence how readily each can agree with the other's viewpoint. A successful conference is one in which there is an exchange and acceptance of various insights, including those that conflict.

Every teacher encounters conference situations that deteriorate as a parent expresses anger, hostility, or blame. If parents have trouble accepting information, it is not uncommon to employ the defense mechanisms of projection—"If only you could teach better he wouldn't have this problem"—or denial—"Don't you dare tell me my son has a problem." If parents become verbally abusive or irrational in anger, it is impossible to communicate effectively. At that point a teacher's task is to diffuse the anger so that communication can begin. To do this, it is crucial that a teacher not become defensive or angry in return. Retaliating verbally, arguing, or retreating from a parent's anger are not helpful responses. A teacher needs to remain calm, speaking softly and slowly; to do some active listening that will allow parents to see their own words and feelings from the other's point of view; and to demonstrate an acceptance of parents' right to their opinions (Rundall, 1982). Handling an expression of hostility this way will help a teacher work with a parent on the areas of disagreement, instead of losing the issues in personal attacks or emotional responses. (Working with hostility will be discussed further in Chapter 15.)

PITFALLS TO AVOID
FOR A SUCCESSFUL CONFERENCE

1. Too technical terminology or jargon

2. Playing the role of an "expert"

3. Negative and destructive evaluations about a child's capabilities

4. Unprofessional conversation—about others
                                                —too personal
                                                —taking sides

5. Giving advice—either unasked for or asked for

6. Trying to solve all problems on the spot or trying to force agreement

---

Conference Evaluation

Soon after a conference is over, it is a good idea to summarize the new information gained and plans made.

1/1/86. Conference with Pete's mother. She is concerned about Pete playing with food at meals.

Plan: 1. Share information with co-teacher.

2. Observe Pete at lunch—move seat near mine.

3. Talk with mother again in two months.

It is also useful, for a teacher's professional growth, to evaluate her participation in a conference, by asking herself questions such as:

- How well did I listen?
- How well did I facilitate parent's participation?
- Did I offer enough specifics?
- Was I positive in beginning and ending the conference?
- How comfortable were we in the conversation?

With experience, teachers grow in their ability to facilitate an effective conference.

It is appropriate for a preschool teacher to hold conferences to discuss developmental progress and goals at least every six months, since change occurs so rapidly at this time. For the needs of particular families and children, conferences may be held more frequently.

It should be remembered that non-attendance at a conference does not necessarily indicate disinterest in a child or the school. Instead, it may be a reflection of different cultural or socioeconomic values, of extreme pressures or stress of family or work demands (Herwig, 1982). A teacher's response to non-attendance is to review the possible explanations of non-attendance, see if different scheduling or educational actions will help, persist in invitations and efforts, and understand that other methods of reaching a parent will have to be used in the meantime.

Summary

Parent-teacher conferences provide the time and opportunity for parents and teachers to consider together all aspects of a child's overall development, including any particular interests, needs or problems that may concern either parents or teachers. Such an opportunity will help further a sense of working together with shared information and common goals.

A teacher has the reponsibility for setting the tone of a partnership in such a conversation by preparing parents for their participatory role in a conversation, guiding a conversation, and encouraging more parent participation by the use of questions and active listening.

Being sensitive to the dynamics of interpersonal relations in general, and more specifically to parental reactions, will help a teacher avoid communication errors that can block real understanding or inhibit the growth of a relationship. Careful planning and evaluation of conferences will help teachers grow in the skills necessary for effective parent-teacher conferences.

Student Activities for Further Study

1. With your classmates, set up a role playing situation in which one of you is a teacher, one a parent. Remember to concentrate on

facilitating a dialogue in the conversation by the teacher's questions and active listening. Your "audience" can help you evaluate and suggest other possibilities. Try these situations and any others you have encountered.

   a. A mother asks how to prepare three-year-old for new baby.

   b. A teacher is concerned about coordinating toilet training efforts.

   c. A mother comments that her four-year-old son is being very "bad" lately.

   d. A teacher is concerned about a recent increase in a child's aggressive behavior.

   e. A father is concerned about his son who is in your classroom; he feels he is not as advanced at four as his older brother was.

   f. Mother asks you what to do about her toddler biting.

2. With a partner, brainstorm many possible teacher responses to these comments and questions from parents. Then decide which is most appropriate, and why.

   a. I honestly don't know how you do it—kids this age drive me crazy.

   b. What I want to know is, when are the kids in your classroom going to do some real work, not just this playing?

   c. Do you think my Sarah is slow—she doesn't seem to me to be talking right?

   d. Well, I don't agree with your soft approach—I say when kids are bad, they should be spanked.

   e. I don't know if I should tell you this, but my husband has left us and I don't think he's coming back.

   f. What's the best way to get a child to go to bed?

3. After reading the following record, develop an outline for sharing this information with parents during a conference.

   Judy is three years and six months, much smaller than the other children in her classroom. She speaks indistinctly, and often not more than two words at a time. She plays by herself most of the time, and in fact seems to shrink back when other children or most adults approach her. She has well-developed fine motor skills and is extremely creative when she paints. Despite the well-developed fine motor skills, her self-help skills lag behind, and she often asks for assistance in the bathroom, and in simple dressing tasks. She enjoys music and often sits for long periods listening to records with the earphones.

Review Questions

1. Identify three of four reasons for holding regular parent-teacher conferences.
2. List five of eight factors that facilitate productive parent-teacher conferences.
3. List four of six pitfalls to avoid in parent-teacher conferences.

References and Related Readings

Anselmo, Sandra. "Vignettes of Child Activity." *Childhood Education* 53.3 (1977): 133-36.

Berger, E.H. *Parents as Partners in Education.* St. Louis: C.V. Mosby Co., 1981.

Bradley, R.C. *Parent-Teacher Interviews.* Wolfe City, Texas: The University Press, 1971.

Briggs, Dorothy C. *Your Child's Self Esteem.* Garden City, New York: Doubleday and Co., 1970.

Carberry, Hugh H. "Parent-Teacher Conferences." *Today's Education* 64.1 (1975): 67-69.

Coletta, Anthony. *Working Together: A Guide to Parent Involvement.* Atlanta: Humanics Press Inc., 1977.

Davis, Donna H. and Donald M. "Managing Parent-Teacher Conferences." *Today's Education* 70.2 (1981): 46-51.

D'Evelyn, Katherine. *Individual Parent-Teacher Conferences.* New York: Bureau of Publications, Teachers College, Columbia University, 1945.

Dodd, J.H. and N.S. "Communicating With Parents." *Academic Therapy* 7.3 (1972): 227-34.

Flake-Hobson, Carol and Kevin Swick. "Communication Strategies for Parents and Teachers." *Dimensions* 7.4 (1979): 112-15.

Freeman, Jane. "Customizing Your Parent Conferences for Better Results." *Learning* 14.6 (1986): 70-74.

Goetz, E. "Parent Conferences Can Work." *Day Care and Early Education* 2.4 (1975): 13-15.

Grissom, Catherine E. "Listening Beyond Words: Learning from Parents in Conferences." *Childhood Education* 48.3 (1971): 138-42.

Hatoff, Sydella H., and Claudia Byram. *Teacher's Practical Guide for Educating Young Children.* Boston, Mass.: Allyn and Bacon, 1981.

Hauser-Cram, Penny. "Backing Away Helpfully: Some Roles Teachers Shouldn't Fill." *Beginnings* 3.1 (1986): 18-20.

Herwig, Joan E. "Parental Involvement: Changing Assumptions about the Educator's Role." *How to Involve Parents in Early Childhood Education.* Ed. Brigham Young University Press. Provo, Utah: Brigham Young University Press, 1982.

Hogan, J.R. "The Three-Way Conference: Parent-Teacher-Child." *The Elementary School Journal* 75.5 (1975): 311-315.

Lawrence, Gerda and Madeline Hunter. *Parent-Teacher Conferencing.* El Segundo, Calif: Theory into Practice Press, 1978.

Kahl, David. "Talking About the Child's Progress." *Today's Education* 62.2 (1973): 34-5.

Kroth, Roger L. and Richard l. Simpson. *Parent Conferences as a Teaching Strategy.* Denver: Love Publishing Co., 1977.

Long, Alan. "Easing the Stress of Parent-Teacher Conferences." *Today's Education* 65.3 (1976): 84-5.

Losen, Stuart, and Bert Diamant. *Parent Conferences in the Schools.* Boston: Allyn and Bacon, 1978.

McCroskey, James C., Carl E. Larson, Mark L. Knapp. *An Introduction to Interpersonal Communication.* Englewood Cliffs, New Jersey: Prentice-Hall Inc., 1971.

Mehrabian, Albert. *Silent Messages: Implicit Communication of Emotions and Attitudes.* 2nd Ed. Belmont, Calif.: Wadsworth Publ. Co, 1981.

Nedler, Shari and Oralie McAfee. *Working With Parents.* Belmont, Calif.: Wadsworth Publishing Co., 1979.

Rathbun, D. "Parent-Teacher Talks: Conferences or Confrontations?" *Learning* 7.2 (1978): 54-58.

Readdick, Christine A., et al. "The Child-Parent-Teacher Conference." *Young Children* 39.5 (1984): 67-73.

Rundall, Richard D. and Steven Lynn Smith. "Working With Difficult Parents." *How to Involve Parents in Early Childhood Education.* Ed. Brigham Young University Press. Provo, Utah: Brigham Young University Press, 1982.

Rutherford, Robert B. and Edgar Eugene. *Teachers and Parents: A Guide to Interaction and Cooperation.* Boston: Allyn and Bacon, 1979.

Simpson, Richard L. *Conferencing Parents of Exceptional Children.* Rockville, Maryland: An Aspen Publication, 1982.

Tizard, Barbara, Jo Mortimer, B. Burchell. *Involving Parents in Nursery and Infant School.* Ypsilanti, Michigan: The High/Scope Press, 1981.

VanderVan, Karen D. *Home and Community Influences on Young Children.* Albany, New York: Delmar Publishers, 1977.

Chapter 11 Home Visits

Chapter 11 concentrates on the occasional home visits made by a classroom teacher as part of the effort to build parent-teacher-child relationships. Varying aspects of home visitation programs or home-based educational programs are described. (See Chapter 8 for a discussion of the initial home visit as part of the orientation process.)

Objectives

After studying this chapter, the student will be able to

1. discuss several purposes for home visits
2. discuss points to consider in undertaking home visits
3. describe advantages and disadvantages of home visits
4. identify the general purpose and techniques of home-based programs

Purposes of a Home Visit

A home visit often presents scheduling difficulties for both teachers and parents and is therefore one of the components of a parent involvement program that is most frequently left out. However, a home visit adds a dimension that is not possible via other methods.

The prospect of a home visit may be frightening for a teacher who has not yet discovered how rewarding this encounter can be for everyone.

John Roberts is frank in expressing some of his reservations to his co-worker. "This whole thing makes me nervous. I'm not all that familiar with the Rodriguez'; the father never drops Tony off, and his mother doesn't talk much. I have a feeling they're pretty old-fashioned. And I never even go over to the side of town where they live. I'm always afraid I'll get lost and hardly anybody talks English over there. Who knows what I could get into when I knock on their door?"

> The Rodriguez family has their own reaction when the note about the home visit first comes home.
>
> "What does Tony's teacher want to come here for?" wonders Mr. Rodriguez. "Has he got some problem, do you think?"
>
> "He said not, but I don't know. You've got to try to be home from work when he comes—my English is too bad for him. I wish we had some better chairs in the living room; I don't know what he'll think."

It is only natural that both participants have these concerns. A home visit takes teachers out of the familiar classroom world for which they are trained and directly into the diverse worlds in which the children live. Parents are in similarly uncharted territory, wondering about their function and perhaps concerned that their home and family "measure up" to a teacher's standard.

With such apprehensions on both sides, it is easy to overlook the reasons for a visit. In *Working Together: A Guide to Parent Involvement,* a letter is quoted from a parent indicating his appreciation of a home visit from his son's teacher. The father writes:

> "I do believe that in the long run it will definitely prove to be the most important step in helping Danny to become more attentive and more progressive in school. . . . I deeply feel that this wonderful gesture . . . will prove fruitful in helping Danny." (Coletta, 1977, Appendix T)

The most important aspect of a home visit, as this father expresses, is the strong evidence that a teacher cares enough to move beyond the territorial confines of classroom to reach out to a child and his family.

> The visit of John Roberts to the Rodriguez family corroborates the value for both parents and teachers. After the visit is over Mrs. Rodriguez comments to her husband, "Well, that was nice. He really does like Tony, doesn't he, and he's not a bit stuck up like I thought he was. Maybe I will go in to the classroom to do some Spanish cooking with the children, like he said."
>
> Her husband agreed. "I'm glad to have had a chance to meet him, since I never get to go to school. He must be a good teacher, to go to such trouble."

One teacher said she had thought of home visits as just another means of talking with parents that was probably not as effective as a conference at school, since one cannot talk as well in front of a child at home. But from the reactions of children and parents after her first visits, she realized

> . . . what should have been obvious all along, that the home visit should be chiefly for the child, and that what could be conveyed to the parents is that the teacher likes and is interested in their child, and therefore would like to see his toys, his cat, where he lives, etc., or to meet other members of his family (Bromberg, 1968, p. 79).

It is difficult for parents to be adversaries of teachers when they show such interest and concern.

For a parent who finds it difficult to get to school because of job or family responsibilities, a home visit offers the only opportunity for face-to-face contact with a teacher. A home visit allows this parent the chance to feel involved in the educational process and offers a reassuring look at teacher and child interacting.

To continue to ally themselves with parents as they indicate their interest and caring for a child is the primary purpose for classroom teachers to make home visits. Their effort to make a visit and their warm concentration on a child during a visit helps to create a sense of partnership with parents.

Of course, a home visit is important to teachers also, in providing firsthand information about a child's physical environment. Information about a home setting and family can be learned by the teacher's observations; this information and its implications is usually not conveyed by a data sheet filled out at a center. Because the home environment is a place where children learn probably more than in school, it is important for teachers to understand that part of a child's life. It helps them understand why he behaves as he does in a classroom (Swick and Duff, 1978). When teachers have a feel for what parents are doing with their children at home and why they are doing it, their own efforts can complement and supplement the home efforts (Gordon, 1976).

John Roberts' experience points out these benefits for teachers.

"I haven't taught many Puerto Rican children. I've been worried about Tony's shyness in the classroom. After I visited his family at home, I realized that their expectations for a preschooler are that he not take the initiative when speaking with an adult. He really does have beautiful manners—I saw that when he was with his parents; it's not really shyness, just the respect he's been taught. I also discovered that only Spanish is spoken at home, which helps me realize some of his language needs in the classroom. It was fun to see Tony at home—he

> was obviously very proud to see me there. All this week since, at school, he's been coming to me more."

For children, home visits offer opportunities to feel very special, with teacher and parent attention focused on them individually. Seeing a teacher in his home helps build greater feelings of trust and intimacy for a child as well.

Undertaking Home Visits

While a home visit can be beneficial for children, teachers, and parents, it is not accomplished without effort and planning. Here are some points to consider.

Explain Purpose in Advance

Parents need to receive a clear explanation of the child-centered purpose of a home visit in advance. Although the parent handbook and orientation discussion should do this, a reminding note from a teacher before a visit is reassuring. Such explanations may decrease the threatening aspects of a home visit, especially with parents who are accustomed to official visitors evaluating or judging their home, financial matters, and functions of family members.

> The reason for this visit is to help the child and parents to get to know the teachers away from the day care center. It also helps to establish a relationship that is both open and friendly. Teachers' visits are mainly social; if you have concerns about your child or the day care center we will be glad to discuss these at another time when your child is not present. (Sample from hypothetical parent handbook)

Arrange Time with Parents

A teacher needs to make clear arrangements regarding the date and time of a visit at parents' convenience by sending a note home with a child and following up with a telephone call. An unexpected visit does not permit parents to feel at ease and in charge of the situation. Some parents like to make a visit a social occasion and prepare refreshments and tidy their house. To be caught off-guard does not facilitate a relaxed atmosphere.

Mrs. Rodriguez reported to her husband, "This is the day Tony's teacher is coming to visit him at 5:30. Can you be sure to be home from work by then? He called and said I should say a time when we'd both be here, so I said 5:30. He said he won't stay long, but I made some pan dulce. This is nice of him to come. Tony's all excited."

Behave Like a Guest

Despite the fact that teachers take the initiative to set up a visit, they are still the guests in another's home. Actually, this puts them in the desirable position of being able to follow another's lead. This aspect of a parent-involvement program gives parents the clear advantage in feeling comfortable, even though both parents and teachers probably experience some discomfort when faced with the unfamiliar. This is a new role for a classroom teacher who is used to being in control. As visitors, teachers graciously accept whatever hospitality is offered by a family. There should be no indication, no word or expression, of surprise or disdain for the family's environment or life-style. They are not there to evaluate, but to support. One of the most essential ingredients for a successful home visit is flexibility on the part of teachers, an ability to accept variations in family behavior and conditions that are different from what they have experienced themselves.

Home visits give parents the advantage of being on their own familiar territory.

A teacher's way of dressing may be important; a style of dressing that is either too casual—old jeans—or too fancy—a new designer suit— may indicate presuppositions about the family's life-style and make all participants uncomfortable.

Teachers should begin a visit in a friendly, relaxed way.

> "I see you have quite a vegetable plot out front, Mr. Rodriguez. Who's the gardener in the family?"

They let parents share whatever family mementoes or anecdotes they'd like, but avoid leading conversation into personal issues themselves.

> "Oh, I'd love to see your pictures of Tony and his big sister."

They listen respectfully to both children and parents.

> "Tony, I do want to see your kitten. Let me just finish looking at these pictures with your Mom."

In short, teachers use all their social skills of tact, sensitivity, and interest to help both themselves and family participants feel at ease with one another and accomplish the overall goal of enhancing a parent-teacher-child relationship.

Be Timely

Teachers need to be sensitive to the demands on a family's time. They should arrive promptly at the designated time. A visit should last from fifteen to thirty minutes, certainly not much longer, unless they have been invited by parents for a particular social event.

Post-Visit Responsibilities

After a home visit, there are several things for a teacher to do to build on what has been accomplished.

Thank-You Note

Send a thank-you note to a family for allowing a home visit to take place. By including positive comments on some aspect of the home environment and comments directed particularly to a child, a teacher further indicates his interest and appreciation of a family (Swick and Duff, 1978).

Dear Mr. and Mrs. Rodriguez and family,

Thank you for making time in your busy schedule for me to visit you at your home on Thursday. I did enjoy the chance to see Tony at home, and to see some of his favorite things. Tony, your kitten is very pretty, and you are doing a good job of looking after him.

Thank you also for those delicious pan dulce, Mrs. Rodriguez. I hope you can come soon to the classroom, and cook with our children.

Sincerely,

John Roberts

Follow-Up

In the weeks and months that follow, a teacher must continue to be in touch with parents with regards to the information learned and issues discussed during a home visit. For example, if a teacher discovered ways that parents can act as classroom resources, a teacher should make an arrangement promptly.

"Mr. Rodriguez, when I visited your home and talked about your garden, we said it would be fun for you to visit the classroom with some of the ripe vegetables. Could you come one day next week? We're talking about harvest season."

Evaluation

A teacher needs to evaluate a home visit to learn how effective it was in strengthening a parent-teacher-child relationship, and how his participation helped meet this goal.

Advantages to Home Visits

Home visits provide positive impetus to a family-teacher relationship. Realistically, there can be both advantages and disadvantages to this method. Let's first examine the advantages.

Increase in Trust

Parents and children usually feel more comfortable and secure in their familiar home environment. In most other aspects of the relationship, a teacher has the advantage as the professional person, of

**Home vists offer teachers the opportunity to experience
a child's home environment and relationships firsthand.**

knowing what to do and how to do it. During a home visit, parents
can take more initiative in furthering the relationship. A young child
who sees his teacher welcomed as a guest into his home gets positive
feelings about his parents' acceptance of his teacher. A sense of trust
is increased among parents, teachers, and children.

Firsthand Insights

A teacher gains not only the rewarding experience of feeling
accepted by a family, but also the firsthand insights afforded by a chance
to see parents and child interact in their home environment. Home
visits can thus enhance and extend the classroom experience, as a
teacher uses his knowledge to modify skills and plans to match individual
children's interests and learning styles, and utilizes parent resources
learned about during his visits.

Disadvantages to Home Visits

Although the advantages are more important, there are definite
disadvantages to home visits that need to be overcome.

Additional Time Involved

Time is no doubt the greatest disadvantage. Not only do home
visits take time, but it is often difficult to schedule a visit during a
teacher's normal daytime working hours, especially in a full-day program.
(In a part-day or part-week program, a teacher can often use some of

his planning and preparation time for visits, when a child is at home.) In a full-day program, even if coverage for a teacher in the classroom can be arranged, parents are often at work and the child at the center. School administrators may offer compensation time to teachers who use some of their own time off.

Both teachers and parents must be convinced that they will gain from a visit before they will give up time after work, during evenings, days off or weekends, to schedule a visit. A teacher's explanations and persistence as he tries to schedule a convenient visit should be an indication to parents of how valuable a teacher perceives this activity to be.

As a parent, the author has been impressed by teachers' evident caring for her children, to care enough to visit in the late afternoon and on Saturday morning. As a teacher, the author's most productive visit came, after weeks of trying to set it up, at 9:30 a.m. before both parents went off to late-morning jobs. After this visit, they consented to visit in the classroom for the first time; their little daughter blossomed. Scheduling time is a definite disadvantage, but one that is worth overcoming.

Possible Negative Feelings

Another major obstacle to overcome for a successful home visit is the negative presuppositions of each participant. Many parents feel suspicious and threatened by an "official" visit, and it takes sensitive, open efforts by schools and teachers to educate parents and remove these fears. It is probably after the experience of a visit that much of this concern is allayed, so teachers must take care to do nothing during a visit that appears to be official scrutiny or judgemental. Teachers' care to focus on the positive is necessary.

Teachers must honestly scrutinize their own attitudes and prejudices. In making home visits, they frequently find themselves in neighborhoods and life-styles quite removed from what they are accustomed to and they must become aware of their biases. When faced directly, personal biases are less destructive than those not admitted, which will manifest themselves in behavior. By focusing their attention on the children and parents' concern for their children, teachers can find positive things in a home situation, rather than focus on those aspects that are different from their experiences. There is no question that emotional responses are complex to deal with, but teachers who are conscious of these dynamics of a relationship are more likely to be effective.

Home-Based Educational Programs

This text assumes that most teachers are part of traditional, school-based learning situation and that they consider home visits to be a useful technique to use in building a parent-teacher working relationship. But it may be interesting to note also that home visitation programs have developed over the last twenty years that focus on teachers educating parents and children in the home.

The goal of most home-based programs is to help parents become better teachers of their children and improve the quality of life for individual families. Typically, disadvantaged families are involved in home-based programs. The home visitors generally concentrate their efforts on working with parents rather than children, often teaching parents how to use everyday care-giving or household situations as opportunities to stimulate learning. When a teacher works with a child, it is a way of modeling appropriate teaching behavior to parents present and involved. All home-based programs assume that parents are the most important teachers of their children during the early years, and the skills they are taught have a long-term impact on all children in a family. Parents are expected to add the responsibilities of learners, and then teachers, to their roles as parents and family members.

The home visitors in these programs require different skills and techniques in addition to those necessary for working with children. In these programs, teachers are parent educators. In several programs, successful home visitors are trained paraprofessionals. (See Gordon and Breivogel, 1976 for a description of Gordon's program in Florida; and Gray, 1971 for the DARCEE program at George Peabody College in Tennessee.) This has several advantages, including the economic factor; it is less expensive to use paraprofessionals. Another advantage to the use of trained paraprofessionals is that residents of the same community may be used. A resident of the community may already have established rapport with a family and understand the values and attitudes of the area (Berger, 1981).

What is taught in each home-based program varies with the goals, but in most programs time and activities are used to build trust and communication between parents and the home visitor, to improve parent-child interaction and learning situations, and to improve home and family life.

Parents who feel isolated and burdened with the demands of young children respond to visitors who treat them with concerned interest. The Home Start guide lists criteria for the selection of home visitors that include the ability to listen with empathy and sensitivity, to relate effectively to many different people, and to adapt one's personality to meet varying needs (U.S. HEW, 1974). Home visitors spend time at each visit talking informally about whatever concerns parents wish to discuss, as well as having sociable chats.

Home visitors are also observant of family needs and spend time helping parents discover resources and methods of improving home practices, such as nutritional information and classes, financial planning, or recreational opportunities in the community. But the majority of time is spent in helping parents become sensitive to the developmental characteristics and needs of their children, and in teaching and demonstrating activities and techniques that parents can use with their children at home. Sometimes home visitors bring toys and books, and demonstrate how these can be used to stimulate communication and creative play. Often these items are left as "gifts" and encouraged to be used between visits (Levenstein, 1971). Home visitors develop activities or help parents improvise toys from the home environment (U.S. Dept. of HEW, 1976; Packer et al., 1976). Home visitors will individualize activities according to the circumstances, often including ideas for younger children, and ideas that other family members can also carry out. They may encourage parents to find their own ways of stimulating learning—perhaps by having a child participate in a household task such as washing dishes or folding laundry, or undertake a routine care-giving situation with an infant in such a way as to create a learning game (Lambie et al., 1980).

The following are some of the well-documented home visitation programs:

1. **DARCEE, from the George Peabody College in Tennessee,** that developed home visitation techniques and activities for mothers of preschoolers, hoping to provide mothers with the coping skills and assurance they need to be their child's sole preschool teacher (Gray, 1971).

2. Verbal Interaction Project by Levenstein, based on the idea that parents can be taught to stimulate their children's intellectual development through verbal interaction about specific toys and books brought by the "toy demonstrator," as these home visitors are called (Levenstein, 1971).

3. Ypsilanti-Carnegie Infant Education Project and the Wisconsin Portage Project, which work with parents of particular children (infants and handicapped preschoolers) (Lambie et al., 1980; Shearer et al., 1976).

4. Home Start Projects, added in 1972 to extend the operations of the center-based Head Start programs, by making the home the base and helping parents become teachers of their children (U.S. Dept. of HEW, 1974 and 1976).

Summary

To summarize, home visits offer to parents, evidence of a teacher's interest and care for their child, and an opportunity to play a more comfortable and dominant role while in their home setting. For teachers, it is another chance to reach out to families and an opportunity to experience a child's home environment and relationships firsthand. For children, it is a chance to build a deeper personal relationship with a teacher in a comfortable home setting. Much has been learned from the home-based educational programs and any community deciding to investigate or institute such a program has an abundance of resource information to draw from. Some of the references at the end of this chapter can help a student who wishes to investigate these programs further.

Student Activities for Further Study

1. Role-play, then discuss the dynamics in the following situations a teacher might encounter during a home visit.
   a. A mother is fearful lest her husband be awakened from sleep— he's a third-shift worker.
   b. A child begins to "show off"—mother is embarrassed.
   c. A mother begins talking very negatively about her child's behavior, as her child sits in same room.
   d. A mother appears very shy—virtually tongue-tied.
   e. The parents keep watching a television program after a teacher sits down.
   f. The parents seem very ill at ease—they keep asking if their child is doing anything bad.
2. Discover whether there is any kind of home-based program in your community. If so, try to arrange to visit along with the visitor.
3. Discover whether there is a Head Start or other preschool program in your community where teachers make regular home visits. If so, try to arrange to visit along with a teacher.

Review Questions

1. Identify several purposes for teachers making home visits.
2. Discuss several points to consider in undertaking home visits.
3. Name one advantage and one disadvantage to a home visit.
4. Identify the general purposes and techniques of home-based programs.

References and Related Readings

Berger, E. *Parents as Partners in Education.* St. Louis: C.V. Mosby Co., 1981.

Bromberg, Susan. "A Beginning Teacher Works With Parents." *Young Children* 24.2 (1968): 75-80.

Coletta, Anthony. *Working Together: A Guide to Parent Involvement.* Atlanta: Humanics Ltd., 1977.

Croft, Doreen H. *Parents and Teachers: A Resource Book for Home, School and Community Relations.* Belmont, Calif.: Wadsworth Publ. Co., 1979.

Forbes, E. "Working With Parents." *Instructor* 89.8 (1980): 52-58.

Goodson, B.D. and R. Hess. *Parents as Teachers of Young Children: An Evaluative Review of Some Contemporary Concepts and Programs.* Stanford, Calif.: Stanford University Press, 1975.

Gordon, Ira J. and William F. Breivogel, eds. *Building Effective Home-School Relationships.* Boston: Allyn and Bacon, 1976.

Gray, Susan W. "The Child's First Teacher." *Childhood Education* 48.3 (1971): 127-29.

Honig, Alice S. *Parent Involvement in Early Childhood Education.* Washington, D.C.: NAEYC, 1975.

Jones, E. "Involving Parents in Children's Learning." *Childhood Education* 47.3 (1970): 126-36.

Karnes, M.B. and R. Zehrbach. " Educational Intervention at Home." *Preschool in Action: Explaining Early Childhood Programs.* Eds. M.C. Day and R. Parker. Boston: Allyn and Bacon, 1977.

Lambie, Delores Z., James T. Bond, and David Weikart. *Home Teaching With Mothers and Infants.* Ypsilanti, Mich.: High/Scope Educational Research Foundation, 1980.

Levenstein, Phyllis. "Learning Through (and From) Mothers." *Childhood Education* 48.3 (1971): 131-34.

———. "The Mother Child Home Program." *Preschool in Action: Explaining Early Childhood Programs.* Eds. M.C. Day and R. Parker. Boston: Allyn and Bacon, 1977.

Nedler, Shari E. and Oralie D. McAfee. *Working With Parents.* Belmont, Calif.: Wadsworth Publishing Co., 1979.

Packer, A., S. Hoffman, B. Bozler, and N. Bear. "Home Learning Activities for Children." *Building Effective Home-School Relationships.* Eds. I. Gordon and W. Breivogel. Boston: Allyn and Bacon, 1976.

Scott, Ralph and Helen Thompson. "Home Starts I and II." *Today's Education* 62.2 (1973): 32-34.

Scott, R., G. Wagner and J. Casinger. *Home Start Ideabooks.* Darien, Conn.: Early Years Press, 1976.

Shearer, D. et al. *Portage Guide to Early Education.* Portage, Wisc.: Cooperative Educational Service, Agency 12, 1976.

Swick, Kevin J. and R. Eleanor Duff. *The Parent-Teacher Bond.* Dubuque, Iowa: Kendall/Hunt Publ. Co., 1978.

U.S. Dept of Health, Education and Welfare. (Office of Child Development) *A Guide for Planning and Operating Home-Based Child Development Programs.* Washington, D.C.: U.S. Govt. Printing Office, 1974.

U.S. Dept. of Health, Education and Welfare. *Home Start and Other Programs for Parents and Children.* Washington, D.C.: U.S. Govt. Printing Office, 1976.

Chapter 12 **Parents in a Classroom**

A valuable method of drawing parents into the educational process of their young children is to involve them in the classroom.

Objectives

After studying this chapter, the student will be able to

1. discuss several advantages and potential problems of working with parents in a classroom
2. identify methods of encouraging parent visitations
3. discuss methods to facilitate parent observation
4. describe methods of utilizing parents as resources in a classroom

Advantages and Potential Problems

There is a lively discussion going on in the teachers' lounge. Jane Briscoe has just announced she has a parent coming in to play the guitar at group time. MiLan Ha says nothing; she's never had a parent in, but Anne Morgan has told her she's just asking for trouble.

"It's a disaster when a parent comes in; the whole routine gets turned upside down, and worst of all, I guarantee you the parent's child will act up dreadfully."

Connie Martinez agrees. "One of my parents last year came in and brought a cake and balloons for everybody when it was her daughter's birthday. When the birthday girl's balloon broke, she burst into tears and her mother slapped her. I was furious, but what could I do? Now I just ask them to have parties at home." Jane looks thoughtful, and a little worried too.

There is no question that bringing parents into a classroom increases teachers' responsibilities as they cope with various aspects of behavior and reactions. Teachers often object to having parents in a classroom for reasons both professional and personal (Tizard et al., 1981).

Involving parents in a classroom for any reason demands extra time and effort from a teacher as there are plans to make and fit into the routine. The best use of parents' time and skills must be determined, and both children and parents must be prepared for their roles in the unusual event.

> Jane Briscoe admits it took several conversations with Mr. Butler to learn of his guitar-playing skill, and then more to convince him that the children would enjoy having him come, and that he would know what to do when he got there! She's also had to reschedule the visit twice to fit around his working schedule, and has spent considerable time helping Sam understand his dad will be coming for a visit, but that Sam will be staying at school and not leaving when his dad goes back to work.

Teachers often have professional reservations about parents' functioning in a classroom. Teachers may be convinced that parents who do not have a professional teachers' education will behave inappropriately with children, especially with their own child, and therefore, put teachers in the awkward position of observing unsuitable adult actions in their own classrooms.

> Connie Martinez sighs. "I could have predicted that child was going to get overexcited with that whole birthday party hoopla. What I didn't know was that her mother would react so angrily. I was embarrassed not only for that child, but also that the other children saw that happen in my classroom."

Teachers may be concerned that parents will behave unprofessionally in other ways, such as discussing children with others outside of the classroom.

Another concern of teachers results from their knowledge of children's reactions when adjusting to changed routines. Some teachers who perceive a child's overexcitement or distress when a parent leaves the classroom after a special event feel the experience is too disruptive to be beneficial.

> "Look, it's a nice idea, but in practice it's too upsetting. Children can't understand why their parents can't stay the whole time, and it undoes a lot of adjustment."

Teachers may also have personal qualms about parents being on hand to observe their actions for an extended period of time. Whether it is true or not, many teachers feel that they are constantly watched and evaluated when parents are present, and therefore feel uncomfortable throughout a visit, feeling the need to perform.

> Mi Lan says, "Frankly, I don't need the additional stress of having a parent watch me through the whole morning."

Considering these objections, are there reasons for including parents in the classroom that outweigh the disadvantages? There certainly are great benefits for parents, children, and teachers.

For parents, spending time in a classroom is the best way to understand what is going on in a program.

> Mr. Butler, the guitar-playing father, helps explain this. "It was good to see what they do at their group time. Those kids are really learning to listen, to take turns talking and participating. Then they had their snack. Several children were responsible for getting the tables set, and they did it just right. And they passed their own juice and not a drop spilled. Then they all tried these vegetables in a dip; at home, Sam would never have touched the stuff, but there with his friends, he did."

Such firsthand knowledge provides a ready basis for discussion with teachers.

In a classroom parents can see how their child is functioning with his peers and other adults. They can also observe typical behaviors and skills for a cross-section of children the same age.

> "You know, it's kind of reassuring to find out that most two-year-olds grab things from each other. I'd been thinking mine was particularly aggressive."

Being in a classroom also gives parents a feeling of satisfaction as they contribute to a program, are welcomed by a teacher, and are recognized as important adults by their child and his or her friends— a real ego boost (Rutherford, 1979).

"I'd never play my guitar for a group of adults, but the kids loved it, I must say."

Children also feel special and important when their parents are in a classroom.

"That's *my* daddy," beams Sam as his dad leads the singing with his guitar.

Such good feelings have a more lasting impact than the transitory distress caused by a parent saying good-bye twice in one morning.

Young children feel special and important when their parents are in the classroom.

Children's feelings of security increase as they see parents and teachers working together cooperatively, each respecting the other's contribution. Children also benefit as parents gain in understanding the process of learning and in children's interaction skills (Taylor, 1967).

Teachers as well as children gain through the expanded opportunities for learning that other adults bring into a classroom.

> "I really like to give them as much music as I can, but I don't have a musical bone in my body. There's no substitute for having a real instrument in the classroom. From me they get a lot of records."

Having an extra pair of hands in a group of young children often allows for activities that just aren't possible without enough adults.

Classroom visitation by parents gives teachers a chance to see parent-child interaction and parental attitudes.

> "It's interesting to me to see Sam and his dad together. Mr. Butler is very comfortable in the nurturing role."

Teachers perceive parent involvement in a classroom as evidence of support for their efforts as parents gain empathy towards a teacher and the problems of working with a group of young children. It is professionally and personally rewarding to deepen a parent-teacher partnership through such cooperative efforts (Breslin, 1975).

> "I really enjoyed having Mr. Butler with us, and I appreciated his interest in sharing some time with us. It makes me feel like I'm not the only one who cares what goes on in this classroom."

It is true there are potential problems when parents are involved in a classroom. Teachers may have professional concerns for the possible reactions of children and/or parents together in a classroom, or they may have personal concerns in regard to performing before an adult audience. And extra time and effort is needed on the part of teachers and parents to plan ahead for the event. However, the following advantages make it worth the effort:

- parents gain firsthand experience of a program, of their child's reactions in a classroom, and feelings of satisfaction from making a contribution,

- children feel special when their parents are involved, feel secure with the tangible evidence of parents and teachers cooperating, and gain directly as parent understanding and skills increase, and

- teachers gain resources to extend learning opportunities, observe parent-child interaction, and can feel supported as parents participate and empathize with them.

Getting Parents Involved

There are many different ways to involve parents in early childhood classrooms. Non-working parents can be regular volunteers assisting teachers in parent-cooperative nursery schools (Taylor, 1967), Head Start programs, or other programs set up to educate both parents and children (Gross, 1977). When parents regularly assume auxiliary teaching roles, it is advisable to prepare them for this experience with a training program. Then, issues of teaching philosophy and goals, children's behavior and learning styles, and appropriate adult guidance and interactive techniques can be explored so parents entering a classroom clearly understand their expected roles.

Many other parents, particularly those who work and whose children are in day-care programs, may visit a classroom infrequently for planned social events, opportunities to observe, or as an extra resource.

An extra pair of hands from a parent helps to make a field trip possible.

There are a number of ways teachers can facilitate parent involvement in a classroom.

Exploring Resources and Needs

Before establishing any plan to bring parents into a classroom, teachers need to gather information about the families to discover which family members can be involved, interests and experiences that can be shared, and time resources. Some of this information can be gathered informally, as teachers learn about families during initial interviews and home visits, during casual conversations with parents and children. Other information may be gathered more formally, by the use of questionnaires and application forms to acquire written responses to specific questions.

A brief background questionnaire may inquire the following:

1. *the names and ages of other children and family members in the home,* to learn whether grandparents or teen-aged siblings are available to come in occasionally, or if younger children keep a parent too busy to visit

2. *occupations,* to learn a little about working hours and days off, to see if there is available time; jobs that are of interest to young children that can provide scrap materials and expertise for classroom use or to help out other parents

3. *interests and hobbies, pets, travel, cultural or religious backgrounds*

A wealth of resources is obtained by these few questions (Miller, 1975). As teachers accumulate information, it is a good idea to organize it into a resource file, with a card or page for each family. This file can be easily updated as new information is accumulated. Tentative plans for using these resources throughout the year can be noted, along with times parents are free to come to school (Swick and Duff, 1978).

Butler, Bill and Joan (divorced)

Other child: Lisa-3, (in center)

Bill: Salesman, Angel Stone, 8:00-5:00 p.m.; can be flexible in morning sometimes; out of town Wed. and Thurs. usually

Joan: Secretary, South West Telephone; 8:30-5:00 Mon-Fri; access to old computer sheets, discarded telephones

Interests: Joan—tennis, needlepoint, Chinese cooking
　　　　　Bill—plays guitar, golf

Possibilities: Bill–play guitar
           –Chanukah celebration (Dec.)

          Joan–ask for paper
           –stir-fry vegetables (Spring)

Note: No social for parents on Wed. or Thurs.

Weaver, Bob and Jane

No other children

Jane: homemaker
Bob: production in furniture factory, 7:30-4:30, Mon-Fri.
Other: **Grandparents in neighborhood, retired. Grandmother likes to cook.**

Interests: Jane–gardening, sewing
         Bob–volunteer fireman

Possibilities: Jane–help with planting (spring)
          –cloth scraps
          –free most days (field trips)
        Bob–wood scraps
         –bring firetruck or uniform (Community Helpers Unit, Feb., late afternoon)
        Grandparents–invite grandmother to cook with us.

Ashley, Sylvia

Terence–9

Sylvia: job training program, 9:00-4:00, for next 9 months

Interests:

Possibilities: Invite for late afternoon time.
         Come in to read informally with children.
         Invite Terrence to throw ball
         with children on playground

Encourage Informal Visits

How do teachers get parents into a classroom? At first, casual, unstructured visits are often best as parents feel no pressure to perform a role and no demands on their time. If allowed to get comfortable in a classroom, they will enjoy interacting with the children, other parents, and teachers.

Reserve Time

One morning or afternoon a week open for visiting creates a welcoming atmosphere. Parents are encouraged to spend an extra few minutes while dropping off or picking up their child—or more if they can stay—to join in or observe some free-play activities and perhaps have a drink or snack prepared by the children. Parents enjoy coming to a center to briefly participate in their child's work (Coletta, 1977). Such a regular occurrence demystifies for children the idea of having parents in a classroom and allows parents to stay occasionally, as their schedule permits. These visitations require little effort on a teacher's part, beyond the usual setting up of free-play choices that require little supervision or assistance, so teachers are free to move about. The casual nature of such visits means that only a few parents at a time are in a classroom, therefore avoiding the overcrowding that may be too stimulating for children. There is also less chance of children feeling "left out" if their own parents are not there, since play activities go on as usual and many other parents are absent as well.

Birthday Celebrations

Most centers have a special way of celebrating children's birthdays. Inviting parents to be present for the celebration can make it even more special. This may mean having the celebration at a time suited to a parent's schedule. Most parents enjoy an event that centers on their child.

Personal Invitations

Specific, personal invitations made to an individual family may include siblings and other family members. The child whose family comes is host for the day, getting chairs for parents and siblings, serving them drinks and snacks, showing them around the room, discussing the art on the walls, etc. (Newman, 1971).

Lunch Invitations

Parents can be invited for lunch in their child's classroom. Most centers do not require too much advance notice to set an extra place for lunch; this offers another chance for a social visit.

Special Occasions

Whether a parent tea party, early morning coffee, or picnic lunch, most parents respond to invitations made to a whole group of parents. With various family structures, it creates problems or discomfort when invitations are made to "fathers only" or "mothers only." Parents with particular work schedules may be unable to accept, and children who do not have the specified parent living at home will feel left out. Certainly special personal invitations can be made to fathers to make sure they are included. Involving children in the party preparations and invitations often gives parents an extra motivation to attend. The time selection should match a teacher's information about work schedules as far as possible.

Zoo Day

A "zoo" day where parents are asked to bring pets provides a good situation for getting parents to share and volunteer their resources (Miller, 1975).

Parents often find their own ways of becoming involved in classroom life when allowed to take the initiative. One center reports that

A "zoo" day when parents bring pets, may help some parents begin to share and volunteer their resources.

when parents come to take their children out of a classroom for appointments or a special lunch, they come back in time for the toothbrushing ritual or to read stories to their own children and some friends before helping a teacher settle everyone for nap—satisfying for everyone. Informal occasions such as these may be the only times some parents come to a classroom. (See additional notes on social occasions in Chapter 13.) Other parents may get involved in additional ways.

Encourage Parent Observations

Parents who are comfortable in a classroom may accept an invitation to spend a short period observing. This is beneficial for all parents, and particularly for parents with special concerns about their child or questions about a program, in anticipation of an extended conversation at a later conference.

Observation periods are most productive when parents and children are prepared for their roles. Teachers may explain to children that parents will be coming "so they can see all the fun things we do in the classroom." Children can also be told that the visiting grown-ups will probably want to sit at one side and not want to play, for a time. (It is ideal to have an observation booth or window where visitors can observe undetected. Since not many schools boast such an opportunity, both parents and children will have to accustom themselves to the others' presence.)

Both parents and teachers should be wary that children act differently in the presence of parents. It is helpful to discuss this openly and

Observing on the playground may help a parent and child become comfortable with the process of observation.

to suggest that parents observe on several occasions, to accustom their child to the practice (Almy, 1975).

Observing during outdoor play is a good first step for both children and parents. Outdoor play may offer more natural opportunities for children to play freely, without feeling they're being watched. Parents who seem hesitant about the observer's role may also be more comfortable outdoors.

Many parents feel uncertain about their role as an observer and may feel more secure when given both verbal and written guidelines for helpful classroom behaviors and points for observation. The following is a sample form that may be used.

Welcome to Our Classroom

1. The children will be delighted to see you, and may need a gentle reminder that you've come to see them play. A crowd could make it difficult for you to observe or jot down questions.

2. Observe your child and as many others as you can. This can be a learning experience about
   - your child and how he relates to other children and the classroom activities,
   - what children are like who are the same age as your child,
   - how the teacher guides each child.

3. Observe your child and several others. Notice how they
   - respond to other children,
   - use language,
   - choose activities and how long they stay with each activity,
   - solve problems and obtain assistance.

4. Observe the teacher in a variety of activities. Notice how the teacher
   - relates to each child,
   - handles difficult situations,
   - prevents problems and guides behavior.

A parent with particular concerns should be given individual guidelines. Parents who observe on several occasions will appreciate having an observation booklet with specific points on each page (Taylor, 1967).

Parents As Classroom Resources

As teachers get to know the families they work with, they become aware of parents' wealth of experience that can be used to deepen children's understanding of the world around them. Parents may be invited to find a time convenient for them to visit a classroom and share an experience. When appropriate, children may be able to visit a parent at work or at home.

Parents are resources in a variety of ways.

Jobs

Many parents' jobs are interesting to young children when demonstrated along with the "tools of the trade." Visitors may be a dental hygienist with a giant set of teeth and toothbrush, a truckdriver complete with truck, a hair stylist, or a carpenter.

Parents sometimes work in places that make wonderful field trips. A tall glass office building with an exciting elevator ride up to see the view, a company next to a construction site, a shopping mall, a neighborhood store, a bus terminal: all may have a cheery parent to greet the children as they explore the different places people work.

Many parents will enjoy sharing their interests with children.

Hobbies

Parents with particular interests and hobbies may offer fascinating substance to a curriculum. A guitar player, an avid camper with back pack and pup tent, a gardener, a cook, an aerobic dancer, a cyclist, rock-hound, or carpenter: all have enthusiasm and skills to share with the children. Most adults, even if initially hesitant, enjoy themselves thoroughly as children respond with zest to the new activities. Sometimes hobbies that appear to be strictly for adults create interesting situations as children relate to them in their own way; one parent who shares tapes of his favorite classical music was delighted to watch children spontaneously improvise movement and dance.

Cultures

Parents can offer firsthand experiences for children in exploring customs, foods, or celebrations of a variety of cultural or religious traditions. Chanukah songs, games, and foods from a Jewish parent; a Chinese parent demonstrating the use of an abacus and chopsticks; Spanish children's songs taught by a Puerto Rican parent; the sharing of some family treasures by a Vietnamese parent; an American Indian parent sharing a craft artifact; mementoes brought back from a vacation trip: such activities woven into a classroom curriculum enrich and stimulate learning for children and provide an opportunity for teachers to demonstrate respect for the diverse family backgrounds in a classroom. Both children and their parents receive a boost to their self-esteem when a representation of their own lives is shared.

Other family members, such as grandparents, may have time to spend in the classroom.

Extended Family

Knowing the makeup of each family will help teachers find resources beyond just parents. A retired grandmother who enjoys reading stories to children, a teenaged brother who can help with ball-throwing on the playground, a baby who can be brought to visit for a bath or feeding (Miller 1975); other family members can provide additional experiences.

Time

One resource provided by many parents is time. A parent coming into a classroom is helpful when an extra pair of hands is needed. Walks or field trips, classroom parties, or more complicated projects are undertaken when teachers can count on additional assistance from parents. Sometimes parents are more comfortable offering to share time instead of demonstrating a talent. As parents interact with children, they are often drawn into an activity they have done as parents—supervising cooking experiences, carving a jack-o'-lantern, playing a game. The parents' presence alone offers a learning experience for children as they see, for example, men nurturing and doing classroom tasks such as pouring juice or cleaning tables, roles more commonly associated with mothers (Hopkins, 1977).

Materials

Parents who are unavailable to come into a classroom may still provide resources in the form of materials to be used in classroom activities. Scraps and throwaways from jobs (computer paper, styrofoam packing bits, spools from a cotton mill), scraps and discards from home (kitchen utensils, dress-up clothes, magazines, fabric pieces), all make a contribution that allows both parents and teachers to feel a sense of cooperation. Some teachers regularly post a list of "Treasures Wanted" via a newsletter or bulletin board.

Parents outside a classroom will feel involved as they prepare materials for classroom use. Tracing and cutting out pieces for teacher-made games is something a homebound mother can feel important doing.

In some communities, it is possible for parents to host an "Open House" for their children's classmates. The children may visit a child's home for a snack or a picnic lunch.

Special Skills

Parents may have skills or knowledge that can be drawn on as resources beyond the classroom, to support a center or to offer to other parents. Architects, builders, or landscape designers can contribute to playground design; accountants or business people can help with budgets, insurance and tax matters; medical personnel can set up first-aid kits and procedures; particularly handy parents can repair toys as needed; "bargain hunter" parents can aid the person who purchases for a center, answering such questions as "Where can we get the best deal on sand?" Knowledgeable parents are possible resources for parent meetings or workshops: a high school counselor leads a discussion on communication techniques; parents who have successfully negotiated divorce and remarriage share insights on stepparenting; a lawyer discusses tax tips for working parents.

Teacher's Role

As teachers invite parents to participate in classroom learning activities, they need to concentrate on their skills of working with adults. Teachers need to be able to relax and enjoy the contribution of others to their classrooms and not feel threatened by any attention transferred from themselves to a visiting adult. It is important to remember that as more specific information is given to parents, the more parents will feel comfortable, knowing what is expected of them. Parents should know what time frame to plan on, and that it is acceptable to leave or stay as their schedules allow. Parents appreciate knowing beforehand exactly what they are expected to do, not vague suggestions that they "join in" (Tizard et al., 1981).

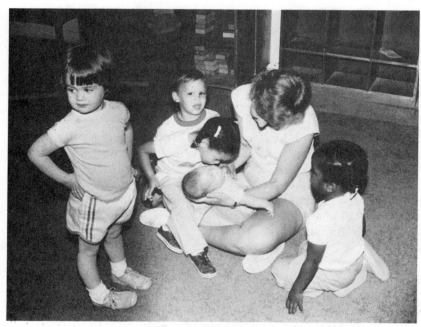

A baby sister may come to the classroom for a visit.

Teachers should immediately greet parents coming into a classroom and make them feel welcome, pointing out an area to sit or begin their preparations. Teachers should watch parents for signs of discomfort or indications of how much they want teachers to help them out in uncertain situations. Occasionally a child of invited parents reacts by showing off, or clinging and being possessive of his parents' attention. It is a good idea to warn parents ahead of time that this may happen, and that a teacher is prepared for it and won't mind. Parents should also be reassured that a teacher will step in if necessary to remind a child of classroom rules, so that parents will not feel that the full burden of guidance is theirs, and perhaps react inappropriately because of embarrassment.

The unusual event may cause a young child to get upset when his parent leaves, even though separation is not normally a problem. A teacher needs to comfort him and to reassure the parent that the classroom visit was still a good idea, even though there were a few tears at the end. The positive feelings for both child and parent far outweigh any brief distress.

Parents like feeling that they're making a valuable contribution to a classroom. Many parents will try to find the time for a visit if they feel truly needed and wanted. A note of appreciation from the teacher and children afterwards, pictures of the event displayed on a bulletin board, a mention of the event as a classroom highlight in the next newsletter—all these convey to parents their time was well spent.

Summary

Parents may become involved in the classroom as

1. casual visitors, to participate in classroom activities, meals or celebrations,
2. observers, to extend their knowledge of children's functioning in a classroom,
3. resources, to extend and enrich opportunities for the children.

Student Activities for Further Study

1. If you are working or interning in a preschool classroom, gather information on parents—family composition, jobs and details of what is involved, hobbies and interests, religious and ethnic backgrounds. Find out if parents have access to any particular materials that are useful in your classroom, or have particular periods of time free. Organize this information into a resource file. (If you are not presently in a preschool classroom, use the fictional family information described in Chapter 1 to make a sample resource file.)

2. Use your resource file to
   a. make a hypothetical plan for how you will use your resource knowledge to invite parents into classroom for particular activities and/or events and/or curriculum topics throughout the year, and
   b. invite three different parents into your classroom, if possible. Remember it will be your role to prepare parents and children for what to expect; play hostess in making parents feel comfortable in the room and guide children's behavior. Use this as an opportunity to observe parents and children in the classroom and the effect of the visit on each.

Review Questions

1. Describe at least one advantage for children, parents, and teachers when teachers work with parents in a classroom, and any one of three disadvantages.
2. List at least two methods of encouraging parental visits to a classroom.
3. Describe at least one method to facilitate parental observation in a classroom.
4. Discuss at least two ways parents can be used as resources in a classroom.

References and Related Readings

Almy, Millie. *The Early Childhood Educator at Work.* New York: McGraw Hill, Inc., 1975.

Beebe, Marian. "Teachers and Parents Together." *Today's Education* 65.4 (1976): 74-79.

———. "An Innovative Early Education Program: Saturday School." *Parent Involvement in the Schools.* Ed. John G. Barclay. Washington, D.C.: NEA. 1977.

Breslin, Deirdre and Eileen Marino. "Parents as Partners." *Childhood Education* 50 (1975): 125-28.

Brock, H.C. III. *Parent Volunteer Programs in Early Childhood Education: A Practical Guide.* Hamden, Conn.: Shoestring Press, 1976.

Coletta, Anthony. *Working Together: A Guide to Parent Involvement.* Atlanta: Humanics Press Inc., 1977.

Fireside, Byrna J. "Use a Parent's Special Talent." *Instructor* 82.1 (1972): 57.

Gilmar, S. and J. Nelson. "Centering Resources for Learning: Parents Get Into the Act." *Childhood Education* 51.4 (1975): 13-15.

Grunbaum, Elizabeth. "Parental Involvement." *Instructor* 84.7 (1975): 72.

Gross, Beatrice and Ronald. "Parent-Child Development Centers: Creating Models for Parent Education." *Children Today* 6.6 (1977): 7-12.

Harris, J.A. "Parents and Teachers, Inc." *Teacher* 96.1 (1978): 85-87.

Hopkins, P. "Every Father Should be a Nursery School Mother at Least Once in His Life." *Young Children* 32.3 (1977): 14-16.

Lipchik, M.A. "Saturday School for Mothers and Preschoolers." *Preschool Education Today.* Ed. Fred M. Hechinger. New York: Doubleday and Co. Inc., 1966.

Miller, Bette L. and Ann L. Wilmshurst. *Parents and Volunteers in the Classroom: A Handbook for Teachers.* Palo Alto: R and E Research Assoc., Inc., 1975.

Nedler, Shari E. and Oralie D. McAfee. *Working With Parents.* Belmont, Calif.: Wadsworth Publ. Co., 1979.

Newman, Sylvia. *Guidelines to Parent-Teacher Cooperation in Early Childhood Education.* New York: Book-Lab, Inc., 1971.

Nielson, Wilhelmina R. "Parents Enrich Classroom Programs." *Childhood Education* 44.7 (1968): 416-419.

Rutherford, Robert B. And Eugene Edgar. *Teachers and Parents: A Guide to Interaction and Cooperation.* Boston: Allyn and Bacon, 1979.

Swick, Kevin J. and R. Eleanor Duff. *The Parent-Teacher Bond.* Dubuque, Iowa: Kendall/Hunt Publ. Co., 1978.

Taylor, Katherine W. *Parents and Children Learn Together.* New York: Teacher's College Press, 1967.

Tizard, Barbara, Jo Mortimer, B. Burchell. *Involving Parents in Nursery and Infant Schools.* Ypsilanti, Mich.: The High/Scope Press, 1981.

West, S. "A Sense of Wonder—Parents and Children Learn Together." *Young Children* 29.6 (1974): 363-68.

Chapter 13 Parents in Meetings

Certain aspects of parent involvement include parents participating in groups, for education or decision making.

Objectives

After studying this chapter, the student will be able to

1. discuss a rationale for parent education
2. identify several assumptions regarding parent education and corresponding implications for planning programs
3. describe ways parents can function as advisors

Anne Morgan and Dorothy Scott do a lot of things differently in their classrooms, but they do agree on one idea: neither of them wants to attend the center's parent meeting next week. Dorothy sounds quite cynical about it: "Look, I've been going to parent meetings for thirteen years and it's always the same thing. A handful of parents show up, and always the same ones, the ones who are already doing a pretty good job and don't need to hear the guest speaker anyway. I'm just getting tired of the whole thing." Anne is also disappointed with the results of the last meeting she attended. "If there's one thing the parents need to understand, it's the terrible effect of television on preschool children. So after they listened to the man we invited to speak on that topic, do you think I noticed any difference in what my children tell me they've watched? It doesn't seem worth the effort." Even their director seems less than certain of the value of the parent meetings she continues to arrange. "It does seem there must be something else we could do to attract more parents."

These comments are frequently expressed teacher attitudes towards the attempts at parent education they have encountered. It would be interesting to hear the reactions of parents involved in the experiences and of parents who stayed at home; in all probability, additional negative responses would be heard.

Traditional parent education consists of various methods for giving to parents information deemed necessary by a professional. The traditional approach stresses information and training that is directly related to parent-child interaction. The model is that of a competent professional dispensing facts to a less competent parent. This one-way model implies a passive audience and a need to overcome a deficit in parental knowledge. Such a stance increases parental self-doubt; it is not surprising that parents frequently engage in these educational approaches with minimal enthusiasm or maximal avoidance!

Such a parent education program can make parents feel powerless and dependent on the advice of professionals. Research on learned helplessness reports that experiences and expectations of failure decrease the ability to learn and take the initiative, and increase the tendency to turn to others for assistance (Hess, 1980). The more parents are treated as if they are not capable, the less they will try to do for themselves. The system through which they are educated is itself an important part of any parent-education program. The usefulness of many informational programs is hindered by procedures that point to the authority of professionals and the incompetence of parents.

In considering models that are more effective, attitudes and practices that support and strengthen parents' sense of competence need to be examined.

What is Parent Education?

For some, parent education holds the promise of an approach to primary prevention (Hobbs, 1975; White, 1980); for others, it is a ruse to avoid acknowledging the failure of compensatory efforts (Schlossman, 1978). For some, it seeks to improve certain families (Bronfenbrenner, 1978); for others, it seeks to improve the institutions with which parents must deal (Gordon, 1977). Although some see parent education as aiding only poor, minority, or special-need families, others see it as of potential benefit for all families (Dokecki and Moroney, 1983). Parent education is typically defined as dealing exclusively with child-rearing, but some widen its scope to include the family as a system and the needs of everyone, including parents as persons, within that system (Wandersman, 1978). Some construe parent education as a process in which experts impose values on families (Keniston, 1977), while others see it as parents defining their own needs and using the expert as a resource (Dokecki, 1977).

This listing of diversity could go on. Some of the divergent opinions involve differences in interpretation of the same phenomena; others seem to address different reference points. Parent education is a complex phenomenon. Its history and development have been and continue to be marked by major shifts in purposes, contents, and approaches (Florin and Dokecki, 1983, p. 23-24).

Auerbach defines parent education as "intervention to help parents function more effectively in their parental role" (Auerbach, 1968, p. 3). Swick expands this to "any effort to increase the development and learning of parents in carrying out the diverse roles they perform," including the personal dimensions of marital roles and relationships, and personal needs as adults (Swick, 1985, p. 4). Such efforts introduce new educational experiences that give parents added knowledge and understanding; cause them to question their habitual ways of thinking, feeling, and acting; and help them develop new methods (where new methods are indicated) of dealing with their children, with themselves, and with their social environment (Auerbach, 1968). The term *education* is part of the problem since it connotes the formal study of facts associated with a narrowly cognitive academic world. In reality, the subject of parent-child relations and education is not so much concerned with facts and knowledge as it is with concepts, attitudes, and ideas (Hereford, 1964). The content of any educational program may be less important than the methods of bringing parents together to widen their horizons and sensitize them to feelings in a parent-child relationship.

A broader consideration of parent education implies a dynamic learning process in which parents are active participants, growing out of parents' interests and needs, and in which parents are able to participate as individuals. Research-based information increasingly suggests that the ways in which parents see their parenting roles and interact with their children directly influence the way young children learn to think, talk, solve problems, and feel about themselves and others. As teachers of their children, parents need the same awareness and skills that teachers have, so they can feel the same confidence in their ability to guide children to the fullest extent (Pickarts and Fargo, 1971). Therefore, parent education needs to offer a broad variety of services designed to complement parents' responsibilities and knowledge, to increase their understanding of children and their competence in caring for them.

The goal of parent education is to facilitate positive additions to parent-child relationships and to a child's functioning; whether or not such a goal is met is difficult to research (Hobbs et al., 1984; Endres and Evans, 1967). One reason why attempts to assess the effects of parent education yield inconclusive results is that many questions related to parent education imply a concern with long-term results of increased knowledge, status, and altered behavior. Most methods used to study the effects preclude the wait for such long-term answers. It is also difficult to correlate the results of one program to another.

Parent education involves making available to all parents the necessary support and attitudes that

1. encourage them to use and depend on what they know,
2. encourage them to share their experience with other parents,
3. support what they are doing, and
4. expose them to new ideas they have not considered (Gordon and Breivogel, 1976).

These ideas eliminate the connotation that parent education is associated only with deficit models of parenting and emphasize the need to support and help all parents.

Assumptions Underlying Parent Education

A philosophy of parent education that involves parents actively in a dynamic situation assumes that

1. parents can learn. Parenting is not a set of instinctive reactions, but a set of learned behaviors. The more parents know about child development and the effects of parent-child interaction, the more they examine what they do and why they do it, and the more skillful they become in displaying appropriate behaviors (adapted from Auerbach, 1968).

2. parents want to learn. Parents do care about their children and will participate when they believe they are helping their children or doing something that makes them better parents (Pavloff and Wilson, 1972). It follows that, if parents do not participate in available education programs, they are not yet convinced of a program's value to their child or to themselves; their caring is present but undeveloped. It must also be considered that specific stresses in parents' lives must be alleviated if parents are to be able to involve themselves in learning and change (Gross, 1977).

3. parents learn best when the subject matter is closely related to them and their children. All parents have unique experiences in the relationships and circumstances of their lives, and need to make specific applications of new ideas to their situations (adapted from Auerbach, 1968). This places the basic responsibility for growth and change within each parent, as each identifies particular needs and motivations.

4. parents can often learn best from one another. A negative expression of this idea is that parents are adults who don't want to be told anything by a stranger, even if he is an expert (Brocker, 1980); parents also frequently resist being told things

by experts they do know. Learning from the common experiences of other adults perceived as peers can be meaningful, as parents remind each other of what they already know and increase their feelings of self-worth as they empathize and understand.

5. parents learn in their own way. Basic educational principles point out individual differences in pace, style, and patterns of learning (Albert, 1962). A dynamic program offers flexible approaches that allow parents to proceed as they feel comfortable, to concentrate on what they find significant, and to participate actively to the extent that they are able (Auerbach, 1968).

These assumptions imply certain practical applications in the planning and implementation of parent-education programs.

Implementing a Parent-Education Program

Parents must be actively involved in planning the educational programs in which they will participate. A collaborative effort in which teachers and parents function as partners in needs assessment differs from the traditional approach of a professional making these decisions alone. There are numerous ways to facilitate this.

Initial Parent Involvement

Parents may come together first for purely social occasions such as pot-luck suppers, bag lunches, or parents' breakfasts. As comfort levels increase and relationships grow, the general discussion among the parents may narrow to particular interests and concerns. Teachers can help parents structure a program evolved directly from the discovery of common needs. Teachers are then acting not as "experts," but as resources, as families define their own needs. It is a natural progression for parents to become involved, because they already feel welcomed as a member of a group of parents (Lane, 1975; Hayman, 1968).

To involve parents directly in the planning of parent education efforts, structure a meeting soon after the school year starts, specifically to generate and discuss ideas that parents are interested in pursuing further. At this initial meeting, parents can take an active role if staff members ask one or two parents to help plan and lead the first discussion (McLelland, 1985).

Answering an assessment questionnaire or survey is one way of receiving input from parents on their interests and needs for future parent programs (Croft, 1979). A sample survey might look like this:

As we plan our parent meeting for this year, your ideas are needed.

1. Rate following topics   Interest

	Great	Slight	None
Discipline			
Sibling Rivalry			
Nutrition and Children			
Getting Ready for School			
Choosing Good Books and Toys			
Sex Education			
Normal Development			

Please add topics of interest to you

2. Circle the day that best fits your schedule:
M   T   W   Th   F

3. Indicate the time of day that is best for you:
Lunch hour
Right after work
Evening 7:00 or 7:30

Thank you for your help. Watch for coming notices.

The disadvantage to using a survey form is that some parents may not take the time for the reading and writing aspects of it, as well as not bothering to return it. The form lacks the personal involvement of individuals in a discussion. But at least a survey conveys the message that parents' ideas are needed and wanted. Parents will pay attention to subsequent announcements of meetings which they have helped to plan.

Teachers are often tempted to plan meetings based on what they believe parents need to learn. But unless parents are motivated by a current need, to gain particular knowledge or skills, they may reject plans imposed by teachers, no matter how important the ideas are. It has been noted that parent-education programs have a greater likelihood of effecting change if they are sensitive to, and design activities around, the basic assumptions and beliefs parents hold regarding child-rearing (Sutherland, 1983). That is, programs should start where the parents presently are, rather than where teachers think parents should be. Only parents can accurately define this starting place by expressing their needs and interests.

When parents help make decisions about topics for meetings, they are more likely to become involved.

Selecting the Style of a Meeting

Group size and style of meeting must be considered when providing for parents' needs for comfort and an opportunity to talk with other parents. Studies find that the most important variable in terms of parent attendance and participation in meetings is group size; smaller groups create feelings of closeness, community, and ownership of the endeavor (Bauch et al., 1973). Other studies indicate that meetings involving parents of just one class are preferable to whole center meetings (Tizard et al., 1981); bringing together a dozen or so parents with children of similar ages facilitates the sharing of experiences and concerns. The advantage to large group meetings is that a timid parent can listen without feeling pressure to participate; the disadvantage is that individual needs are often not met, as all parents will not have the opportunity to ask questions related to their particular situations or gain the satisfaction of sharing with other parents (Karnes and Zehrbach, 1972).

Since parents learn from each other as well as from professionals, the style of a meeting should encourage such interaction. Greater changes may occur in parents' behavior and attitudes following discussions within a group of parents than following lectures (Kelly, 1981). This requires a reconceptualization of the roles of directors, teachers, and parents in parent education, emphasizing the importance of parents speaking to each other and putting professionals in the role of consultants, supporting instead of instructing (Hess, 1980). In some instances of successful parent education, nonprofessionals function well as group leaders (Hereford, 1964). When parents identify a need that requires an expert, teachers can help locate and invite suitable resources.

A teacher's role in a parent discussion group is first to provide a structure that helps establish a warm atmosphere of informality and friendly sharing, and then to function as a facilitator of group discussion. Such a leader displays acceptance, support and encouragement for each parent in a group to express themselves; objectivity, to avoid taking sides in most discussions; tact, to protect each parent's right to discuss in a non-threatening environment; alertness to both verbal and non-verbal responses of group members, using that feedback to guide a discussion and maintain group morale.

It is only possible for a teacher or director to function this way when they have relinquished the attitude that only they know about young children. Such an attitude shows clearly in their interaction with parents and inhibits the formation of any informal group discussion. Heavy utilization of media or lecture techniques do not allow parents to participate as do group discussions or workshop formats.

Teachers can structure the initial meeting of parents to ease interpersonal communication. Name tags, with reminders of whose parent this is, help parents make initial connections.

Icebreaking games or activities may start a conversation. It is important to remember, however, that teachers are now dealing with adults, not children, so an early childhood teacher must learn techniques that are appropriate for adults.

Teachers can demonstrate the philosophy that parent meetings are another way of working with the whole family by involving children in making refreshments or decorations during a classroom day, or asking parents to make a picture at the meeting to leave in a child's cubby for him to find the next morning.

Parents may choose previously developed modes of parent education, such as P.E.T., STEP, or Active Parenting programs. All these concepts emphasize parent-child communication skills and are explored well in group discussions.

The prior existence of a social network of friends and relatives correlates with a lower level of attendance at regular group sessions and special events for parents (Powell, 1983). In other words, parents without reciprocal ties with other adults are more eager for the support and interaction with adults in parent-education settings. This may be especially true for single parents. The opportunities for social interaction and new relationships provide incentives for some parents to become involved in such a parent-education group. Some groups function primarily as parent–support groups, with education a secondary consideration.

Selecting a Time for a Meeting

Other stresses and concerns of daily life may prevent some parents from involving themselves in parent-education activities. Teachers need to be conscious of any accommodations they can make to help alleviate some of these problems.

Meetings are more convenient if parents help select the dates and times. Sometimes parents' attendance is precluded by child-care demands; providing baby-sitting may alleviate that problem. Transportation difficulties may keep parents from participating; parent committees can set up carpools or arrange meetings in more central locations. Such assistance enables parents to become involved and is evidence that teachers understand some of the problems.

For working parents, evening meetings are often difficult to attend; after a long day at the job, then taking children home to prepare supper and getting through the evening routine, going back to school becomes quite unattractive. Many centers find success in providing an evening meal—a covered dish supper, or a spaghetti dinner—when parents come to pick up their children. Parents, children, and teachers relax together after a work day, enjoying a social occasion without parents having to worry about hurrying home with tired, hungry children. The children can play in another room while parents continue to more serious discussion. Parents and children are able to get home still early in the evening, after a pleasant and productive time for all.

Schools centrally located to parents' workplaces find that asking parents to "brown bag" it occasionally for a lunch meeting brings parents together while children are cared for in the center. Such meetings recognize the many demands on parents' non-working time.

Busy, weary parents are more likely to attend meetings where the time frame, announced in advance, will not be much more than an hour and will begin and end promptly. It is helpful to announce meetings well in advance (a month minimum), with weekly, then daily, reminders. Coordinating plans and arrangements takes time, so staff should assume parents are not able to come on short notice. Attention to physical comfort, with adult-sized chairs, refreshments, and a relaxed, uncrowded atmosphere creates optimum conditions for concentrating on a discussion.

As parent-education discussion groups evolve, their purposes and goals will be more strictly defined by the participants. It is important to the ongoing success of such programs that parents and teachers occasionally evaluate whether or not activities are meeting the intended goals. It is important to remember that the effectiveness of any parent-education program is not measured by how many people come, but by the effect the program has in changing attitudes and behaviors, and increasing parental competence. An evaluation should center on how a program works for those who come and what additional steps can be taken to include others.

For teachers like Anne Morgan and Dorothy Scott, who have been part of a traditional professional-giving-information type of parent-education program, it may require a determined effort to accept the concept of parents choosing, guiding, and actively participating in a discussion. But such forms of education give strength and power to parents as they gain "confidence in their own impulses and their own competence" (Katz, 1980).

Parents as Decision Makers

Some programs involve parents as advisors and policymakers. Parent membership on parent councils or policy boards brings them into decision-making positions that may affect their children and the community they represent. The exact roles of decision makers may vary according to the regulations of the school or agency involved.

Federally funded programs, such as Head Start and Title 1, have federal guidelines and local regulations to govern parental roles on advisory councils that have 50 percent parent membership. These roles are active, with the power to decide on budget matters, curriculum, and hiring positions.

Parent-cooperative schools generally allow their parent boards to make all policy decisions.

Other parent councils in some public and private educational settings may function as purely advisory bodies, with decision-making powers vested in professional personnel.

Many parents are eager to have a voice in their children's schools. One study indicates 82 percent of respondents were interested in serving on an advisory council (Berger, 1981). Effectively involving parents in cooperative decision making can benefit everyone. Children benefit as programs shape their offerings to fit community character and need. Parents assuming leadership roles develop skills that benefit themselves and their communities, and increases their confidence in their abilities to shape their children's lives. They also may demonstrate

Parents are involved as decision makers in some programs.

more support for a school or center, as they perceive a closer connection between its functioning and their own goals. Parents who feel they have a vehicle to voice their concerns will not withdraw or resort to negative methods of making themselves heard. As parents learn more about how a school functions and why, they learn more about children's needs. Directors and teachers benefit by the expansion of their viewpoints with the addition of parents' perspectives. They also may find their efforts are strengthened with the addition of parent understanding and support.

In poorly planned parent-advisory situations, a variety of problems may surface: conflicts on how to conduct the organizational process; power struggles between parents vying for control of a group; confusion about the responsibilities of group members; and disagreements over institutional philosophies and goals (Berclay, 1977). But when an organization develops a trusting relationship among its members and helps develop group communication and planning skills, parents participating in the decision-making process develop important relationships between home and school. Specific guidelines for, and clear understandings of, parent action are most helpful. For example, rather than vague phrases like—"the director will decide in conjunction with the parents"—a more specific statement is desirable like—"the director will screen job candidates and present three choices, without recommendation, for final selection by the parent council" (Schram, 1975).

Summary

Each early childhood education program has its particular characteristics, goals, and client populations and each school or center must consider how it brings parents together for education, support, and/or advisory purposes in the total effort of parent involvement. Some early childhood programs even involve parents in the decision- and policy-making process. The following are assumptions that can be made if a philosophy of parent education is to involve parents actively:

1. parents can learn

2. parents want to learn

3. parents learn best when the subject matter is closely related to their particular circumstances

4. parents can often learn best from one another

5. parents will learn at their own pace, in their own way

Teachers can structure meetings with parents in such a way as to facilitate parent participation, where parents will define for teachers their individual needs and wants. Meeting times should be decided according to when parents are available.

Student Activities for Further Study

1. Attend a parent meeting at your own, or any other, preschool. Notice: efforts made to promote social comfort and interaction; physical arrangements and services, such as baby-sitting, seating, refreshments; planned activity and parents' response to it. Find out how and when the meeting was publicized. Discuss your findings with your classmates.

2. If you are working or interning in a preschool, devise a survey form to assess parents' interest and needs for making future program plans. After you obtain the responses, analyze the information and then devise several plans that match parents' expressed needs and wants. If you are not currently in a classroom situation, work in pairs to devise a questionnaire, then answer it as each of the hypothetical families in Chapter 1 might. Analyze the information and devise several education plans that match those needs and wants.

3. Plan a simple "ice-breaking" social activity for the beginning of a meeting. Share with your classmates.

4. Contact several preschools in your area, including a Head Start or other federally funded program if one exists in your community. Find out whether parents participate in any advisory capacity.

Review Questions

1. Discuss a rationale for parent education.
2. Identify three of five assumptions regarding parent education.
3. For each assumption, describe a corresponding implication for planning parent-education programs.
4. Describe how parents may act as advisors in a program.

References and Related Readings

Albert, Gerald. *"Learning Theory and Parent Education: A Summing Up."* Marriage and Family Living 24.3 (1962): 249-53.

Almy, Millie. *The Early Childhood Educator at Work.* New York: McGraw Hill, Inc., 1975.

Auerbach, Aline B. *Parents Learn Through Discussion: Principles and Practices of Parent Group Education.* New York: John Wiley and Sons Inc., 1968.

Bauch, Jerold P. et al. "Parent Participation: What Makes the Difference?" *Childhood Education* 50 (1973) 47-53.

Berclay, G. J. *Parent Involvement in the Schools.* Washington, D. C.: National Education Association, 1977.

Berger, E.H. *Parents as Partners in Education.* St. Louis: The C. V. Mosby Co., 1981.

Bjorklund, Gail and Anne Marie Briggs. "Selecting Media for Parent Education Programs." *Young Children* 32.2 (1977): 14-18.

Braun, L., J. Coplon, P. Sonnenschein. *Helping Parents in Groups—A Leader's Handbook.* Boston: Resource Communications Inc., 1984.

Brocker, Tobias H. "Towards New Methods in Parent Education." *Parenting in a Multicultural Society.* Eds. Mario D. Fantini and Rene Cardenas. New York: Longman, Inc., 1980.

Croft, Doreen J. *Parents and Teachers: A Resource Book for Home, School and Community Relations.* Belmont, Calif.: Wadsworth-Publ. Co. Inc., 1979.

Endres, Mary P. and Merry J. Evans. "Some Effects of Parent Education on Parents and Their Children." *Adult Education Journal* 18.2 (1967): 101-111.

Florin, Paul R. and Paul R. Dokecki. "Changing Families Through Parent and Family Education." *Changing Families.* Eds. Irving E. Sigel and Luis M. Laosa. New York: Plenum Books, 1983.

Gordon, Ira J. "Parent Education and Parent Involvement: Retrospect and Prospect." *Childhood Education* 54.2 (1977): 71-79.

Gordon, Ira J. and William Breivogel, eds. *Building Effective Home-School Relationships.* Boston: Allyn and Bacon, 1976.

Gross, Beatrice and Ronald. "Parent-Child Development Centers: Creating Models for Parent Education." *Children Today* 6.6 (1977): 7-12.

Harman, D. and O.G. Brim. *Learning to be Parents: Principles, Programs and Methods.* Beverly Hills, Calif.: Sage, 1980.

Hayman, Hannah L. "Snap Judgement: A Roadblock to Progress on Parent Involvement." *Young Children* 23.5 (1968): 291-3.

Hereford, Carl F. *Changing Parental Attitudes Through Group Discussion.* Austin: University of Texas Press, 1964.

Hess, Robert D. "Experts and Amateurs: Some Unintended Consequences of Parent Education." *Parenting in a Multicultural Society.* Eds. Mario D. Fantini and Rene Cardenas. New York: Longman, Inc., 1980.

Hobbs, Nicholas and Associates. *Strengthening Families.* San Francisco: Jossey-Bass Publishers, 1984.

Karnes, M. and R. Zehrbach. "Flexibility in Getting Parents Involved in the School." *Teaching Exceptional Children* 5.1 (1972): 6-19.

Katz, Lilian. "Mothering and Teaching: Some Significant Distinctions." *Current Topics in Early Childhood Education.* Vol. 3. Ed. Lilian Katz. Norwood, New Jersey: Ablex Publishing Corp., 1980.

Kelly, Francis J. "Guiding Groups of Parents of Young Children." *Young Children* 37.1 (1981): 28-32.

Lane, Mary B. *Education for Parenting.* Washington, D.C.: NAEYC, 1975.

Larson, R.G. "Can Parent Classes Affect Family Communication?" *The School Counsellor* 19.4 (1972): 261-70.

Lillie, David et al., eds. *Teaching Parents to Teach.* New York: Walker and Co., 1976.

Lombana, Judy H. *Home-School Partnerships: Guidelines and Strategies for Educators.* New York: Greene and Stratton, 1983.

Marland, S.P. "Education for Parenthood." *Children Today* 2.2 (1973): 3.

McLelland, Donna. "Getting Started With Parent Involvement." *High/Scope Resource* 4.2 (1985): 9-10.

O'Connell, Christine. "Helping Parents with Their Children." *Today's Education* 65.4 (1976): 43-44.

Pavloff, Gerald and Gary Wilson. *Adult Involvement in Child Development for Staff and Parents: A Training Manual.* Atlanta: Humanics Inc., 1972.

Pickarts, Evelyn and Jean Fargo. *Parent Education: Towards Parental Competence.* Englewood Cliffs, New Jersey: Prentice-Hall, Inc, 1971.

Powell, Douglas R. "Individual Differences in Participation in a Parent-Child Support Program." *Changing Families.* Eds. Irving E. Sigel and Luis M. Laosa. New York: Plenum Press, 1983.

Schram, Barbara A. "Building Blocks of Parent Decision Making." *Day Care and Early Education* 2.5 (1975): 8-11, 20.

Sutherland, Kay. "Parents Beliefs About Child Socialization: A Study of Parenting Models." *Changing Families.* Eds. Irving E. Sigel and Luis M. Laosa. New York: Plenum Press, 1983.

Swick, Kevin. "Critical Issues in Parent Education." *Dimensions* 14.1 (1985): 4-7.

Tizard, Barbara, Jo Mortimer, B. Burchell. *Involving Parents in Nursery and Infant Schools.* Ypsilanti, Mich.: The High/Scope Press, 1981.

Section IV: Making a Partnership Work

Chapter 14 Working with Parents with Special Needs

Every parent's situation is unique in its history, emotions, and demands. Teachers find themselves working with parents who have special needs at particular times. This chapter examines several of these circumstances, and discusses helpful teacher responses.

Objectives

After studying this chapter, the student will be able to

1. describe behaviors in children and parents associated with the stress of divorce and/or remarriage and discuss ways teachers can be helpful

2. describe possible emotional responses of parents of exceptional children and discuss ways teachers can work effectively with them

3. describe some responses of parents of infants and discuss ways teachers can work effectively with them

4. discuss factors that create an abusive situation, indicators that suggest abuse or neglect, and teachers' responsibilities in working with these families

Working with Families Undergoing Change Due to Divorce

> Dorothy Scott has recently noticed some disturbing behaviors in one of the children in her classroom. He has been quite out of bounds, almost defiantly breaking the group rules, and striking out aggressively at other children. She's also bothered by the quiet sadness she sees in him at other times. She knows his parents' divorce is now final, and she wonders what she might do to help the family at this time of change.

The family that concerns her is not alone. According to Census Bureau predictions, nearly half of all children born in 1979 will spend a significant portion of their childhood with only one parent. Currently about half of all marriages end in divorce, and more than 60 percent of these divorces involve children living at home. Because about 50 percent of all divorces occur in the first seven years of marriage, the children of divorced parents are often quite young (Skeen and McKenry, 1980). One researcher has predicted that single-parent families and stepfamilies will outnumber nuclear families by 1990 (Visher and Visher, 1979). Such large statistics have led to the societal acceptance of divorce; divorced persons are no longer as much stigmatized or considered deviant since "no-fault" divorce laws refrain from naming a wrongdoer (Hunt, 1977). Nevertheless, the many myths and real concerns that prevail about the functioning of a "broken home," and the corresponding behaviors of children, may work to the detriment of many families undergoing this transition. An important first step for teachers working with such families is to be informed of the facts concerning divorce and examine their own attitudes and expectations to avoid stereotyping.

Research evidence does *not* support three common generalizations regarding children of divorce: (1) that boys whose fathers do not live in the home have trouble identifying with a strong masculine role; (2) that these children do less well in school; and (3) that they are more prone to delinquency (Herzog and Sudin, 1972). Despite evidence to the contrary, studies indicate that teachers' expectations lead them to perceive the behavior of children from father-absent homes more negatively than the same behavior in children from two-parent homes (Santrock, 1978). While there is some evidence that a stable two-parent home with harmonious and warm relationships provides a better environment than a one-parent home (Herzog and Sudin, 1972), the crucial factor is probably the emotional climate, rather than the structure of the family unit (Lombana, 1983). Unhappy parents have unhappy children (Atlas, 1981). However, 75 percent of single-parent families consider that they and their children are doing well.

Divorce, the second most stressful experience for families after death, is a critical experience for an entire family, affecting each member differently. The disruption usually extends for a period of time; most evidence of disturbance in children is still present one year after a marriage breakup (Wallerstein and Kelly, 1975). To some degree, divorcing family members experience abandonment, trauma, rejection, loss of income, and a lower standard of living. Most adults, lacking an adequate model for single parenting, are confused in how to go about daily life. A single-parent family is not the same as a two-parent family minus one adult. The entire family system is strained (Hunt, 1977).

This is a time of bereavement for everyone in a family; the family they knew is gone. One parent usually leaves the home and is less available to a child, and sometimes siblings leave as well. A mother's working pattern may increase and a family's living standard is likely to change with increasing economic stress (Skeen and McKenry, 1980). Each family member grieves in different ways peculiar to their role and age. The stages of grief are similar to the Kubler-Ross model for dealing with loss in death, with initial denial, followed by anger and then bargaining to find a happy way out. Depression follows as ultimate realizations are made. The final stage is acceptance of the loss (Skeen and McKenry, 1980). It is important to be aware of patterns, but not to expect all children and parents to react similarly to divorce due to individual personalities, experiences, and outside supports, as well as varying developmental levels in children.

Children react with a variety of behaviors, related to their dependent position in a family and level of intellectual development. It is interesting to note that 50 percent of children are most upset by the initial parental conflict in the pre-divorce phase; 8 percent are most upset at the actual time of transition—when the announcement is made and the father leaves the home. (This study was of fathers leaving, as is most often the case.) Another 25 percent are most upset during the adjustments of the post-divorce phase (Luepnitz, 1979). Boys appear to be more vulnerable than girls (Heatherington, 1979).

In preschool children, their self-concept seems to be particularly affected. Their view of predictability, dependability, and order in the world is disrupted (Wallerstein and Kelly, 1975). In their anxiety to be sure their needs are met, preschool children may show an increase in dependent, whining, demanding, and disobedient behaviors (Heatherington, 1979). Other noted behaviors are: regression to immature behavior; separation anxiety and intense attachment to one parent; and guilt, shame, and anxiety about abandonment, loss of love and bodily harm (Anthony, 1979). In their play, preschool children may be less imaginative, exhibiting less associative and cooperative play and more unoccupied and onlooker play. More aggression is frequently noted (Heatherington, 1979). Preschool children, because of the egocentric nature of their thinking, often feel responsibility for the divorce and behave "better than good," fearing to lose the remaining parent's love through more "bad" behavior. Sometimes the exact opposite behavior is seen as a child tries literally to test every limit, to see what it takes to lose the other parent. Even infants show behavioral changes such as sleeping and feeding irregularities, clingyness, and lack of trust, as they react to tensions felt at home.

School-aged children may show great sadness, fears and phobias, anger, loneliness, shaken identity, and an inability to focus attention on school-related tasks (Wallerstein and Kelly, 1976). Other school-aged behaviors may be nervousness, withdrawal and moodiness, absent-mindedness, poor grades, physical complaints, and acting out behaviors (Allers, 1980).

Parents, at the same time, have their own difficulties. They often feel a double sense of failure for not living up to the American dream of happily-ever-after, and for their unsuccessful efforts to make a marriage work (Braun, 1976). This decreases their confidence, self-image, and feelings of competence, while increasing feelings of anger, guilt, terror, and helplessness. Some of these feelings directly relate to their children as they worry that they have endangered their children by their actions (Braun, 1976). In most cases, there is disorganization in the household; even meeting rudimentary needs is overwhelming when an exhausted and anxious parent takes on more roles. A parent's preoccupation with personal distress makes for poor parenting in the year or more following a divorce. Frequently unavailable to a child, parents exert less consistent and effective discipline, communicate less well, may be less nurturant, and make fewer demands for mature behavior (Heatherington, 1979).

Working With Children in the Classroom

A family overwhelmed by its own turmoil is greatly helped by the understanding and support of teachers and others outside the family. A teacher can help a child within the classroom and provide information and supportive guidance to a parent in a variety of ways.

Maintain Structured Environment

Children whose lives are in a state of transition are helped by the maintenance of a relatively structured and predictable environment. Some certainty is provided when a child's classroom world is unshaken. Keeping to familiar activities and a scheduled routine will lessen some of the negative effects of a stressful home environment. As a child perceives that his basic physical and emotional needs are being met, he may come to feel personally safe. Part of an environment's stability is demonstrated by consistent expectations. Teachers who firmly and gently maintain limits enhance a child's sense of certainty during this uncertain time.

Encourage Expressions of Feelings

Teachers' knowledge of specific areas where these children need attention comes from observing and listening to them in the school setting, rather than making assumptions about problems. A teacher can help children work through feelings by opening up an area for discussion, and understanding and accepting a child's reactions.

"It can be pretty scary not to have both your daddy and your mommy living in your house together anymore."

"Sometimes children get pretty mad at their mommy and daddy when they change a lot of things in their family."

Teachers who use active listening skills to listen empathetically can help a child release many pent-up feelings.

Teachers can also provide classroom activities and materials that offer acceptable opportunities to work through feelings: clay, water and sand play, paint, family figures and props for dramatic play, and books about various family styles may help. (Several dozen children's books about divorce have been published in the past decade; a list of books for preschool children and information on others is included at the end of this chapter.)

Privacy and additional opportunities to be alone may help some children.

Teachers may offer concrete evidence that a child is loved, with touch, hugs, smiles, but must be careful that a child does not become too dependent on them (Skeen and McKenry, 1980).

Teachers may discover that some children need additional help in understanding a family's changed situation; repeated, clear explanations of information supplied by the family may be appropriate.

Encourage Acceptance

Teachers can guide children in accepting their changed family structure. In words and actions, teachers demonstrate their respect for each family, stressing how unique each family is. Books or pictures that show stereotypical family groupings are not helpful. Teachers want to avoid activities for an entire group that make some children feel uncomfortable, such as making Father's Day cards or gifts. As a teacher becomes knowledgeable about family patterns, adjustments will need to be made.

Be Aware of Group Reactions

Teachers may find that other children in a group may express or experience anxiety that their own parents may also divorce or leave.

It is best to remind children that all families are different; that when grownups have problems, they still love and look after their children; and that they need to tell their parents what they're worried about.

Working with Parents

As teachers become aware of parents' probable emotional reactions they will understand some puzzling behaviors.

> "Honestly, I don't understand the woman. Every time I ask how Danny has been at home, like if he's having trouble sleeping there too, she changes the subject. Doesn't she even care that her own son seems upset?"

Because of the feelings of guilt and isolation, parents may be evasive or hostile when asked innocent questions about a child's daily routine (Braun, 1976). Often parents are so preoccupied with their own concerns that they are unavailable to teachers, as well as to their children. Teachers must remind themselves frequently that this does not mean they are disinterested.

When teachers are aware of parents' emotional state, they are less likely to become angry at parents' behavior and seeming indifference to their children's problems.

Reassure Parents

Teachers who empathize and demonstrate their caring are in a position to encourage parents in helpful actions with their children. Teachers can remind parents that an open and honest discussion of adult and child feelings will help, as will clear statements of the facts of divorce and a new living situation. Teachers can reassure parents about the amount of time needed for families to adjust; giving information regarding the grief process and positive outcomes may help alleviate parental guilt (Skeen and McKenry, 1980).

Teachers can provide books about divorce for both children and adults. (See the list at the end of the chapter.) Having a lending library of such books readily available in a center is useful.

Be Aware of Legal Agreements

Teachers should know the legal and informal agreements between parents regarding their child's care (Briggs and Walters, 1985). It is important that teachers release children to only those persons authorized to take them.

Know Available Community Resources

Teachers should refer parents to community resources that can help families in times of stress. It is important that teachers remember their professional expertise is in working with young children. However caring and concerned they may be about family situations, their only role here is to provide emotional support, information, and an accepting, listening ear. When parents need professional counseling to work out their problems, teachers should refer them to appropriate community agencies. Many communities have family and children's service agencies with qualified family therapists and counselors. United Way agencies may offer this information; teachers should be familiar with the appropriate agencies for referral in their own communities.

Teachers also may refer parents to agencies that help families in severe economic stress.

Another helpful referral is to organizations that provide support and social opportunities for isolated parents and children. One example is Parents Without Partners, an international organization of more than 200,000 full- or part-time single parents, with many local chapters that provide social opportunities for single parents and their children, and single-parent education and support. Many churches offer similar programs. (For more information about Parents Without Partners, the national headquarters is 7910 Woodmont Ave., Suite 1000, Washington, D.C. 20014.) Parents may also be interested in discovering if their community offers an organization of Big Brothers and Big Sisters, that provides opportunities for children of single parents to form relationships with interested adults to supplement possible missing relationships in a family.

Teachers should be knowledgeable about their specific community resources and have information ready for referral if the opportunity arises.

Keep Requests Light

Teachers must be especially conscious of any requests they make. Asking stressed, single parents to "bring in two dozen cookies tomorrow" or "send in a new package of crayons" may be overwhelming in light of the new strains on both time and budget.

In working with families undergoing divorce, teachers need to be conscious of their own attitudes, values, and emotional reactions. These personal aspects can influence a teacher's ability to function well with parents and children and may cause a teacher to expect more problem behaviors than are really present. Truly helpful teachers do not get caught up in assigning blame or evaluating families negatively.

Working with Stepfamilies

A teacher notices that whenever Pete Lawrence's stepbrothers visit for the weekend, the Monday after is a disaster. Pete is frequently whining and demanding, and his mother always looks frazzled and exhausted. And when he was asked to draw

> his family last week, he drew his mother and sister, then his
> stepfather, then his "other" father, and then lost interest in the
> project. She doesn't know if she should be concerned with this
> behavior or not.

About 250,000 families are "recycled" every year—created after the breakup of old families; between one-third to one-half of these have children from either or both former marriages. Such family structures can be complex as the number of possible relationships is multiplied. This complexity is the source of both the positive and negative aspects of a "blended" family.

One of the major difficulties is that the parents often feel ambiguity in their roles, unsure of when to step in or stand back. Here again, the only role models offered are distinctly negative—everybody remembers Cinderella's very unattractive stepmother! Parents often expect to make up for the upset in the original family by creating a close-knit happy family (Lombana, 1983). However, friction, differences in child-rearing beliefs, conflicts with other parents, and children testing the entire situation result in a good deal of stress; 40 percent of remarriages end in divorce within four years (Lombana, 1983).

Teachers may need to remind stepparents and themselves that there are positive aspects for the children involved: they have multiple role models and an extended kin network; they may have happy parents, additional siblings, and a higher standard of living; a new family may offer a model of conflict resolution and flexibility (Coleman et al., 1984). Teachers also can be influential in affirming that everything parents do to take care of a marital relationship is a priority.

In working with stepfamilies, teachers can provide similar kinds of emotional support and information that they offer to adults and children undergoing the transition of divorce. It is helpful to reassure parents that adjustment takes time, usually years, and to provide children with a secure, stable classroom environment.

Teachers need to be sensitive to family name differences. If John Smith is the stepfather of Billy Jones, he may not appreciate being called "Mr. Jones." Again, teachers also need to learn the legalities in each family situation, including who has the right to pick up children or give permission for their care.

Teachers can help a child adjust by accepting the multitude of family styles represented in a classroom. Attention to language and the message it conveys to children is important; what does it imply to talk about "real" parents? (Coleman et al., 1984). Teachers should not put stepchildren in awkward positions by promoting activities that cause confusion. "Mothers' tea parties" or "fathers' breakfasts" can cause problems about who gets the invitation. Designating "Parent" events might remove this awkwardness. (If teachers are concerned that fathers will be left out, they can make this clear through personal conversations.) If children are making Christmas gifts for mothers, encourage stepchildren to provide gifts for as many mothers as they'd like!

Working With Parents of Exceptional Children

Sylvia Rodriguez presently attends the Cerebral Palsy Kindergarten in the mornings, but her mother has asked the daycare center if she can go there in the afternoons if Mrs. Rodriguez begins to work full time. The teacher in the afternoon program is rather concerned about this, as she has not worked with a physically handicapped child before.

Since the passing of the Education for All Handicapped Children Act of 1975 (PL-94-142), which directed that all children from ages three through eighteen must be provided with free and appropriate education in the least restrictive setting, many teachers besides those trained in special education are working with the exceptional children mainstreamed into their classrooms. The same law directs educators to involve parents in the development and implementation of educational programs for their handicapped children (Ehly et al., 1985). Since 1974, Head Start has been mandated by Congress to have 10 percent of its children be those who are handicapped (Community Services Act, PL 96-644). Working with parents of children with special needs offers particular challenges to a preschool teacher, who must learn to understand the common emotional reactions, anxieties, and problems that these families face.

Emotional Reactions

Parents of exceptional children undergo an adjustment process that is lifelong; its emotional stages resemble the process of grieving. The shock of learning that one's child is handicapped is frequently followed by feelings of guilt, of somehow being responsible. Many parents undergo feelings of denial that may take the form of shopping from one professional to another, always looking for a more optimistic opinion or magical solution (Lombana, 1983). Sometimes denial takes the form of projecting blame onto others (Grossman, 1978). Anger often follows, before acceptance finally takes place. Although most parents of exceptional children entering a preschool have probably been aware of their child's special needs since birth, entering a classroom with children who do not have similar problems may be another reminder that the problem will always exist.

For many parents, the realization that their child is handicapped is a blow to their sense of self-worth. They are in difficult parenting situations with many unknowns and may feel less than capable. Most parents of exceptional children live with increased amounts of stress in their lives due to the increasing amount of time and energy spent parenting a handicapped child; the economic strain of medical expenses, therapy, and treatment, the strain of living with complex emotions and shattered dreams; the isolation that results as families either anticipate or experience social rejection, pity, or ridicule (Lichter, 1976).

No parent is ever prepared for a handicapped child (Barsch, 1969). There are no role models, no guidelines to assist parents in modifying their child-rearing practices to match their child's special needs. Parenting is a task that can make people feel shaky, even under the best of circumstances; parents of exceptional children often feel most insecure in their position.

Parental reactions can best be understood by hearing them in the words of a parent of a handicapped child talking to a group of professionals.

"It's a strange life, because I don't consider myself an unhappy person, and I'm doing okay, but there's a part of every parent who has a child who is damaged which is in perpetual mourning. . . . What happens to a family when you have a handicapped child? I think that really it is a myth that tragedy brings families together. It does not. We grieve very, very privately, and men and women grieve differently. . . . There is a certain animosity that is just *there* between parents and professionals that will *always* be there because you have these intervention programs, . . . but you can't make our kids better. And when push comes to shove, that's what we really want. . . . The bottom line is, he can't be fixed. And that always makes a parent sad. And as a professional that's something you have to understand. . . . As a professional you should keep in a part of you the idea 'I don't know what it's like. I have not been in this parent's shoes.' And make yourself a little less judgemental. But there is this anger that we parents have because we're in the know, but you're writing out the IEP's (Individual Educational Plans), and you're making the judgements and you're the one who's determining things. . . . There is a free-floating anger that has to do, very simply, with our children not being whole, and there's nothing really that you can do about that. . . . So sometimes when parents are aggressive and upsetting, I don't think you should take it personally. . . . I never had so many people (helping me). . . . And I can remember feeling that I didn't like it, that

this was a real intrusion on my life and who I was as a mother
. . . (but still) I really needed help. I need a great deal of help.
. . . People who are in your profession have chosen it, and
it is a profession that gives you a lot of self-esteem and a lot
of good feelings. . . . *The parents have not chosen this.* No
parent would choose to have a child that is anything less
than normal and whole. And so while we both want the best
for our child, the best program, we also have to realize that
we're coming from different places. You're coming from a
place that gives you a lot of self-esteem. A parent of a
handicapped child does not have that self-esteem (Kupfer,
1984).

Parents of an exceptional child find themselves trying to maintain
the family's integrity as a group with its own developmental tasks while
providing for the distinctive needs of their exceptional child. These
parents must find an appropriate educational program for their child.
They must also undertake the process of letting go, especially difficult
when complicated by a desire to overprotect their handicapped child,
a frequent reaction due to guilt feelings (Grossman, 1978).

When teachers increase their awareness of these particular emotional reactions and tasks, insensitive responses can be avoided.

Parent Relations with Professionals, Teachers, and Others

Many parents of exceptional children already have an established
history of relationships with professionals by the time they encounter
a classroom teacher. Families of children with special needs learn to
allow professionals into their lives to provide the help and knowledge
they need. These parents also have learned how to enter a professional's
world in order to equip themselves to better help their child (Seligman,
1983).

Some of these earlier experiences with professionals may not have
been positive. Parents of exceptional children relate stories of being
shuttled from one professional to another and of finding a confusing
lack of integration between these professional evaluations. Sometimes
they feel they have only been partially informed of the findings and
prognosis, and have not been given complete knowledge of the available
resources. Such experiences may predispose these parents to be suspicious or hostile when interacting with a teacher who is still another
professional. Yet a partnership between parents of an exceptional child
and a preschool teacher is crucial to the child's optimum functioning.
Only when teachers interact with these parents do they gain valuable
information on the developmental and medical history, social and emotional history. In addition, teachers can assist parents in obtaining the
skills and information necessary for directly working with their children
in the home. Continuity between home and school is crucial for the

optimum development of an exceptional child; efforts to learn and coordinate similar techniques that can be used throughout a child's life are important.

How can a preschool teacher work effectively with these parents? Several ideas are important.

Treat Parents as Individuals

Parents of exceptional children want most to be given the "status of individual personality" (Barsch, 1969). They do not want to be categorized, but treated with dignity. Teachers who know and respond to parents as individuals show such respect.

Teachers who examine their attitudes towards special-needs children and their parents will avoid treating them as stereotypes.

Focus on the Present and Future

Teachers must be aware of parents' tendencies to project blame and feel guilty for their child's problems. Teachers should avoid discussing the past, the source of a child's disability, and focus conversations and plans on the present and future; what actions can best help a child and parents now and in the time to come (Grossman, 1978).

Clarify Information

Teachers may have to reinterpret or reinforce earlier communications from other professionals. Parents who are uncomfortable with medical and/or educational terminology may use a teacher to clarify the information. Teachers should remember that their function is to clarify, not comment on, the diagnosis. Preschool teachers working with children mainstreamed into their classrooms need to communicate regularly with other members of the professional team who are planning the overall care and methods of treatment.

Be Hopefully Realistic

Parents value a teacher's realistic approaches. It is only natural to want to comfort parents with optimism, but raising false expectations is cruel. Teachers should offer hope whenever possible and help parents rejoice in the small successes. Specific and frequent reporting to parents is helpful here.

Increase Parent Involvement

Recognizing that parents of exceptional children often feel impotent, teachers should provide opportunities for parents to contribute meaningfully in the process of helping their child. Opportunities to observe and participate in a classroom help a parent feel included, as well as provide firsthand knowledge of his child's functioning and a

Teachers will help parents of exceptional children see the small successes and rejoice with them.

teacher's methods of working with him. As teachers help parents devise and follow through on plans for home training, parents are able to function more effectively with their children.

Know Available Community Resources

Teachers must be familiar with all community resources that can be helpful to families of exceptional children. Parents who don't know where to turn for assistance will need teachers' knowledge for referrals.

Help Reestablish Self-Confidence

Recognizing the social and emotional isolation of many families with exceptional children, teachers should make particular efforts to help them establish social linkages with the outside world (Swick, 1984). Introducing and involving them in work or discussion projects with other parents, arranging for other parents to take the initiative in approaching them, are methods for helping parents of exceptional children reestablish self-confidence in relating to others.

Teachers who recognize the emotional reactions and needs of parents of exceptional children are best able to support and strengthen these families' abilities to function optimally for their children.

Working with Parents of Infants

Another group of parents that have special needs requiring special consideration are parents of infants.

> "Honestly, that Mrs. Black! Doesn't she think I know anything at all? You should see the list of instructions she left with the baby this morning—how much to feed, when to feed, what to do if she doesn't finish it all, what it might mean when she cries. I'd be furious, if it wasn't so funny."

There are often strained feelings between the caregivers of babies and their parents. The inherent tension that exists between the individualized focus of parents on the well-being of their child and the generalized focus of a program on the well-being of all children is exacerbated by the particular aspects of parental development that are at work in the parents of infants (Lurie and Newman, 1982). Teachers who are working with parents of infants need to consider the particular emotional responses characteristic to the first stages of parenting.

Reactions of Parents of Infants

The important process of attachment in the first two years of a baby's life is mutual; adults are becoming attached to their special babies, just as babies are becoming attached to the adults who care for them. This means that not only do they care for each other deeply, but they also feel more secure and comfortable in each other's presence. It is this feeling of special closeness and relationship with their babies that is crucial to the beginning parent-child relationship and the optimum development of the baby. But this is also the cause for parents' possessive feelings toward their babies. They do not want to be away from them for too long and are convinced that their baby isn't safe with anyone else (Galinsky, 1982). This is the reason that, for example, mothers leave long, explicit lists of directions that a caregiver may find insulting to her intelligence, or demand exactly detailed accounts of every minute of the babies' day away from them. Such behaviors may also mask other emotions: feelings of rivalry or jealousy in relation to a caregiver; fears that their baby might not still love them if someone else is caring for him.

Given the fact that babies can also produce similar feelings of possessiveness in their supplemental caregivers, it is not surprising that tension between parents and teachers in an infant room is present.

Another factor to consider is that new parents are often anxious and tentative as they approach the unfamiliar tasks and decisions of

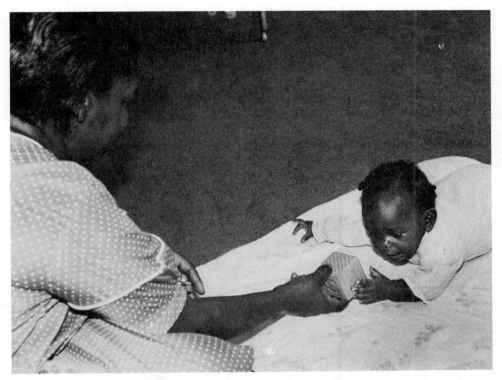

The relationship between infants and parents needs to be supported by the staff.

caring for an infant. Parents are unsure of how they measure up to the expected standards in their new role. The confident behaviors of a very experienced caregiver may increase the parents' feelings of incompetence by contrast.

There are many life adjustments necessitated by adding a baby to a household: new demands on time and money; disruptions in the marital relationship and the smooth running household and careers; physical exhaustion from attending to a baby's needs twenty-four hours a day, as well as returning to work outside the home. The parent of an infant is often emotionally and physically stretched with the stress of the new life style.

> The growth spurt associated with the first year of parenting is probably the most intense, compact and pressurized period of growth in a young adult life (Joffee and Viertel, 1980, p. 319).

Teacher Relationships with Parents of Infants

Recognizing the emotional responses and needs of new parents, caregivers can do several things to form an effective partnership with these parents.

Support the Attachment Process

Teachers can make sure that infant room practices facilitate the attachment process. The function of good infant day care is to support a family's developmental needs, and attachment is the primary need for both infants and parents.

Parents should feel welcome to drop in whenever they want. Many parents of infants will come and feed their baby during lunch hours or other free times during a day, if they feel welcomed. Mothers who want to nurse or offer a bottle should be provided with a comfortable chair and as much privacy for a one-to-one time with their baby as they would like. This is not an intrusion into an infant room routine, but an important time for parent and baby.

If parents feel that routines and regulations are not separating them from their baby, they will feel less possessive in their relation with a caregiver and reassured that their baby's care is satisfactory.

Standardize Informational Procedures

Procedures for passing information back and forth between parent and caregiver must be standardized and clear. Many centers keep a written record of daily occurrences such as feedings, naps, diaper changes, activities, and behavior, as well as recording developmental progress. They offer parents additional forms and a chance to record information that can help a caregiver, such as the last feeding time, amount of sleep, unusual behavior, or home routine. Keeping this individual form conveniently located—on top of a baby's cubby, perhaps—means that its use is routine for all adults. When parents are convinced that an infant room staff wants to share with them fully and that the information they offer as parents is important to their baby's day, feelings of anxiety and rivalry often decrease.

Remain Objective

Caregivers of infants need to be conscious of their own feelings towards the infants in their care. This relationship is warm and nurturing on a caregiver's part, but brief, probably lasting only through the months of infancy. What these babies most need from a caregiver is support warmly offered to a total family unit, as a baby and parents work through the process of attachment. There is no place in this relationship for caregivers who think how much better a job they do for a baby than his own anxious, inexperienced parents do. With connotations of rivalry among adults, a baby will only suffer. Loving caregivers realize that the best way they can help an infant is to support his parents' growth.

Introduce New Parenting Techniques

Teachers of infants should offer information and ideas to new parents. During their infants' first year, first-time parents are most open to learning basic parenting behaviors that have a lasting effect on themselves and their children (White, 1980). As their relationship develops, teachers should have frequent conversations in which it is appropriate to introduce ideas and answer questions subtly. At the same time, teachers must guard against overt behaviors that suggest parental incompetence, contrasted with professional expert knowledge. A readily available stack of articles and books is appropriate for some parents. A teacher in an infant room educates gently, as a friend.

> "Wow, we should really have a celebration today. When I noticed how hard it was for her to say good-bye to you this morning, I realized this was the first time she's done that. That crying when you leave is a good sign that she loves you very much, that all your hard work these past few months has paid off and she's become attached to you. That's a very special day."

As an increasing number of infants are cared for by other adults outside their homes, these teachers will have important opportunities to support families and act as resources at this crucial point in their lives.

Working with Abusive or Neglectful Parents

> Every time Dorothy Scott reads an article in the paper about child abuse and neglect in her city, or any other, she shudders. "What kind of parents could do a thing like that?" she wonders. "Thank goodness we'll never have that problem in our school— not with our kind of parents."

Many teachers believe that in their communities, with their particular populations, they will never have to face this problem. But this is simply not so. Child abuse occurs in every segment of society, among families who are just like everyone else. Teachers must understand the dynamics of abusive families and the indicators that suggest a problem may exist, as well as the legal obligations and possibilities for helping a child and his family.

The Child Abuse Prevention and Treatment Act of 1974 defines abuse and neglect as "the physical or mental injury, sexual abuse, negligent treatment or maltreatment of a child under the age of eighteen by a person who is responsible for the child's welfare, under circumstances which indicate that the child's health or welfare is harmed or threatened thereby." Adults who are entrusted with the care of children are responsible for their well-being. When this well-being is at risk, the law enables others to intervene on a child's behalf.

What forces cause parents to abuse their children? Three conditions need to exist for child abuse to occur (Helfer, 1975): (1) parents must be capable of abuse; (2) a child must be perceived by his parents as being different; and (3) a crisis comes in a stressful situation. A fourth condition may be that there is no lifeline or rescue operation available to parents—no close friends or relatives who could relieve the situation (Kempe, 1974).

Characteristics of Abusive Parents

Abusive parents usually acquire the potential to abuse over a period of time. Generally they were reared in a way that precluded the experience of being nurtured (Justice, 1976). Regardless of present financial or social status, they are deprived individuals who have difficulty experiencing pleasure, often distrustful, emotionally and socially isolated, even from their own spouse. They usually have a sense of personal incompetence, are frequently immature and dependent (Polensky, 1977). These parents are generally looking for love from their child and want it in the form of obedience and conformity (Stolk, 1974). So preoccupied are they with their own neediness that they don't see their child's needs (Polensky, 1977). These parents believe in the value of punishment and are fearful that too lenient behaviors will "spoil" a child.

These parents usually see their child, in a special, unrealistic way, often with excessive or unrealistic expectations. In some instances, these children are difficult children, with developmental or behavioral problems.

Precipitating Circumstances

In most cases, the personality potentials for both parent and child are present, but a crisis event is needed before a parent loses control and abuse occurs. Often a family undergoes too much change too fast, with no time to recover before hit by a new crisis (Justice, 1976). The crisis may be economic—loss of a job, financial problems; it may be personal—desertion by a spouse or other marital problems, death of a family member or other transition events; it may be environmental—a move, inadequate housing, the washing machine breaking down. Whatever it is, however remote from the child himself, this event is the last straw and a parent loses control. Because these are circumstances that know no barrier of socioeconomic background or culture, abusive situations are found in every stratum of society.

Indicators of Abuse and Neglect

An alert teacher is often the person who first notices that a family needs help. There are both physical and behavioral signs that should trigger questions in a teacher's mind.

Physical Signs of Abuse

- bruises or contusions, especially those in places where a child's physical activity cannot account for them: backs of knees, upper back; those that are bilateral (matching on each arm); or those that indicate some agent made the mark (a belt buckle or loop of electric cord). Sometimes long-sleeved clothing inappropriate for the season may attempt to cover up such marks.
- injuries reported to be caused by falling, but that do not include hands, knees, or forehead.
- burns, especially small burns such as those made by a cigarette or match.
- trouble sitting or walking may indicate physical or sexual abuse.
- frequent injuries.

Physical Signs of Neglect

- need for medical attention, even after conditions have been drawn to a parent's attention.
- clothing inadequate for weather, unwashed or uncared for.
- physical hygiene unattended to.
- child excessively fatigued or hungry, missing breakfast constantly.

Behavioral Indicators

Abuse or neglect may be indicated by a variety of behaviors in children. The following are some behaviors that should trigger teachers' watchful concern:

- deviant behavioral systems, such as aggression, destructiveness, and disruptive behaviors; or passive, withdrawn, extreme quiet
- daydreaming
- fearful of adults and of parents
- unusual, sophisticated sexual acting-out (contrasted with curious, exploratory behaviors usually associated with preschoolers)

Teacher's Role

When a teacher suspects abuse or neglect in a family situation, there are several courses of action indicated.

Report to Proper Agencies

Teachers are mandated by law to report cases of suspected abuse in all states, and day-care workers in most. Preschool teachers should check their own state regulations for current laws and the appropriate agency to whom to report. The burden of proof is not on teachers, but on the protective services agency to whom teachers must report; if a report of suspected abuse or neglect is made in good faith (contrasted with the malicious intention of a parent who is trying to discredit another in a custody battle, for example), the reporting adult is protected from liability.

There are instances of teachers and centers who try to close their eyes to the problems they suspect or see in families, perhaps fearing reprisals or parents' anger if they involve themselves in "family matters." Teachers need to accept their responsibility as perhaps the only people who know what is going on with some children and their families, and as the only advocates a child might have. Teachers need to realize their own legal and moral responsibilities, if they discover their center's policies discourage such active advocacy roles.

Document Evidence

When teachers become aware of possible abuse and neglect, documentation of what they see must be kept. Such records substantiate any suspicions with evidence and are useful to an investigator. Simple, dated descriptions are all that is required.

Nov. 18th. Two large bruises, on each upper arm, including distinct finger marks.

Dec. 3rd. Bright red welts on backs of legs. Child reports father was very angry previous night.

Examine Personal Attitudes

Teachers need to examine their own attitudes to be able to work with these families. Many teachers feel great anger towards parents who are hurtful to their small children. It is important to recognize the existence of this anger and to work especially hard to get to know parents and the circumstances of their parenting, in order to develop true empathy for their situations. It is more appropriate for teachers to release some of their negative feelings in conversation with colleagues, rather than with parents, since parents are themselves in need of nurturing and acceptance, not expressions of anger. It is important to remember, however, that confidential material or statements that have not yet been confirmed must be treated professionally.

Create an Atmosphere of Trust

Teachers' concern and caring for children in these troubled families enable them to support children through very difficult times. It helps these children to know teachers care for them, are dependable and trustworthy, and are concerned enough to help them and their parents. Such an atmosphere of trust may free children to confide their problems and allow them to feel confident in the ability of other adults to help them and their parents. These children do not need to hear condemnation of their parents, who are the most important people in their lives, no matter how troubled at this time. Teachers can also comfort themselves in the knowledge that they are providing an important model for children, helping them to realize that not all adults are abusive.

Refer Parents to Support Groups

Many communities offer agencies and groups to support parents under stress. If teachers know these community resources, they can refer parents on a preventative basis or reassure them after a court's referral. Many agencies, such as the Family Support Center in Charlotte, North Carolina, offer support to parents in the form of therapy, a twenty-four-hour stress telephone line manned by trained volunteers, and reparenting education for parents who have abused. One method found very effective is to give families a "parent aide," a parent who makes home visits and models positive and appropriate ways to interact with children.

In recent years, there have been tendencies for courts to be less punitive with parents and concentrate on efforts to help parents learn alternative methods of discipline and appropriate expectations. Teachers can wholeheartedly support such struggles. There are benefits for an entire family when parents learn new methods of parenting.

Support for these efforts can also come from parents who have experienced similar problems. Many communities have a local group of the national Parents Anonymous organization, whose members are formerly abusive parents who come together to encourage each other in their attempts to change their behavior. For more information about this organization, write: Parents Anonymous, 2810 Artessia Blvd., Suite F, Redondo Beach, CA 90278.

The reality is that child abuse and neglect is a problem many teachers will encounter. The best scenario is for teachers to be able to recognize signs of distress and problems, to know their legal and moral obligations and their community resources, and to support families through the agonizing process of evaluation and reconstruction. Building a caring relationship with parents is the best gift a teacher can give an abused child.

Summary

Some parents with special needs include parents experiencing separation, divorce, and remarriage, parents of exceptional children, parents of infants, and abusive or neglectful parents. Teachers working with parents with special needs will be challenged to develop new sensitivities in understanding the dynamics and emotional responses of both parents and children in each situation. Teachers must also incorporate necessary classroom behaviors that can help children and skills and knowledge to support parents. In the process of such professional growth, teachers will be able to reach out to help the families who need them most.

Student Activities for Further Study

1. Investigate and gather referral information and brochures on any agencies that exist in your community to:
   - assist or support parents and/or children undergoing separation and divorce, such as counseling services, Parents Without Partners, Big Brothers and Big Sisters, etc.,
   - assist parents and their exceptional children, or help in the identification and early intervention process,
   - offer support to new parents, and
   - assist, treat, and/or support in abusive family situations.

   If there are a large number of such agencies, it is useful for each class member to visit one to gather information and report back to the class.

2. Find the state law that defines the legal responsibilities for professionals and paraprofessionals in preschool and child care in your state regarding reporting abuse and neglect. Learn your local reporting agency. It is helpful to invite a representative of that agency to visit your class.

3. Investigate your library resources for parents and children with special needs. Compile a list of these to have available for parents.

4. If exceptional children are mainstreamed in preschool classrooms in your community, plan a visit to these classrooms or to any specialized

schools. Learn what their parent-involvement policies and practices are.

5. Role-play, and discuss the following situations:

   a. You are concerned by a four-year-old's aggression and regression in your classroom. The father moved out of the home two months ago. You want to discuss the child's behavior with his mother.

   b. A mother wants to tell you all about how terribly she and the children were treated by her ex-husband.

   c. A child in a recent divorce situation seems totally withdrawn and sad. Your conversation with the child?

   d. A child who tells you, "He's not my real daddy, he just married my mother. I hate him." Your response?

   e. A child tells you, "My daddy hit my mommy hard. He scares me when he's so mean to us." Your response?

   f. A child has been observed in explicit sexual activity (not exploration). You want to discuss this with parent.

   g. A mother of a cerebral palsy child says, "The doctors say he'll never walk or talk right, but he seems so much better in your class. What do you think?" Your response?

   h. A mother of an infant says, "My mother visited this weekend and says for me not to pick the baby up so much, just to let him cry, so you shouldn't either." Your response?

Review Questions

1. List several behaviors in both children and parents associated with the stress of divorce or remarriage.

2. Discuss three of four ways teachers can be helpful to children experiencing divorce or remarriage.

3. Discuss three of four ways teachers can be helpful to parents experiencing divorce or remarriage.

4. Identify three of five possible emotional responses of parents of exceptional children.

5. Describe four of seven ways teachers can work effectively with parents of exceptional children.

6. Discuss typical responses of parents of infants.

7. Identify three of four helpful behaviors for teachers of infants.

8. List two of three factors that can create abusive situations.

9. List any six indicators of abuse and neglect.

10. Identify three of five responsibilities of teachers in situations involving abuse and neglect.

References and Related Readings

A. *On Divorce and Remarriage (for teachers' understanding, and to offer to parents.)*

Allers, Robert D. "Helping Children Understand Divorce." *Today's Education* 69.4 (1980): 26-29.

Anthony, E.J. "Children At Risk from Divorce: A Review." *The Child in His Family.* Eds. E.T. Anthony and C. Kampernils. New York: Wiley, 1979.

Atlas, S.L. *Single Parenting: A Practical Resource Guide.* Englewood Cliffs, New Jersey: Prentice-Hall, 1981.

BelGeddes, Joan. *How to Parent Alone—A Guide for Single Parents.* New York: Seabury Press, 1974.

Biller, Henry V. "Father Absence, Divorce and Personality Development." *The Role of the Father in Child Development.* Ed. Michael E. Lamb. 2nd Ed. New York: John Wiley and Sons, 1981.

Braun, Samuel J. and Dorothy M. Sang. "When Parents Split." *Day Care and Early Education* 4.2 (1976): 26-29.

Briggs, Beverly A. and Connor M. Walters. "Single-Father Families: Implications for Early Childhood Educators." *Young Children* 40.3 (1985): 23-27.

Burden, S. et al., eds. *The Single Parent Family.* Iowa City, Iowa: The University of Iowa Press, 1976.

Coleman, Marilyn, Lawrence H. Ganong, and June Henry. "What Teachers Should Know About Stepfamilies." *Childhood Education* 60:5 (1984): 306-309.

Francke, Linda Bird. *Growing Up Divorced.* New York: Linden Press/ Simon and Schuster, 1983.

Galper, Miriam. *Co-parenting: A Source Book for the Separated or Divorced Family.* Philadelphia: Running Press, 1978.

Grollman, Earl. *Talking About Divorce: A Dialogue Between Parent and Child.* Boston: Beacon Press, 1975.

Heatherington, E. Mavis. "Divorce: A Child's Perspective." *American Psychologist* 34 (1979): 857.

Heatherington, E. Mavis, Martha Cox and Roger Cox. "Effects of Divorce on Parents and Children." *Non-Traditional Families: Parenting and Child Development.* Ed. Michael E. Lamb. Hillsdale, New Jersey: Lawrence Erlbaum Assoc. Pubs., 1982.

Herzog, Elizabeth and Cecilia Sudia. "Fatherless Homes: A Review of Research." *Childhood Education* 48.4 (1972): 175-81.

Hunt, Morton and Bernice. *The Divorce Experience.* New York: McGraw Hill, Inc., 1977.

Jacobson, D.S. "Stepfamilies." *Children Today* 9.1 (1980): 2-6.

Luepnitz, Deborah A. "Which Aspects of Divorce Affect Children?" *Family Co-ordinator* 28.1 (1979): 79-85.

Lombana, Judy H. *Home-School Partnerships: Guidelines and Strategies for Educators.* New York: Greene and Stratton, 1983.

Klein, Carole. *The Single Parent Experience.* New York: Avon, 1973.

Noble, J. and W. *How to Live With Other Peoples' Children.* New York: Hawthorn Books, 1979.

Quisenberry, James D., ed. *Changing Family Lifestyles: Their Effects on Children.* Wheaton, Maryland: ACEI, 1982.

Salk, Lee. *What Every Child Would Like Parents to Know About Divorce.* New York: Harper and Row, 1978.

Santrock, J.W. and R.L. Tracy. "Effects of Children's Family Structure Status in the Development of Stereotypes by Teachers." *Journal of Educational Psychology* 70 (1978): 754-57.

Sinberg, J. *Divorce is a Grown-up Problem: A Book About Divorce for Young Children and Their Parents.* New York: Avon Books, 1978.

Skeen, Patsy and Patrick C. McKenry. "The Teacher's Role in Facilitating a Child's Adjustment to Divorce." *Young Children* 35.5 (1980): 3-14.

Skeen, Patsy, Bryan Robinson and Carol Flake-Hobson. "Blended Families: Overcoming the Cinderella Myth." *Young Children* 39.2 (1984): 64-74.

Visher, E.B. and J.S. Visher. *Stepfamilies: A Guide to Working With Stepparents and Stepchildren.* New York: Banner/Mizel, 1979

Wallerstein, J.S. and J.B. Kelly. "The Effects of Parental Divorce: Experience of the Preschool Child." *Journal of Child Psychiatry* 14 (1975): 600-616.

Wallerstein, J.S. and J.B. Kelly. "The Effects of Parental Divorce: Experience of the Child in Later Latency." *American Journal of Orthopsychiatry* 46 (1976): 256-69.

Books for Preschool Children

Adams, E. *Mushy Eggs.* New York: C.P. Putnam's Sons, 1973.

Boegehold. *Daddy Doesn't Live Here Any More.* Racine: Western Publishers, 1985.

Caines, J. *Daddy.* New York: Harper and Row, 1977.

Goff, Beth. *Where is Daddy? The Story of a Divorce.* Boston: Beacon Press, 1969.

Kindred, W. *Lucky Wilma.* New York: Dial Press, 1973.

Lexau, J. *Emily and the Klunky Baby and the Next-Door Dog.* New York: Dial Press, 1972.

Perry, P. and M. Lynch. *Mommy and Daddy are Divorced.* New York: Dial Press, 1978.

Roy, Ron. *Breakfast with My Father.* Boston: Houghton Mifflin Co., 1981.

Seuling. *What Kind of Family is This? A Book About Stepfamilies.* Racine: Western Publishing Co., 1985.

Stein, S.B. *On Divorce: An Open Family Book for Parents and Children Together.* New York: Walker and Co., 1979.

Stinson, Kathy. *Mom and Dad Don't Live Together Any More.* Annick Press Ltd., 1984.

(For a list of books for school-aged children, see Skeen and McKenry, 1980.)

B. *On Parents of Exceptional Children.*

Barsch, Ray H. *The Parent-Teacher Partnership.* Arlington, Virginia: The Council for Exceptional Children, Inc., 1969.

Chinn, P.C., J. Winn, R. H. Walters. *Two Way Talking With Parents of Special Children.* St. Louis: C.V. Mosby, 1978.

Featherstone, H. *A Difference in the Family: Life With a Disabled Child.* New York: Basic Books, 1980.

Feldman, M.A. et al. "Parents and Professionals: A Partnership in Special Education." *Exceptional Children* 41.8 (1975): 551-54.

Gallagher, J.J., P. Berkman, and A.H. Cross. "Families of Handicapped Children: Sources of Stress and Its Ameliorization." *Exceptional Children* 50.1 (1983): 10-19.

Grossman, Bruce. "Closing the Parent-Professional Gap." *Developmental Disabilities of Early Childhood.* Eds. Barbara Feingold and Caryl Bank. Springfield, Illinois: Charles C. Thomas Publishers, 1978.

Heward, W.L., J.C. Dardig, Allison Russell. *Working With Parents of Handicapped Children.* Columbus: Charles E. Merrill Publ. Co., 1979.

Kupfer, Fern. "Severely and/or Multiply Disabled Children." *Equals in This Partnership: Parents of Disabled and At-Risk Infants and Toddlers Speak to Professionals.* Washington, D.C.: National Center for Clinical Infant Programs, 1984.

Lichter, P. "Communicating With Parents: It Begins With Listening." *Teaching Exceptional Children* 8 (1976): 66-71.

Lillie, David, Ed. *Teaching Parents to Teach.* New York: Walker and Co., 1976.

Lombana, Judy H. *Home School Partnerships: Guidelines and Strategies for Educators.* New York: Greene and Stratton, 1983.

Michaelis, Carol. *Home and School Partnerships in Exceptional Education.* Rockville, Maryland: An Aspen Publication, 1980.

Seligman, Milton. *The Family With a Handicapped Child.* Orlando, Florida: Greene and Stratton, Inc., 1983.

Stewart, W.E., J.C. Conoley, D. Rosenthal. *Working With Parents of Exceptional Children.* St. Louis: Times Mirror/Mosby College Publication, 1985.

Swick, Kevin J. *Inviting Parents into the Young Child's World.* Champagne, Illinois: Stipes Publ. Co., 1984.

C. *Working With Parents of Infants*

Brazelton, T. Berry. "Cementing Family Relationships Through Child Care." in *The Infants We Care For.* Rev. Ed. Laura L. Dittmann,

Ed. Washington, D.C.: National Association for the Education of Young Children, 1984.

Galinsky, Ellen. "Understanding Ourselves and Parents." *Caring for Infants and Toddlers: What Works, What Doesn't.* Vol. 2. Eds. Robert Lurie and Roger Neugebauer. Redmond, Washington: Child Care Information Exchange, 1982.

Joffe, S. and J. Viertel. *Becoming Parents: Preparing for the Emotional Changes of First-Time Parenthood.* New York: Atheneum Books, 1984.

Lurie, Robert and Kathy Newman. "A Healthy Tension: Parent and Group Infant-Toddler Care." *Caring for Infants and Toddlers: What Works, What Doesn't.* Vol. 2. Eds. Robert Lurie and Roger Neugebauer. Redmond, Washington: Child Care Information Exchange, 1982.

White, Burton L. *A Parent's Guide to the First Three Years.* Englewood Cliffs, New Jersey: Prentice-Hall, 1980.

D. *Working With Abusive Parents*

Berger, E. *Parents as Partners in Education.* St. Louis: The C.V. Mosby Co., 1981.

Helfer, R. and C. Kempe. *Child Abuse and Neglect: The Family and the Community.* Cambridge, Mass.: Ballinger Publishers, 1976.

Helfer, R. *The Diagnostic Process and Treatment Programs.* U.S. Dept. of Health, Education and Welfare. Washington, D.C.: U.S. Govt. Printing Office, 1975.

Justice, Blair and Rita. *The Abusing Family.* New York: Human Services Press, 1976.

Kempe, C. Henry. "Battering." *Raising Children in Modern America: Problems and Prospective Solutions.* Ed. Nathan B. Talbot. Boston: Little, Brown and Co., 1974.

Meddin, Barbara J. and Anita L. Rosen. "Child Abuse and Neglect: Prevention and Reporting." *Young Children* 41.4 (1986): 26-30.

Polensky, N.A., C. Desaix, S.A. Sharlin. *Child Neglect: Understanding and Reaching the Parent.* New York: Child Welfare League of America, Inc., 1977.

Reed, J. "Working With Abusive Parents: A Parent's View—an Interview with K. Jolly." *Children Today* 4.3 (1975): 2-10.

Schmitt, Burton P. "What Teachers Need to Know About Child Abuse and Neglect." *Childhood Education* 52.2 (1970): 58-62.

Shanas, B. "Child Abuse: A Killer Teachers Can Help Control." *Phi Delta Kappan* 61 (1975): 479-82.

Spinetta, J. and D. Rigla. "The Child-Abusing Parent: A Psychological Review." *Psychological Bulletin* 77 (1972): 296-304.

Swick, Kevin J. *Inviting Parents Into the Young Child's World.* Champagne, Illinois: Stipes Publishing Co., 1984.

Chapter 15 Working with Particular Attitudes and Behaviors

Encounters with some parents may be so discouraging or threatening that teachers withdraw from other efforts to work with parents. Chapter 15 considers reasons for parents' behavior and strategies for approaching them.

Objectives

After studying this chapter, the student will be able to

1. discuss reasons for hostile reactions and considerations in dealing with them
2. discuss reasons for apparent indifference and considerations in overcoming it
3. discuss over-involvement of parents and ways of dealing with it

As professionals, teachers have the responsibility to keep working towards effective relationships with parents, even under very difficult conditions. Perhaps the most difficult circumstances arise when teachers and parents view a situation quite differently. These differences may center on pedagogical issues: differing opinions on appropriate educational goals, curriculum, teaching or discipline methods. Parental expectations and behaviors may conflict with a teacher's view of her role. Differences arise when teachers try to help parents recognize a characteristic or need of their child that parents don't wish to accept. The uncomfortable feelings that develop in both teachers and parents may make it hard to continue the dialogue to the point where real communication or problem-solving can take place.

In general, as a teacher contemplates such situations, it is important to analyze a situation critically from both teacher and parents' viewpoints; define and break a problem into its component parts to see how each person perceives a situation. In some cases, there may be no solution to the vast differences in perspective or emotional response of teacher and parent; but in others, a careful analysis of the dynamics and facts of a situation may help the parties find common ground on which to work together.

Hostility

> In a recent conference, the parent angrily burst out at the teacher, "My son has never had this problem before. If you ask me, there's something wrong with a teacher who can't get a young child to obey her. Don't tell me he needs limits! I think your director should watch *you* more carefully!"

As a teacher responds to this attack, it is important to consider several points.

Hostility as a Mask

Teachers need to realize that everything that seems like hostility may not really be so. Sometimes parents are motivated by genuine concern for their child and questioning the practices or evaluation is a form of healthy self-assertion. Individuals who are not used to being assertive may err and appear aggressive instead (Rundall and Smith, 1982). Sometimes parents who feel powerless attempt to grab power inappropriately.

Another emotion that may be masked by hostility is the grief parents feel when realizing that their child has a developmental problem or handicap (see Chapter 14).

> Bearing in mind that a parent may be overwhelmed or upset by the staff's findings or interpretations, one should view parents' defensive reactions more as their method of coping with aroused anxiety than as an attempt to obstruct the proceedings (Losen and Diament, 1978, p. 150).

It is essential that a teacher think about a parent's position before automatically labeling a response as "hostile."

True hostility appears as an individual reacts with anger when dealing with a person seen to be "in authority." A hostile person is defensive, suspicious, assumes that others have unfriendly intentions, and therefore feels impelled to strike the first blow (Jersild, 1955). Such hostile reactions often indicate a carry-over of childhood attitudes or earlier experiences with authority.

Hostility Inhibits Communication

When parents are verbally abusive or irrationally angry, it is impossible to communicate effectively. It is a teacher's task to defuse the anger so that communication can begin (Lombana, 1983). The first step in working with an angry reaction is to accept it. An expressed feeling is real, no matter how distorted the perception of facts that caused the feeling. Accepting someone else's feelings does not mean giving up one's own perspective, it simply means being more sensitive to that of the other. By taking a parent's perspective, a teacher is able to show genuine concern and is more likely to respond appropriately. As a teacher reflects an understanding of a parent's point of view through active listening, a parent realizes that his feelings are recognized.

> "You're really very upset by my comments about Roger's behavior, aren't you?"

Such feedback may eliminate a parent's need to show more anger because a teacher clearly has picked up on the message, and may elicit a response that can clarify a concern in terms of specific details.

> "You bet I'm upset, and I'll tell you, I don't think it's fair to be talking about making him keep rules after all that kid has had on him. With his dad being so strict with him, and then leaving last year, he's had enough to get used to, without you being strict too."

When active listening does not evoke an opportunity to hear the reasons behind the anger, a teacher should continue to reflect back her empathic perception of a parent's response.

> Parent: "Of course I'm upset—anybody would be, to hear a teacher say such things about their child."
>
> Teacher: "It really troubles you to hear the kind of comments I made."
>
> Parent: "It certainly does. It's just not fair—what do you know about it anyway?"

> Teacher: "I know there's a lot about Roger I don't know, and I'm counting on you to help me understand. What can you tell me that would help me?" and so on.

Remain Calm

To be able to work through the anger, it is vital that a teacher remain calm in every way. The louder and more vehement a parent's voice, the softer and slower should a teacher speak, being careful that her body language remains open and positive. It is very important that a teacher not become defensive or argumentative, and not retaliate verbally such as the following:

> "Look, don't you talk to me about my teaching. If you were doing a halfway decent job with parenting I wouldn't be having these problems in my classroom."

Defensive behavior suggests that the attacker is right and tends to escalate the tension. Responding to a parent's emotion with a teacher's emotion can only lead to an explosive situation. Remaining calm may not be an easy task.

> Professional skins are not significantly thicker than anyone else's. And there are limits to one's ability to remain non-judgemental in the face of persistence in irrational or inappropriate behavior, despite our best efforts to understand it or tolerate it (Losen and Diament, 1978, p. 150).

Nevertheless, a teacher must continue to maintain composure and the best chance of doing so is to try to perceive a situation from a parent's perspective, and identify with the emotional responses of a parent without taking the situation personally. Learning to support parents nonjudgementally, without losing emotional control, is crucial. Professionals do not have the right to lose control with parents. By taking on the role of teacher, they commit themselves to working constructively with those who need assistance.

It is necessary for a teacher to analyze her own emotional responses, determining whether this has become a power struggle and why she feels so strongly about an issue; are there facts involved or only emotional responses?

It is also important that a teacher not retreat from the anger by suggesting "We'll talk some other time," or "You'd better talk to the director." The potential for communication and learning more about a problem is available here and now. As teachers help parents express feelings and perceptions, they both have an opportunity to see the issues from a different perspective.

Adhere to Facts

As a conversation proceeds, teachers must be careful that any disagreeing statements concern facts and issues, not personalities. In discussing different viewpoints, participants should use descriptive statements, not evaluative ones. It is easier to deal with descriptions, rather than labels (Stewart et al., 1985).

NOT: "Roger is a very undisciplined, out-of-bounds child."
RATHER: "I'm noticing that it's hard for Roger to keep the rule about hitting others. This week when he was angry with Eddie on three different occasions, he hit him. Do you notice hitting at home?"

Teachers need to remember that angry outbursts may be triggered if they approach parents with problems so directly that the only recourse is to attack back in order to protect themselves. It is effective to use more palatable methods, such as "sandwiching" the meat of a problem between two slices of supportive statements regarding a parent's interest and concern (Rundall and Smith, 1982). For example:

I appreciate how deeply concerned you are for Roger. There's no more important thing for a child than to know his parents care. I'm concerned about his ability to develop some self-control, and I feel sure this is an area that we can work on to come up with some things that might help him."

Respect Parents' Concern

It is important that angry parents know their concerns are taken seriously. These problems are important to a parent and must not be minimized by a teacher.

One way to indicate respect for parents' problems is to write down every complaint and suggestion for a solution (Lombana, 1983). This action says that the concerns are important and parents are being listened to. It is also valuable to state that educators don't have all the answers and need all the help they can get.

Reschedule Meeting

On those occasions when all attempts to reduce the amount of anger and initiate communication fail, it may be wise to reschedule another meeting.

> "I'm not sure we can accomplish anything more today. Could we meet again next Wednesday at this time? Maybe some new ideas will occur to us in the meantime."

It can be useful to invite a colleague or supervisor to sit in on the next conference, since some participant at every conference needs to be free of emotional responses and have skills to help the other participants deal with their emotions quickly and fully (Stewart et al., 1985). Checking out a situation with a colleague may help a teacher see it from a different perspective.

Anger is a powerful emotion, destructive if allowed to rage unleashed, but potentially a strong motivation to examine a situation and work together for understanding and change.

Indifference

> Connie Martinez is concerned about a different kind of behavior. There are a couple of parents in her classroom that she simply can't reach. They seem apathetic, uncaring about their children's needs or the teacher's attempts to involve them in any way.

There are several possible reasons behind apparent indifference. One may be that the overwhelming pressure in parents' lives prevents them from focusing much attention on their child, as much as they care for him. Too many concerns about basic physical needs may crowd in. A parent who worries that her resources will not stretch to cover both food for the rest of the month and the electric bill has little emotional energy left to care about higher emotional or social needs.

Pressure in parents' lives can also come from having two sets of career demands and the problems of meshing two schedules, relocating households when told to, and continuing to push up the ladder of success (Holmstrom, 1972). Sometimes there is little time or energy left for personal relationships or development. Such parents are often more than willing to entrust child care to the professionals and to withdraw to more obviously gainful career pursuits.

Parents who feel particularly uncomfortable due to differences in social class or cultural backgrounds may withdraw from a situation and appear indifferent. These parents may have a high regard for teachers and education, but feel that education is a one-way street and that they have nothing to offer.

Still other parents who seem indifferent may be adults who missed childhood, who are themselves products of abnormal parenting. Such parents spend their grown-up years attempting to have their own lost needs met by their children, and by doing so raise children whose needs are never met (Rundall and Smith, 1982).

Whatever the reason for parents' lack of interest or involvement, most teachers don't like not being able to reach them. As is human nature, teachers who feel unsuccessful in reaching particular parents often withdraw from them, thereby increasing the distance between them. It is common for teachers to shift the blame from themselves to parents (Rundall and Smith, 1982).

These responses do not improve a situation. It is more helpful to adopt an attitude that parents are not unreachable, but that teachers have not yet found ways to reach them.

Teachers must assess the reasons for parents' unapproachability and consider various ideas to overcome it.

Personal and Economic Pressures

For parents overwhelmed by economic and personal pressures, there is little probability of their becoming involved or less "indifferent" to their children's needs as long as these external pressures exist. The most positive action for a teacher is to be an advocate for these parents, referring them to appropriate agencies for assistance. Such concern and help will lay the basis for trust in a relationship that may develop as these parents' other concerns are lessened.

Career Interests

For parents busy with their own career interests, teachers may emphasize particular techniques to reach them—newsletters that can be read at their convenience, occasional bag lunches with their children issuing the invitation and planned with plenty of advance notice. Opportunities to talk with other upwardly mobile parents may be appreciated as a source of support.

Cultural Differences

With parents who may remain distant because of discomfort with social or cultural differences, teachers must be warm, friendly, and casual in their contacts. It may be important to consciously simplify speech styles and vocabulary.

Other parents from similar backgrounds who are more comfortable in a school setting can be helpful in making contact with these parents and personally inviting and accompanying them to informal events. Casual social activities or hands-on workshops (making toys for their children or materials for the classroom) provide less threatening experiences.

Through genuine indications that a teacher needs and values parent participation, those parents who feel they have nothing to offer may see that preschool education is not as formidable as they had believed. Persistence can pay off here.

Emotional Pressures

Perhaps the greatest challenge to teachers comes in attempting to reach those parents who are less sensitive to their child's and a teacher's needs because of their own overwhelming emotional needs. This can be any parent at any particular time of their life. Teachers must realize that their expectations for these parents to understand and be involved are often unrealistic. A truly helpful stance is

> to be prepared to accept these parents as they are and to offer them, not what we need in the way of their involvement in our programs or what their child needs in parenting, but what the parents need themselves to grow (Rundall and Smith, 1982, p. 73).

What they need is nurturing. These parents need to be accepted for what they are, encouraged for whatever they have done, reinforced for any strength and efforts, and helped to feel understood. As teachers slowly establish a climate of trust with these parents, they should recognize that this relationship may help lessen parents' neediness.

In conversation, teachers focus the discussion on a parent, his concerns and interests. Whenever possible, teachers should provide services for parents—a cup of coffee when they're looking tired, an opportunity to trade outgrown clothes with another family—as an indication that teachers care for parents and understand their needs. In fact, teachers are creating a dependent relationship, not for the professional's needs, but as a way to assist a parent in establishing a trusting relationship (Rundall and Smith, 1982). Once a parent exhibits trust in the relationship, a teacher can gradually begin to set limits and demands that would have been too frightening before the relationship was secure.

It may be a long and trying struggle, but by responding to parent's needs, teachers may be able to reach parents who are "unreachable" in ways teachers had first expected to involve them.

Over-Involvement

To teachers struggling to get parents involved in a program or even indicate an interest in their children's welfare, the predicament of over-involvement might seem a lesser problem. But a parent who is too involved in a school situation may hinder his child's move towards independence or do the wrong thing at the wrong time, disrupting his child and the class. This is sometimes the parent who "knows it all," and is full of recommendations or criticisms, or doesn't want to hear a teacher's observations of his child. Sometimes this parent just gets in the way of orderly classroom procedures as he lingers to talk indefinitely, despite a teacher's need to care for the children or set up activities. How does a teacher respond to these behaviors?

Understanding a parent's behavior is a first step to tolerating or dealing with it. A teacher must get to know a particular parent to assess the individual situation and motivation.

Reluctance to Separate

Many parents are overwhelmed because of their own reluctance to separate from their children. Being uncomfortable with separation is a natural experience in the developmental stages of parenthood, but a positive resolution of the conflicting feelings is important for both child and parent.

These parents need particular reassurance that their child is being well cared for. Regular and specific reporting of information helps, as will personal notes and phone calls to share personal anecdotes about their child. This communication reassures parents that individual attention is paid to their child, and that they are not losing contact with him.

Empathizing frankly with a parent's feelings brings separation right into the open.

> "I know there must be a lot of mixed feelings about seeing her grow up—rejoicing at all the new things, sadness at the idea of the baby left behind. It must seem to you sometimes like you're not as close as you once were. But it's just different, isn't it? Believe me, you're still the most important person in her world. Why, just the other day . . . ."

Teachers should encourage parents to share their feelings and thoughts, and such communication allows teachers the opportunity to reassure and subtly remind parents of a growing child's needs.

> "Hard as it is for you, the most loving thing a parent can do is to allow a child some room to move on, feeling stronger about being able to function without you. She needs to know you have enough confidence in her that she can be all right, for a while, without your presence."

When presented with the idea that it is for their child's welfare, many parents try harder to let go.

Unmet Personal Needs

A parent who is over-involved because of unmet personal, social, and emotional needs benefits when a teacher responds with genuine appreciation and praise for their efforts. It is counterproductive to try to stop this involvement, since it is so important for a parent's emotional health, as well as potentially helpful to a school or center.

When a parent's over-involvement in a classroom becomes a problem to a child and teacher, his efforts can be redirected to other areas that are less disruptive (Swick, 1978)—another classroom; working to involve other parents; preparing materials.

The particular strengths of parents should be identified and utilized fully, always with sincere appreciation for the value of their contribution. Positive ways to contribute may be found—an extra pair of hands at lunch time in the infant room, a cozy lap for an upset toddler, gathering dress-up clothes that need refurbishing, or calling other parents to remind them of an upcoming meeting. Such efforts are not disruptive to a child's independent functioning and allow a parent to feel important to a program.

Insecurities

For a parent who "knows it all" and wants to share his knowledge, a teacher may need to indicate frequently that she considers a parent to be the real expert on his particular child. Sometime a parent acts this way out of insecurities caused by real or imagined perceptions of a teacher's competence and dominance in a situation. When a teacher emphasizes partnership and defers to a parent's knowledge of his child, parental feelings of unimportance may diminish.

> "You know, parents really know their own children best. I need to know all I can about Johnny, and I appreciate your sharing your knowledge. What can you tell me about his playing in the neighborhood at home?"

Sometimes a parent's information can be acknowledged and shared with others.

> "That's a good tip about those children's books. Could you write that down so I can add it to next month's newsletter? I think a lot of parents would like to know."

When the "know it all" parent is unable to hear a teacher's points, a teacher must exercise skills of assertiveness and state her position clearly without belittling a parent's ideas or antagonizing and hurting. Teachers who recognize the complexity of human behavior know that a situation may be perceived in a variety of ways and it is healthy to air all perspectives. This realization often prevents becoming too aggressive in presenting one's views. Assertiveness in a discussion may be helpful; aggressiveness will likely be destructive.

If reluctant to accept the validity of another's viewpoint or information, a parent may be more susceptible to information conveyed by less personal means. Making pertinent articles available to parents allows them to absorb the ideas and make them their own; an exposure to new ideas is accomplished without the resistance that can be inherent in personal discussions.

Lingering to Talk

For a parent who lingers on indefinitely to talk, a teacher should draw clear limits while still making the parent feel welcome.

Teachers may find it valuable to keep a journal to record feelings, perceptions, and experiences working with parents.

> After a few minutes of talk, when other responsibilities press, the teacher can say, "I enjoy talking with you, but right now I need to get over to those children at the water table. We'd love to have you stay if you have a few extra minutes. Perhaps you'd like to sit near the book corner—there's always someone looking for a story to be read."

This reassures a parent that his presence is welcomed and provides a chance for him to be useful in classroom life. If he is uneasy about leaving his child, it allows him to observe a teacher and see how busy she really is.

If such patterns continue, a teacher may need to say frankly

> "I really want to talk with you, Mr. Jones. It's important to me to hear from you. But arrival time is so busy I'm not able to give you my full attention. Let's see if we can find some time to talk that's less hectic for me. I can be free at naptime, or at my break this afternoon at 3:30."

Specific guidelines help a parent realize the many facets of a teacher's responsibility.

Summary

Teachers may encounter troublesome behaviors and attitudes that are personally annoying and professionally discouraging. In each case, a teacher's first step should be to attempt to identify the feelings or circumstances that might be the cause. A stance that is directed towards solutions, rather than accusations, is important. Meeting these needs constructively will eliminate some of the destructive reactions, including teacher frustration.

For a teacher who makes genuine efforts to understand and problem-solve, and still finds situations that seem to have no solution, remember that you are not alone. Any teacher has had similar experiences that sometimes linger in the memory long after forgetting more positive experiences. It is important to learn as much as possible from these negative experiences, and to keep on trying!

Many teachers find that recording their feelings, perceptions, and experiences in working with parents is an invaluable tool for their own growth. Informal notes or journal entries document concerns, needs, and progress, and pinpoint areas that need attention. Such personal notes, meant purely for a teacher's use, provide both an emotional release and evidence that her efforts are effective.

Student Activities for Further Study

1. Role-play, and then discuss with your classmates, the following situations where teachers are faced with hostile reactions.

    a. Mother says, "I refuse to talk to you any more. You're just plain wrong about Sarah—she's a very bright child."

    b. "How dare you ask me so many questions about my child? It's none of your business."

    c. "I want to talk to your director. If you were doing your job properly, there would be no problem with Melvin. She should know how really incompetent you are."

    d. "If you ask me, you want me to do your job for you. You can't handle him in the classroom, so you want me to get tough with him at home."

    e. "As long as I'm the one paying the bill for child care, I want things done as I ask. I insist that you get busy and teach Barbara to read this year before she goes to kindergarten. Are you saying I don't know what's best for my own child?"

Review Questions

1. Discuss possible reasons for apparently hostile responses.

2. Describe three of five considerations for teachers dealing with hostile reactions.

3. Discuss three of four possible reasons for apparent indifference; for each, identify a consideration for teachers' overcoming indifference.

4. Discuss three of four possible reasons for over-involvement; for each, identify ways of working with these parents.

References and Related Readings

Holmstrom, Lynda Lytle. *The Two-Career Family.* Cambridge, Mass.: Schenkham Publ. Co., 1972.

Jersild, Arthur T. *When Teachers Face Themselves.* New York: Bureau of Publications, Teachers College, Columbia University, 1955.

Lombana, Judy H. *Home School Partnerships: Guidelines and Strategies for Educators.* New York: Greene and Stratton, 1983.

Losen, Stuart M. and Bert Diament. *Parent Conferences in the Schools.* Boston: Allyn and Bacon, 1978.

Rundall, Richard D. and Steven Lynn Smith. "Working With Difficult Parents." *How To Involve Parents in Early Childhood Education.* Ed. Brigham Young University Press. Provo, Utah: Brigham Young University Press, 1982.

Stewart, W.E., J.C. Conoly and D. Rosenthal. *Working With Parents of Exceptional Children.* St. Louis: Times Mirror/Mosby College Publications, 1985.

Swick, Kevin J. and R. Eleanor Duff. *The Parent-Teacher Bond.* Dubuque, Iowa: Kendall/Hunt Publ. Co., 1978.

Working With Parents. Eric ED 133960. Florida Learning Resources Systems/Crown. Jacksonville, 1975.

Chapter 16 Looking at Parent- Involvement Programs that Work

The text has offered a rationale for working as partners with parents in preschool education and considered numerous strategies and practices that may open and enhance the communication process. It remains for teachers and programs to create their own parent-involvement programs, to respond in ways that are most appropriate to the particular needs of their populations.

Objectives

After studying this chapter, the student will be able to

1. understand the ways various preschool programs function to involve parents in their program

Some of you may already know of good programs for children and their families that exist around the country. Child-care programs vary a good deal in the way they look and function, depending on the needs of the populations they serve, amount of funding and staff available, philosophy, and goals. Each center must create its own patterns that work well for the staff and families concerned. As centers consider ideas to try, it may be useful to look at some programs that work effectively with children and their parents.

Open Door School, Charlotte, North Carolina

Located in the building of its sponsor, the Unitarian Church of Charlotte, the Open Door School offers a rich, creative program for preschool children. The school was established in 1966 as a morning program for three-, four-, and five-year-old children at a time when no public kindergarten and little preschool education existed in the city. When no integrated schools of any kind were available, Open Door encouraged the enrollment of children of all races, religions, economic levels, and ethnic origins. As community needs evolved, so did the structure of the Open Door School. Several years ago, a parent-cooperative program for two-year-olds was added, as was a full-day program for three- and four-year-olds, who came together for lunch, nap, and afternoon activities from their morning classrooms.

From the beginning, working with parents has been a part of the Open Door philosophy, and now parents who want to be actively involved in their children's preschool experience deliberately seek out Open Door, for themselves as well as their children. As one parent said, "We feel like it's our place too."

How does this good feeling come about? The director says, "We work at it." For parents, Open Door's written philosophy states that the school "acts as a resource on a professional level: teacher to parent; educates parents about child development through workshops, discussion groups, and two-year-old's Parent Co-op classes; alerts parents to events related to children, parents, and education; maintains a library of child development information of interest to parents; provides a support system of other parents: a basis for friendships; assists with tuition through Open Door's scholarship program for low-income families." For teachers, it is a stated part of their job descriptions to "establish and maintain an open and healthy relationship with parents; to visit at his/her home, each child in the class before school starts or immediately thereafter; to hold parent/teacher conferences twice a year, one in the fall and one in the spring; to attend parent meetings." New staff members undergo an orientation week before school opens for each of their first two years that includes discussions on working with parents and a workshop on parent-teacher conferences. In fact, many of the staff are former or current parents.

The two-year-old program, meeting two consecutive mornings per week, involves parents initially by requiring them to participate in the classroom on a rotating basis along with paid teachers. Both fathers and mothers actively participate with teachers and children in the classroom, setting a pattern for a high level of involvement that carries over into following years when regular participation is not required, only invited.

Before they enter the two-year-old classroom, these participating parents are given a three-hour workshop that covers topics such as typical developmental behaviors of two-year-olds, what to expect in the classroom, what is forbidden in the classroom, and who does what, including who will step in if a child of an involved parent has a problem (the parent). Despite this preparation, many participating parents later admit they approached the experience with hesitation, wondering if it would work—would they know what to do, or get in the way, or do something wrong in front of the teachers. But after being in the classroom, the questions vanished. The director says she is frequently asked how it works to have the parent co-op aspect to the two-year-old program—"Don't you find the children cry or are clingy?" "Sometimes," she responds, "and that's OK." Parents and children together are learning to trust and be comfortable.

Open Door is a very comfortable place. Teachers, parents, and children are all on a first-name basis and there is a drop-in atmosphere. When parents bring children in or pick them up, they linger and chat—with teachers, other parents, and other children. A teacher new to the staff commented on how impressed she'd been in the beginning of school to hear parents comment—"Look how he has grown" or "Hasn't she settled down!"; their frequent contacts have brought them to know and care for each child. Parents form an extended family between families and the school, with parents arriving at the same time in late afternoon for relaxed conversation on the playground or to pick up another child with their own to take to a Children's Theater matinee, much as a relative would.

Casual as it seems, there is careful thought about what will work well for children and their families. Before children enter the program, teachers make a brief, informal home visit to get to know them. Parents

Open Door is a comfortable place, where parents feel free to sit and chat awhile with teachers.

fill in an acquaintance sheet with space for both mother and father to answer such questions as "What do you enjoy most about your child?" "What is your method of setting limits for your child?" "Where do you experience your greatest difficulty with your child?" Parents have a group meeting before school begins to introduce them to the school's philosophy and practices, and discuss issues of separation.

Open Door's gradual easing-in program allows enough time for children and parents to become comfortable before parents move away. On the first day, the session is shortened and parents stay the entire time. There are several more shortened, small group sessions before the whole group comes together and stays for a full session. A coffee room is there for parents to meet each other and to be available if they are needed. Teachers are sensitive to parents' concerns and come out of the classroom to let them know how the children are doing: "He's crying, but I think he'll be OK," "It's not him you hear," " I think it might be a good idea for you to come back in the classroom for a while." One parent commented that this kind of experience really helped build her trust in the teacher, the idea that she could count on the teacher to tell her the truth. Teachers are also sensitive to

An effort is made to make even the car-pool drop-off a time for relaxed communication.

parents who are just not ready to leave their children and allow them to take as much time as they need.

Communication is worked at. Although most children arrive by car pool, parents escort the two-year-olds and all–day children into their classrooms every day, as the school feels it is important to have a direct transition for these children. The car-pool pace is relaxed enough to allow for some interchange, and most parents come into the classroom two or three times a week. The school feels it is important that parents make this connection and encourages them to do so. Parents are given teachers' home phone numbers and encouraged to call. The school sends out newsletters, individual teachers send out newsletters (often quite elaborate ones with wonderful anecdotes of what children have said and done). One teacher sends home personal letters about each child that are much appreciated.

> On February 11th we looked out the nap room windows while getting up and saw rain drops forming as ice on the bushes. Brendan announced decisively, "Those are called ice berries."
>
> We got new sand. Jonathan proclaimed, "It's almost like corn-bread."
>
> Jonathan's dad, Dean and Uncle Jack set up a small tent and the next day we figured out how to make one with our old bedspread. Rae's dad, Brad, brought Otis, his synthesizer; we each improvised a tune and sang a cool round of "Rudolph" and "Jingle Bells."
>
> We are creating a collection of pictures to look at each time we recall or plan for a trip. Seth and Andrew have promised pictures of their mountain homes and Jonathan will get us one from his Wrightsville Beach first-time-in-a-motel-trip. When you travel away, please bring us a folder with a picture or mail a postcard or share a spare photo. If you have a picture (photo or something from a brochure, etc.) of a place your family is planning to go, please send it in ahead of time even; we want to share the anticipation as well as the memories.

Teachers convey the message that they care about each child and his family, and value the communication with them. Parents respond by growing closer, by sharing information voluntarily—as one teacher said, "not because I'm the expert, but because I'm a member of the family."

This emotional response is reciprocal. As one teacher said, "I find myself investing lots more in individual children than I have at other places I've worked. Everything I do with William matters—I can't get rid of William in six months, he's not mine alone. I've got the whole family. I know the family is committed; these parents belong to the school. The parent is no longer an 'it,' but has become a person. It becomes really hard when they're no longer with us."

Most of the commitment to working with families is demonstrated informally, on a day-to-day basis. Organized events tend to be fairly low-key: a December holiday party for parents only, for which the children make cookies and punch and gifts; a Thanksgiving feast, again prepared by the children, which parents may attend; an end of year pot-luck lunch on the playground. The parents in the full-day program have standing invitations for lunch and also have a pot-luck supper in the summer, which families who are both leaving and entering the program attend. Parents are invited to classrooms to share interests, time for field trips, etc.

Parent education meetings vary according to a needs assessment each year. Each class has an in-class evening parent meeting in October that continues the discussion of philosophy and practices, and helps the individual teacher emphasize involvement.

One teacher found that by emphasizing the importance of father involvement at the fall meeting, she later had 100 percent of her fathers appear for conferences. Conferences are scheduled twice a year, fall and spring, at hours during the day and early evening that fit parents' schedules. One teacher scheduled conferences over a cup of coffee in a local restaurant when it proved to be a more convenient place to meet.

Parents volunteer labor for workdays. The director tells of a project a year or so ago when the playgrounds and equipment had to be moved due to an addition on the church. Most of the parents worked for four consecutive Saturdays in temperatures over 100 degrees. At the end of one of these back-breaking days, one parent thanked the director, saying it was the closest he'd ever been to a barn-raising, a wonderful experience of being together with others who have a common goal—"our children."

The staff at Open Door is forthright about letting parents know how and what they can do—a "Talent" list and a "Wish" list hang in the office along with volunteer sign-up sheets. A newsletter jokes every third sentence—" We can use anything."

Rae spent a large part of the afternoon dragging a ragged, stringy rope. (We use absolutely everything.) . . . Heath invented a game of rolling hickory nuts through the big black plastic tube. (We make use of highly unlikely objects.) . . . Janelle stirred silently in the beat-up cooker that has no handle. (We can find a use for . . .)

Open Door let parents know how they can help—and parents respond.

A booklet of loving, funny, and serious anecdotes about their children was sent home by the full-day program last summer. "The News from Late Afternoon," organized under slightly tongue-in-cheek headings as "Scientific Achievements," "Family and Society," and "Business and the Economy," must have delighted every parent, with the evidence of observing and listening to the children with loving care. It concluded with words that seem to speak for Open Door: "There is much more, but by now you should have gotten the message: you have enriched our lives by sharing your children and yourselves with us. That's why, instead of just "Good-bye," it's fun to be able to say, "We'll be right here tomorrow."

Open Door is finding ways to see parents and teachers as partners in the process of child-rearing.

Henderson County Child Development Center, Hendersonville, North Carolina

A town in the Blue Ridge Mountains in North Carolina is home for an innovative program that works hard to have an impact on the families it serves. Originally a center for the children of migrant workers who spend the summer and fall months working in apple orchards, vegetable fields, and packing houses, the program now operates year-round with several population groups, expanding to full capacity at two different centers from July to December when the migrant families return to the area.

The main center is located in the Education building of the First Presbyterian Church in Hendersonville and offers full-day developmental day care for children from ages three months to five years, year round. Many of the children served are referred and paid for by the Department of Social Services, perhaps 25 percent are children from the community with the reasonable fees paid by their families. This program is greatly expanded by the migrant children, from infants to five-year-olds, who are supported by funding from the East Coast Migrant Head Start Project that the center serves as a delegate agency for six months of the year. When the center in town is filled by migrant children, a second center in the country is opened to care for three- to five-year-olds in full-day care.

The commitment to parent participation has been there from the beginning. The center is now incorporated as a private, nonprofit organization, with a board of directors composed of eight parents and seven other community members; during the six months the migrant parents are involved, four migrant parents are included on the board. Using the Head Start guidelines for parent participation, there is also a parent committee that involves all parents from both centers, with their own elected chairman and secretary. This group decides on the education they want for themselves, participates in decisions regarding the program, and elects a representative to the Parent Policy Council of the Head Start Project in Washington.

One of the staff positions paid for by the Migrant Head Start funds is a recruiter. Although in the first year the recruiter had to "beat the bushes," visiting orchards and camps to get families involved, the continuity and quality of the program now do the recruiting for him and his time is spent in important liaison and support relationships with families. He functions as a "sounding board," a person who listens to and supports families under the stress that comes from a migratory life of change and hard conditions. He helps families get food stamps, accompanies them to the office to translate for Spanish-speaking workers, transports families for medical needs, helps with paper work at the Social Security office, reads letters and makes phone calls. He sorts out the complicated interrelationships among families and passes along this information to teachers to help them understand the families they work with. He works in parent-support groups and meetings, and generally responds to the many different requests, often conveyed by the bus drivers each day—"Tell Chris there's two new families in the camp with babies." "The Sanchez' pipes burst."

Despite the demands of long working hours, parents are encouraged to communicate with teachers and staff as much as possible. At least half of the children are transported by bus, with complicated arrangements for where to be picked up or dropped off that may change daily. Nevertheless, most parents frequently come into the classroom and see the teacher. The director estimates there are one or two contacts daily between each parent and the staff. Teachers make home visits to each child at least once during the six-month period. Newsletters, with a page for each classroom, the director, the nurse, and the recruiter are sent out monthly. Newsletters usually contain recipes and practical activities to do at home. The parent handbook, printed in both English and Spanish, includes information on goals and regulations, symptoms of illnesses, accident prevention, general developmental information, and community resources for assistance with clothing, health, and housing.

There is a team approach to communicating and working with parents that conveys to parents that there is a multitude of united staff members who care. One parent commented that this absence of tension among the adults makes her feel good about the center and helps her child's sense of security. The bus drivers, having daily contacts twice with parents, are important parts of the communication process. A staff member at the center said, "I trust the bus drivers to let us know if there's anything going on we should know about." The bus drivers remind parents about parent meetings and go beyond normal duties in helping families, such as taking out kerosene heaters when the weather suddenly turns cold.

Another part of the team is the pediatric nurse-practitioner at the migrant clinic who does the physicals for the children before they enter the center. Over a period of time, she has gotten to know the families and helps other staff with this understanding. The center is justifiably proud of the medical component of the program, having a full-time

The staff respect the migrant parents as people who have a good deal to offer their children.

nurse on the staff, and uses it as another vehicle for educating parents. Parents are encouraged to go with the nurse when she takes their children to doctors and dentists, as a way of educating and helping parents to see what they can do.

From the staff comes a feeling of respect for the parents they work with. Parents are not viewed as migrants, as victims, as poor people, but as people who have a good deal to offer their children. Staff respect the way their children come first with these families who frequently chose this life as offering more positive opportunities than their past. The staff knows these parents are eager for knowledge that will help their children, that they don't want "hand-outs" but work hard, pay their bills, and do what they can.

The eagerness to learn things that will help their children is measured by the success of the monthly parent meetings at the center. The center helps by providing baby-sitting, transportation, light refreshments, and numerous reminders—notes, newsletters, invitations from busdrivers, teachers, and the recruiter. They ask parents for their ideas, needs, and interests in topics, knowing that if parents are sure they will leave the meeting with something that will benefit their children, they will come. One popular meeting was to make toys and materials that could help in a child's development. Fathers sawed and sanded blocks, and were enormously proud to have something like this to show for their efforts. At another meeting, a local manufacturer donated sample clothing so parents had new garments to take to their children.

The staff's sensitivity to parents' individual needs was shown by the decision to change the parent meetings from the original format of mixed Spanish and English with an interpreter translating English into Spanish, with much confusion. Now all the parents come together at first for a welcome, perhaps a little business, then separate for the program in the individual languages. The staff has found many more are attending, feeling freer and more comfortable. There is an emphasis on being comfortable with each other; staff are called by first names and attempts are made to remove any professional barriers that might cause apprehension.

This is demonstrated by the involvement of parents in understanding the developmental screening of their children. The children are given a thorough screening each year using the LAP (Learning Accomplishment Profile), a standard tool in Head Start and other programs. Before the LAP screening, a parent meeting is arranged to discuss what the LAP is, show some of the areas to be tested, and some of the expected behaviors at each age. The screening becomes a pleasant experience for the children, set up like a carnival, with stations for each skill to be tested (fine motor, language, etc.), and each child getting a little related gift to take home from each station (crayons, a book).

The center works hard to make sure they are reaching parents who speak both English and Spanish.

After the screening, conferences are set up to discuss with parents their children's individual needs. The teacher of four- and five-year-olds was busy in the spring doing pre-kindergarten conferences with parents. As one of their rights the parents are made to understand the assessment. When additional testing needs to be done, parents are encouraged to observe the doctor or psychologist from behind a one-way mirror and discuss the findings that same day. The assumption is that fully informed parents are less apprehensive and more involved.

Some events are planned mostly for social contact and family enjoyment. At the beginning of the six-month program, a picnic offers an opportunity for families and staff to get to know one another and to talk about what they will do together in the coming months.

The center makes Christmas a big event, knowing that many families might not have Christmas without their help. But here again, there is sensitivity to letting the families make their own decisions about how they will use the help. Money raised by staff bake sales, raffles, and community donations is used to buy appropriate gifts for each child such as clothing or simple toys. A wrapped gift is given to each child by Santa, who visits the evening party, planned for after work hours so parents may attend. Other gifts are labeled and placed in a bag where parents pick them up and give them to their child when they choose to. This avoids having it seem as if the center is the only one providing Christmas gifts for the children.

Spring graduation is another big event that brings out many family members and relatives. The oldest children leave the center complete with cap, certificate, and family pride. Building good feelings for parents and their children is an important center goal.

Perhaps some of the most unique services offered by the center come through a close working and contractual relationship with the Trend Community Mental Health Services. The professionals there work closely with the center in the comprehensive developmental screening processes and in the establishment of groups for parent education and support. In addition, a Parent Assistance Program (PAP) was developed to provide diagnostic and referral services for parents of children in the center. The program recognizes that parents who are under stress for any reason—whether alcohol- or drug-related, marital or family distress, emotional instability, financial or legal problems—cannot live effectively with the children the center is committed to serve. The PAP program is designed to motivate parents to seek help in the earliest possible stage of a problem for diagnosis and referral. If mental health services are required, the program provides three individual or family therapy sessions for each problem, at no additional charge to the parent. (Fees for sessions beyond three are charged on a sliding scale related to income.) Since the supportive connections are already there, it is assumed that parents feel comfortable in seeking this assistance, either by self-referral or referral by the center staff.

Another important service offered by the Early Childhood Intervention Program at the Mental Health Service is training for the center's staff in helping them to understand child development in light of a migrant worker's life style, principles of therapeutic day care, and to become more knowledgeable about games and educational toys for the home. The contract also provides for an employee assistance program to help identify problems and refer staff members for appropriate assistance.

The training and staff support systems combine to help the staff continue to grow in their demanding work and to maintain staff continuity and stability. Most of the staff have been with the program for a number of years, increasing the sense of continuity and familiarity with the families.

These methods of working with parents produce grateful feelings of support for the center and its staff. One mother said, "You know, I hear parents griping, but when you come to the center and get involved in the meetings, you start to understand some of what's going on here. I don't know how they do it. Four kids at home can be pretty hard—and these teachers have fifteen, all day long. I'd never have made it through if it wasn't for them. It's a good feeling not to have to worry about your kids when you're at work, and to trust the teacher. The kids know I trust her too—that helps. That and the PAP—I learned so much from them."

She had indeed. She had stopped by the office to share a success story. Her child, who had left the center and was in a public school kindergarten, was getting a lot of negative feedback from the teacher. "Every day there'd be something more bad he'd done that the teacher would tell us. So I got tired of it. I asked for a conference, and told the teacher that no wonder he wasn't changing his behavior, he was getting all that attention for being bad. I told her from now on I wanted to hear some good things he'd done."

The parent was a little surprised at herself and very pleased. "I wouldn't have known that, if it weren't for the center, and I wouldn't have known what to do." A staff member agrees. "Our parents have developed a habit and expectation of talking with the teacher, and now feel they have a right to communicate."

The parents of the Henderson County Child Development Center are offered support, knowledge, and the power that comes with that

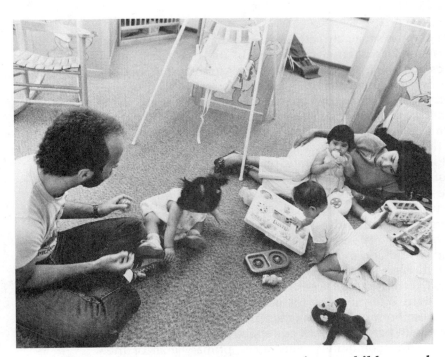

The center is determined to offer young migrant children and their families a positive head start.

knowledge, and the belief in their ability to do good things for their children. One concrete way they can affect things that happen for their children is by the "continuity records" they are given to pass along to other Head Start Migrant centers, recording their educational, developmental, and medical records. These records prevent children from having the same things done to them repeatedly—screenings and immunizations—and from having their needs overlooked when they move on.

Other parents are starting to see the choices and settle outside the migrant stream. Two of the staff members are former migrants.

The director summed it up. "You can work with a child in the center, but for the total child, the family has to be involved. We have to impact on the family, and that's a hard thing to do. And we're not trying to change them; we're just trying to show them some other ideas, ways they can do things differently, to help themselves and their children." A dedicated staff is committed to supporting families in their own individual growth.

The University of Southern Maine, Child Care Services, Portland, Maine

Portland, Maine is an small, attractive city bursting with the energy of rebirth and change. This energy is reflected in the day-care center and other services to families offered under the sponsorship of the University of Southern Maine. From a small center serving about two dozen children, the center has grown to an enrollment of about two hundred at two separate locations in less than a year. Some children are served full time, some only part time, and some only during the semesters when their student parents are enrolled at the university. Some of the children are in a temporary on-campus center, awaiting the completion of a beautifully designed campus building; others are in a house in the remodeled downtown area. These locations reflect the different populations served by the centers: students, faculty, and staff at the university; alumni and others related in some way to the university; and community residents, including both two-career professional families and a number of slots paid for by social services and Title XX funds. Children from six weeks to six-years-old are cared for; a developmental day camp for ten weeks in summer and winter camp during school vacations offer services for parents of six- to fourteen-year-olds as well. These options, plus some adaptations of the traditional methods of working with parents, as well as a spectrum of other services offered to families in the community, illustrate a primary goal of the center: to find out and provide what parents want and need. As the director expresses it: "Child care has changed so much. In the sixties

The center tries to respond to the needs voiced by the parents it serves.

and seventies, it was primarily a service for the indigent. Now we serve primarily middle-class parents who know what they want, and are in fact very demonstrative in expressing their needs. We have had to shift our whole thinking about what they need and what services to provide."

There is a good-natured acceptance among the staff that parents involved in professional careers or busy lives as university students already have many demands on them. One teacher, asked why she thought parents who had expressed the wish for a parent group still did not turn out for an evening meeting, stated simply—"Exhaustion." But, rather than interpret this negatively or give up, the staff continues to try to find new ways of communicating.

Parents seek out the center in large numbers. Day care, particularly for infants and toddlers, is a fairly recent and scarce commodity in Maine. Parents are attracted by the quality of the program, which offers excellent adult-child ratios with professionally trained teachers supplemented by work-study students and interns from nursing, social work, and psychology programs. The university does not have an early childhood program so the center is not technically a lab school; it sees its role as a model in a small state where day care is not well developed. The university is supportive of the center and sees it as a marketing tool for students and employees.

The center's admissions director works with parents during the initial information exchange and decision process. The first contact may be an individual appointment or an evening group meeting of five to ten couples to discuss the program and look around the center. Most often there is a second visit, sometimes to sit down with both the admissions director and the head teacher of a particular classroom. In the infant rooms there may be several visits, with parents watching everything and asking questions. Parents fill in information forms that are different for preschoolers and infants and toddlers, and deal with specifics: "How does child react to these social activities: rocking, kissing, cuddling, mild roughhousing?" "What is position while napping?" "Mood upon awakening?"

Parents are urged to make the day-care decision carefully and are encouraged to observe at different times during the day, so they know it all. Said the admissions director, "We have nothing to hide. We want them to see exactly what goes on. For example, at twelve o'clock, things can be pretty hectic, with morning children leaving, afternoon children arriving, children eating lunch and getting ready for nap, parents stopping by on their lunch hours. I want them to know the facts of busy group care, so they can decide if they're comfortable with it." With the same matter-of-factness, parents are encouraged to shop around if they hesitate over the fees, that are about the national average. "We tell them good day care costs and that we'll hold the application for a week to let them look around and see what else they can get." (There are scholarship funds to assist student parents.) Helping parents make responsible decisions is important to the center.

After parents decide on the center, parent and child come together for a visit. An individualized plan is made for managing the beginning experiences. Depending on the reactions of a child and his parents, a child may be part-time for a day, a week, or even longer in the infant and toddler areas, with freedom for parents to stay, call, or drop back in unannounced. The emphasis is on what helps best in each situation.

Because the majority of children served by the program are infants and toddlers, special attention is directed towards understanding and empathizing with these parents. "In most cases the children are doing well, and what we're dealing with is the parents who aren't, because of such guilt as they grapple with their own feelings about leaving such a young child with people they [parents] don't really know." The staff recognizes that these feelings often produce initial negativity, where the parents seem to be looking for any negative aspect; teachers accept these behaviors and recognize there is nothing personal involved, but rather a reaction that diminishes as a parent builds a sense of trust and attachment with the caregivers.

In building this relationship, every staff member obviously devotes much effort, taking care to initiate conversation daily. One teacher spoke of "welcoming the parents into my house," meaning she recognized it as her responsibility to take the initiative to help parents feel comfortable. Everyone is on a first name basis. In most classrooms teachers work as a team with one member of the team recognized as

As parents build a sense of trust and attachment with caregivers, it becomes easier to leave their infants.

the person who is most responsible for parent contact. It is considered necessary in a situation where there are many adults to give parents one stable person with whom to talk frequently. In one of the infant rooms, each caregiver is most responsible for her own special group of babies and is therefore most familiar with the details of their lives. This helps her concentrate her attention on a particular group of parents. Parents may call any time throughout the day. With the youngest children, information is recorded daily by parents and a daily care log with specific details is given back to parents at the end of the day. It is emphasized to parents that their knowledge and plans for their child are important. They make the decisions about when new foods will be introduced or toilet training begun, and teachers will listen and follow their directions. Parents are asked to fill out a monthly update sheet on their infants, specifying anything new in the baby's routine, likes and dislikes, their home plans and procedures. There are parent suggestion boxes and frequent opportunities to talk.

And how do parents respond to these initiatives? "We teachers become part of the family. Many of the young professional parents have moved to Maine for its desirable life-styles and are far from a network of family supports, so they come to depend on us for advice, support, and to tell us things. They can't wait to tell us what he had for supper last night, and how he played before bed." And teachers listen, knowing the importance of all this. A young mother spoke of the comfort in the center, of being able to sit on the floor and play with all the babies, and of being able to talk with other parents. Mothers come throughout the day to breast-feed and create a "Kaffeeklatsch" group for discussion and enjoyment. The center recognizes this as an opportunity for teachers to educate parents subtly during the conversation. Teachers also benefit from these close relationships, and speak of feelings of support and recognition from parents.

Communication is accomplished through a variety of other methods. The halls are lined with shoe bags, each "parent pocket" labelled with a parent's name. Memos, newsletters, notes, and informative articles frequently fill the pockets. There are parent bulletin boards in the classrooms. One teacher plans to implement two recent suggestions from parents: more frequent newsletters as substitutes for meetings, and a picture board, to help parents put a face on the names of part-time teachers they hear from their children. There is a "hot line," with certain times of day available for telephone conversations. One innovative idea is an "electronic report card"—videotaped segments on each infant highlighting developmental accomplishments.

Conferences are held at least twice a year. For the few parents

Mothers can be free to come and spend time with their babies.

who do not respond to invitations or follow-up calls for setting conference appointments, a written assessment and invitation to discuss is sent home.

The staff accepts parents' choices of whether or not to participate in other communication efforts. Informal luncheons are held each month. "We just announce we'll get a table in the university cafeteria and be there from 11:30 until 1:00, if parents want to bring a bag lunch and come chat about whatever they'd like." Evening meetings are held three or four times a semester, sometimes with dinner and child care, with the groups divided into the age group classifications—one night for infant and toddler parents, another for preschool parents. As mentioned previously, evening meetings do not meet the needs of professional parents, so a survey was conducted to discover what parents prefer. They will try the early morning coffee and the late afternoon get-togethers as suggested by the parents.

Parents act as resources to the program to some extent, although volunteers in the classroom are rare because of work schedules or because there are a number of adults already present. Parents act as consultants on medical, legal, nutritional, and architectural issues. The new playground will be built largely by parent volunteers. Material resources, rather than time, are often the way these parents choose to participate. A wish list is offered and parents fill these tangible requests promptly. Parents from all of the population groups served—students, employees, and from the community—are represented on an advisory committee that meets once every two or three months and helps in the decision-making process of the center.

What is exciting about the center is the new ideas for outreach to parents of children in the center and to parents in the community at large. This year the center has received a grant from the Junior League for a parenting center that will be located in the new child-care center on campus. The Parenting Center, under its own director, will offer a variety of services to parents: a library of parenting materials, classes, workshops, and seminars on a variety of child development and family related topics. These offerings also will be made available at lunch time in various companies around the city. The University Child Care Services has already established a Child and Family Institute that does the in-service training for Head Start and Title XX programs in the state. The vast library from the Institute will supplement the library for the Parenting Center, as will a grant for books from the local IBM office.

Another service for parents is evolving from the existing counseling bureau at the university, that is underused by the student parents. Counselors will now be available at the day-care center, ready to counsel "on the run," much as teachers do. It is hoped that from this relationship a support group will develop. The director states the idea clearly, "If this happens, the support group will evolve, instead of us saying 'We're

The Parenting Center will offer child development education for parents, right at the center where their children are cared for.

going to be running this group, please come.'" It is believed that parents should define their needs and the center should be ready to meet them.

Another outreach to community parents is a series of commercial television programs, a pilot project of one hour a day for a week during prime time, including a series of family vignettes, guest commentators, and opportunities for parents to call in. A future plan is to package some of these vignettes into parenting programs that can be used by corporations or individuals, perhaps available for VCR loan from the Parenting Center.

It is recognized that with modern working parents, some traditional ways of educating parents may need to be dropped and less traditional forms of child care may be called for. A grant proposal to establish sick child care centers is hoped to go into effect next year. The plan is to open two family day-care homes the first year during the flu season from January to April, and six centers the following year. The idea is to make sick care affordable at $2.00 an hour. The center hopes this is a model other communities may adopt.

The center will also act as a treatment center for sexually abused infants and toddlers under a state program established to give therapy and education to parents as well.

There is a possibility of implementing evening and Saturday care in response to parents' needs. As the director said: "We try to be all things to all people—which means we sometimes might overextend ourselves."

The center clearly believes that busy contemporary families need all the help and support they can get, and that families help define the ways the center should be prepared to help. There is an air of excitement around this new program as ideas develop and possibilities become realities to children, their parents, and the community.

Thorndike Street School, Inc., Cambridge, Massachusetts

Located in a building filled with community service programs in the heart of Cambridge, Massachusetts, the Thorndike Street School offers a quality program of full day care for twenty-nine toddlers and preschool children. There are two distinctive aspects of the center's philosophy and functioning that contribute to the sense of community in which parents and teachers work together closely.

Thorndike Street's educational philosophy has been clearly articulated through discussion by staff and parents, and refined over a ten-year period. Basic to the definition of quality child-care service for children and families are the numerous aspects of learning for both adults and children. "We begin with the premise of believing in and respecting the rights and dignity of children, thus those of adults, individually and collectively (educational philosophy, TSS)." The philosophy continues to state that a basic goal is for "children to develop a positive self-image of who they are in a diverse world, with an appreciation of similarities and differences between themselves and others." This goal is translated into a program that emphasizes racial, economic, and cultural diversity. Discrimination in any form is not tolerated, including sex-role stereotyping. (The center's cook is presently a male.) A multicultural curriculum is an important part of this plan; traditions, holidays, and rituals from many cultures around the world are celebrated. Books, records, and puzzles that foster non-sexist and anti-racist attitudes are carefully sought out. Conscious choices in enrollment create a family population that reflects the racially diverse community in which the center is located: Hispanic, Haitian, Afro-American, and Caucasian families are presently part of the center. Two-thirds of the families are assisted by DSS funds for low- and moderate-income families, while one-third of the families are middle–income families paying private fees. The staff composition also reflects the population served, and hiring is set at a goal of at least 50 percent teaching staff of color.

When families apply to the center, they are choosing the center deliberately because they know what the center is about with its multi-ethnic emphasis and they want to be a part of it, for themselves and their children. "It's so rewarding for us all," says the director, "for staff who see that children are having a chance to really start fresh, before they've learned any negative attitudes from the world at large, and for parents who see their child having a best friend from another culture. We have so much to learn from children about appreciating the differences."

The staff works hard at implementing affirmative action in both hiring and enrollment, and it is the way staff members work together to make decisions that is the other distinctive feature of the Thorndike Street School. The staff works as a collective for decision making by consensus regarding the enrollment, hiring, and curriculum of the school as a whole. There is no hierarchical structure; everyone's vote is equal and is encouraged to make sure that he/she is heard from before a final compromise is reached. A staff member points out that this is quite an expedient system; when the whole group feels it has a say in what happens, it is possible to avoid the undercurrent feelings that might keep them from moving on. In order to function as a collective, the staff meet daily for one hour while another paid employee supervises the nap room. The center has two teachers in each room for both morning and afternoon hours, and this staff meeting is part of the time overlapped by this schedule. Any staff member may propose an issue to be discussed at each meeting. Though this seems like an astonishing amount of time for communication, teachers comment it is still not enough to cover the number of issues regarding the school's functioning, as well as specific understandings of children and families. A consultant joins them one day a week to help with specific behaviors of children and classroom practices. Such time for staff communication builds up great respect for the different perspectives and experiences offered by each staff member. One teacher spoke of how they had learned from a teacher from Ghana, whose approach to communicating was different in that as she often told anecdotes from her true life experiences; they discovered they would learn something relevant to an issue being discussed. Parents notice and value the closeness of the staff.

The decisions made about adding new staff members who appreciate and value the multi-ethnic basis of the center and the staff collective are important. Parents are involved closely in staff hiring and are kept informed of each step of the process. As resumes of prospective candidates arrive, they may be read by all parents and staff for ideas

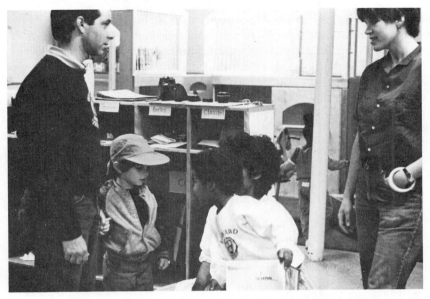

Families choose the center because of its multi-ethnic emphasis.

on which candidates to consider further. Parents are invited to attend the preliminary interviews. After a preliminary interview, the group decides if a candidate should be invited back to work in the classroom with children, for observation by parents and staff. If this goes well, an evening interview is scheduled and parents are asked to attend. Final decisions about employment are made by a consensus of both parents and staff after this interview.

Parents are involved in budgeting decisions also; as the director put it, "Without their approval of the budget, we don't act." Biannual meetings review the budget for the past six months and plans the budget for the next six. No tuition increases are imposed without parents agreement.

Other decisions are made by a parent-staff board composed of the entire staff of nine, plus eight invited parents. Both the president and vice-president of the board are parents.

From the beginning, parents and staff members closely collaborate on the children's behalf. Everything is carefully defined in both printed and spoken communication; no misunderstanding is left to chance. A typical entry procedure includes at least two phone conversations with the director before an initial interview in which the school program and philosophy are discussed and printed materials describing these are offered. A copy of hiring, enrollment, and educational philosophies are given, along with a paper entitled Parents' Rights. Thorndike Street School makes very clear at the outset what they stand for, so parents may choose this or not.

Parents are encouraged to observe a classroom, then bring their child to play and interact. This allows parents to see how the staff relate to the children and to each other. Parents are asked to complete an information form which was, in fact, designed by parents, and includes developmental and home information useful for teachers. ("In general, is your child fairly quiet, fairly talkative, or fairly average?" "In a stressful situation [examples] does your child cry, withdraw, throw a tantrum?" "How do you usually comfort your child?")

The form also includes a segment on parent involvement.

PARENT INVOLVEMENT

As has been explained, the parents at TSS take turns (about twice a year) cleaning up the school on weekends. That same weekend, we are asked to bring in fresh fruit for the week. Aside from clean-up weekends, we are expected to spend a couple of hours during major clean-up and repair on our Spring and Fall Renovation Days.

How much time will your schedule/interests permit for you to become involved sharing ideas, planning meetings, fundraising?

Will you be able to attend monthly Parent/Staff Pot-Luck Supper Meetings regularly?_____

Would you be willing to serve on a committee?_____

Are there any special areas in which you have particular interests or abilities that you would be willing to share with the Parents/Staff of TSS?_____

The director says, "Our perception of the day-care center is that it be a support to families, not just another place where they are expected to perform a role, so we try not to make demands beyond the attendance at parents' meetings and the occasional committee." Nevertheless, because of the parents' caring, many are involved in additional ways.

The staff collective makes the final admissions decisions based on the affirmative action factors of age, race, sex, and economic status. When a child is to be enrolled, parents are asked to bring their child for at least two visits—one in the morning and one in the afternoon—and parents stay with their child during those visits. On the first day without his parents, a child stays for four hours, including lunch. After this experience, teachers and parents discuss how it went. If all went

Teachers and parents will discuss how each phase goes for the first few days.

well, the second day will be for six hours, through nap. The next teacher-parent conversation decides whether to move to full days or continue the part days. Teachers ask parents to adhere to a strict schedule, telling children when they will return and to be sure to call if there is any change so children can be reassured.

Communication is the key to reaching the Thorndike Street goals. Monthly parent-staff meetings are held in the evening, except during July and August. Since dinner and child care is provided, attendance is generally good. Meetings are informative to parents: in September, staff members present school policies which are discussed; in October, parents divide into groupings of toddlers and preschoolers to discuss classroom activities and curriculum. Parents help devise classroom policies; for example, at a recent parent meeting, teachers proposed that no props from home be brought for superhero play, and teachers and parents discussed this idea before implementing it together. In December, a huge multicultural holiday celebration is held along with a brainstorming session to generate and prioritize ideas for future workshops with invited guest speakers. One year the important topics that parents selected were television, nutrition, helping children deal with grief and loss, and war play. This last topic proved to be of such great interest that teachers and parents organized another session. The director reports these sessions as extremely vital events where every parent present contributes and communicates. The last meeting of the year is a big picnic, attended by families including older children who have "graduated," and extended families. The director comments that at these parent-staff get-togethers she feels both wonder and satisfaction that such an incredibly diverse group of people are getting along together.

There are warm feelings of comfort during the daily comings and goings. Parents and teachers linger for a while, talking and joking. One father brought his toddler son very early so he could play with him for a while before going off to work. In the toddler room, teachers enhance daily communication by keeping a notebook on top of the toddler's cubbies and writing a sentence or two about each toddler daily. This lets the afternoon teachers know a little about how a child's day has gone, and provides for parents another personal connection with a teacher and child. Teachers recognize that with parents of very young children there are frequently feelings of guilt, but these feeling are lessened when parents perceive their children are in a positive situation.

Teachers respect the fact that parents really do know their own children best through living with them, but recognize that help with behaviors related to children's group experiences is needed, as when

Parents and teachers linger and chat together.

children become resistant at pick-up time. The teachers at Thorndike Street respect parents' dignity as well as children's, and therefore, rather than stepping in and taking over, they talk with a parent in advance, strategizing what they can do to help a situation. Teachers privately confront parents about hitting children, inside the school or on the way out, stressing that this is not allowed as part of the school's philosophy of children's rights and needs for dignity. Generally, staff have found parents to be responsive when they are given methods to regain their control.

Conferences are held regularly. With a mandate from the Office for Children to have written evaluations in children's files, conferences are generally tied in to reporting this assessment to parents, giving them a copy, and talking about future goals and directions to work together. Conferences may be held at any time at a parent's request. Both teachers attend a conference, and the director may sit in if there is a problem. Conferences may be held at school during nap time or during a home visit. During a home visit, both teachers will go for dinner and visit with a child and his family. The conference is held after the children go to bed, so a visit may last two to four hours. Teachers are paid for doing home visits and the evaluations.

On rare occasions when communication breaks down, staff do what they can to reestablish dialogue. One instance was a meeting of two teachers, the director and a parent who brought along a friend— "and this all helped."

Such comfort with each other brings a willingness to volunteer. Parents assist the staff and center in many ways including helping with newsletters, helping to write a grant to get funds for classroom equipment, collaborating with staff to write a new parent handbook (a parent who is a graphic artist is designing it), and typing and photocopying necessary papers for the center. Parents and staff saved the center $3000 by working together to lay the tile floors in the new center.

Parent volunteers are also classroom resources. Music is provided by parent volunteers, as well as some memorable ethnic cooking experiences. Recently an Ethiopian family prepared a native dish and had lunch with the children, showing how to use their fingers to dip the pancakes. Parents may accompany children on trips away from the center.

Parents at the center are valuable advocates for children. The staff has drawn up flyers about the latest in the state budget, asking parents to call their legislators to lobby for day care in the state budget. There has been a dual lobbying effort on affordability and wages for staff and parents' advocacy has helped turn the tide.

Thorndike Street School is an exciting place. The mutual support works to the benefit of everyone: teachers say that when parents believe in them, it gives them energy to do more; parents feel important and comfortable in knowing they are listened to and have an impact. Parents

Parents and staff have chosen Thorndike Street School as a place where each person can have an impact.

and staff together chose the school as a place where they can work together, committed to a community that supports the right for growth in children and adults.

Summary

From these accounts of four different programs, it is evident that there is more than one method of working with parents. The common thread is the philosophy that parents deserve support and respect as they undertake the massive and vital tasks of parenting, and that teachers can work most effectively with children when they work closely with parents. Each center has worked to find the particular methods that best suit their program, with its specific goals, needs, and perception of the needs of the families served. There are some things that work well; in general, methods of working to ensure the fullest communication possible are important. The challenge is always there as teachers and centers continue to reach out to the families they serve.

Suggested Activities for Further Study

1. Visit a local day care center and/or preschool half-day program. Arrange to interview the director, a teacher, and a parent about

their perceptions of how the parent-teacher relationship is developed and how each participant feels about the degree of communication established. Learn what methods of communication exist and how parents become involved in the program. How do your findings compare with the descriptions of the four programs in the chapter?

2. Draw up a chart, with a column for each of the four programs described. Summarize the information given in the descriptions, under: Philosophy of Working with Parents; Orientation Procedures; Communication Methods; Parent Involvement in the Program; Parents as Decision-Makers. What similarities do you discover? What differences?

3. Draw up a similar chart for the center where you are involved as a student, or where you work, and for the center you visited in Question 1. What similarities do you find with the chart of the four programs from the chapter? What differences?

Review Questions

1. Using the chart you drew up in Question 2 above, compare and contrast the four programs, regarding the ways each involve parents in the programs and in relationships with classroom teachers.

2. List those components and philosophies the four programs have in common.

References and Related Readings

Note: Due to the nature of this chapter, the information was gained firsthand by interview or by reading the hand-outs from each center. Students may be interested in reading descriptions of several other types of programs, including the ways they involve parents. Such descriptions may be found in:

Galinsky, Ellen and William H. Hooks. *The New Extended Family: Day Care That Works.* Boston: Houghton Mifflin Co., 1977.

Index